TWIN VOICES

Having experienced first hand the devastation that can be inflicted by polio, Janice Flood Nichols knew she had to tell her story and push for further efforts to vaccinate all of the world's children...

From Susan M. Heim, author of *Twice the Love: Stories of Inspiration for Families...with Twins, Multiples and Singletons.*

"In Twin Voices, Janice Nichols transports us back in time, allowing us to once again hear the voices of those whose lives were forever changed by polio. Her heartbreaking story of loss, including the death of her brother, reminds us of the many heroes we left behind in the war against polio."

Paul A. Offit, MD, author of *Autism's False Prophets Bad Science, Risky Medicine, And The Search For A Cure*

TWIN VOICES

A Memoir of Polio, the Forgotten Killer

Janice Flood Nichols

iUniverse, Inc.
New York   Bloomington

Twin Voices
A Memoir of Polio, the Forgotten Killer

Copyright © 2007, 2008 by Janice Flood Nichols

iUniverse books may be ordered through booksellers or by contacting:

iUniverse
1663 Liberty Drive
Bloomington, IN 47403
www.iuniverse.com
1-800-Authors (1-800-288-4677)

Because of the dynamic nature of the Internet, any Web addresses or links contained in this book may have changed since publication and may no longer be valid. The views expressed in this work are solely those of the author and do not necessarily reflect the views of the publisher, and the publisher hereby disclaims any responsibility for them.

ISBN: 978-1-60528-030-1 (pbk)
ISBN: 978-0-595-63272-5 (ebk)

Printed in the United States of America

To all who made this journey with us

Contents

PART ONE: TOUGH TIMES

PART TWO: PROGRESS

PART THREE: LOOKING BACK, LOOKING FORWARD

APPENDIX

Acknowledgments

Without the love and support of my husband, Dave, and son Kevin, the story of a little boy named Frankie and his twin sister, Janice, would have remained half locked inside my heart. Thank you for your love, for believing in this story, and for respecting my need to bring meaning in a broader context to my life's journey. I love you both.

To the members of my family who have given voice to this story: Betty Coolican Wightman, Pat Marshall Coolican, Bonne Paltz Hall, and Bob Paltz, as well as to my college roommate Mary Jane Reid Maidment. I love you all. To Uncle Tommy, thanks for the newspaper photo ops that you and Buddy always finagled when Frankie and I were little kids. I love you.

It has been gratifying to meet or reconnect with the following individuals whose lives were impacted by our polio story: Dr. Alice Jaros Turek (retired pediatrician and public health official), Louise DeMartino, Alan DeMartino, Gary DeMartino, Brett Sagenkahn, Esther and Chet Sagenkahn, the "voice" of Betty Anne Read supplied by her daughter Carol Read, the "voice" of Jeanne LaVoy supplied by her daughters Pat LaVoy Harris and Marty LaVoy Hahn and her daughter-in-law Jean LaVoy, and Mr. and Mrs. John Kalamarides, son and daughter-in-law of Dr. John Kalamarides.

I will be forever indebted to members of the SUNY Upstate Medical University staff, including: Dean Hugh Bonner, Eric and Diane Luft, Annette Sharkey, Bob Fluck, Deborah Rexine, Carol Plumley, Sharon Kitchie, and Renee Gearhart Levy. Your role brought our polio story full circle.

The following individuals added invaluable historical context to this work: Christine Scott of the March of Dimes, Joan Headley of Post-Polio Health International, Dudley Ericson, Carol Anthony, and David Mazur of Rotary International, Molly Elliott and Kellie Caimano of the *Syracuse Post Standard*, Kathy Hadley at the Onondaga County Medical Society, Sarah Kozma at the Onondaga County Historical Association, the Syracuse Office of Vital Statistics, the National Oceanic and Atmospheric Administration, the University of Pittsburgh, Sona Bari and Oliver Rosenbauer of the World Health Organization, Benoit Rungeard, Virginia Steckel, and Scott Eden of Sanofi Pasteur,

Dr. Alice Kendrick and Linda Schellinger of the Jamesville DeWitt Central School District, Maxine F. Kidder, RN, PNP, and Jann Hartman. Technical and editorial support was provided by David Hall, Mary Anne Sacco, Kimberly Petsch, and L. Edward Purcell.

To Michele Moore Ridge, my college friend and grad school roommate, thanks for the copy of the *Rotarian*. I'm sure Frankie knew that the article on Rotary's PolioPlus program would help me see the importance of telling our story, a story you always encouraged me to tell.

My special friends Mary Jane Reid Maidment, Cheryl LaFex-Maestri, Karen Gates Konefal, and Lenore Gripp Highet have provided me with continual feedback and much-needed encouragement. Only true friends would have found it "pleasurable" to read a new draft of this book every few weeks. I'm certain that I would have abandoned this project long ago if it had not been for your support. Thanks so much for your faith in me and for loving Frankie, though none of you ever knew him, as much as I do. God has blessed me with many special friends who always remember the anniversary of Frankie's death. Thank you, Mary Jane Reid Maidment, Karen Konefal, Pam Budny, Carol Read, and Pat LaVoy Harris.

To the staff at City Hospital in Syracuse, New York, and the private physicians and therapists who cared for us and comforted our parents, thank you— Love, Jan.

I hope that if the family of the little girl who died from bulbar polio in City Hospital on May 11, 1953, ever reads this book, they will contact me. I derive comfort from the thought that the two Syracuse children who died of polio in 1953 are united in Heaven. Likewise, I like to picture my friends, Patty and Cheryl Munson, united with the young Syracuse gang.

On January 10, 2007, my orthopedic surgeon, Dr. John Kalamarides, left his earthly home. By now, I imagine that he has received his heavenly orders and is busy assuming the role of special guardian to the numerous physicians around the world who care for the acute and chronic needs of polio patients.

I continue to cherish my special friendship with retired pediatrician and public health official, Dr. Alice (Jaros) Turek. In February 2007, my husband and I flew to Florida to meet her.

List of Illustrations

Foreword

by
Alice (Jaros) Turek, MD, MPH

When I completed my medical school and specialty training in the early 1950s, we were in the throes of the worst polio epidemics ever experienced in our country. While I was an intern and first-year pediatric resident in Pittsburgh, Dr. Jonas Salk and his University of Pittsburgh team worked tirelessly to develop the vaccine that would signal the beginning of the end of worldwide polio epidemics. In 1965, I earned a master's degree in public health, with a concentration in epidemiology, from Yale University. I was fortunate to be involved in President Johnson's Great Society initiatives. My last position was as Director of Health for Manchester, Connecticut. I retired in 1983 and moved with my husband, Victor Turek, to Florida.

Enjoying retirement, I was certain that my days as a physician were behind me. How surprised I was when I received a call in early March 2006 from a woman who introduced herself as Janice Flood Nichols. She explained that both she and her twin brother had suffered from polio in 1953 and that they had received care at City Hospital in Syracuse, New York. Sadly, her brother had died two days after admission. She indicated that she had decided to write a book about polio and that, as part of her research, she had requested a copy of her twin's death certificate. After noting that the certificate had been signed by Alice Jaros, MD, she immediately contacted Dr. Eric Luft, Curator of the Health Sciences Library at SUNY Upstate Medical University. Within minutes, we were speaking on the phone.

Although the number of yearly polio cases worldwide has been drastically reduced from 350,000 in 1988 to 1,997 cases in 2006, failure to contain and eradicate the deadly polio virus remains an important public health concern. We need look no further than the temporary vaccination boycott in parts of northern Nigeria in 2003–2004 to appreciate the necessity of continued immunization. By 2006, the disease had spread to twenty-four countries in Asia, Africa, and the Middle East that had been previously certified polio-free. Fortunately, diligent public health officials marshaled the resources to contain the spread, but we are still playing catch up. As of June 2006, ten of the twenty-four countries still reported new cases.[1]

Unvaccinated individuals in both endemic and polio-free countries remain susceptible to the disease. Anyone who carries the virus has the potential to spread the disease to *unprotected* individuals anywhere he travels. In spite of the fact that over 95 percent of people infected with the polio virus remain asymptomatic or develop only mild flu-like symptoms, nearly 3 to 4 percent develop what is referred to as "true polio." Unvaccinated individuals also run a small risk of contracting polio from a person who has recently received the oral polio vaccine.[2]

I pray that I will live to see the eradication of polio, a virus that has brought unimaginable suffering to countless patients and families. Polio vaccines have provided the necessary tools; personal will and political fortitude are required to accomplish the goal.

I am pleased to lend my voice to this story and welcome the opportunity, in coming pages, to discuss the history of polio, the progress that has been made in prevention strategies, and the global challenges that still remain.

True, Frankie's and Janice's story is only one story and a unique one at that. But, their story represents the deadly face of polio. Who would have thought that a death certificate, signed more than fifty years ago, would become the basis for a new adventure and a special friendship?

Preface

For those born before the early 1960s, your memories of polio may well include stories of friends, neighbors, or relatives who suffered from the world's greatest crippler. You may even be a survivor.

For those born later still, your memories may be limited to recollections of a polio vaccine that you received as a child via a sugar cube saturated with the serum or through droplets placed directly on your tongue.

For many children and adults living in Third World countries, polio remains an active killer and crippler. For many present-day polio survivors living in developed countries, polio has disrupted their lives once again in the form of a condition called post-polio syndrome.

Polio is the story of people just like Frankie, just like me. Frankie was a spunky six-year-old who loved playing baseball, collecting bees in jars, and climbing trees with his friends. Polio robbed him of his breath and his life in less than three days. Polio left his twin, fortunate to recover, determined to share this story. Sadly, polio may strike yet another child as you turn these pages—sadder still because a child can be protected, with vaccination, for as little as sixty cents. Polio can be eradicated. We're almost there.

It's up to you. It's up to me.

Introduction

The narrative in this book is factual and drawn from my personal experiences and from conversations with the real-life characters who lend their voices to this story. My own story is told from an adult perspective, looking back as best I can.

In the book, you will meet many people: Frankie (my twin), Dorothy and Frank (our parents), Dr. Alice Jaros Turek (a resident physician at City Hospital in Syracuse, New York, in 1953), Betty Wightman and Pat Coolican (my aunts), Bob Paltz and Bonne Paltz Hall (my cousins), Betty Anne Read, Jeanne LaVoy, Louise DeMartino and Esther and Chet Sagenkahn (our friends and neighbors in DeWitt, New York), Dave (my husband who speaks as my spouse as well as a physician who trained under my childhood orthopedic surgeon, Dr. John Kalamarides), Brett Sagenkahn, Alan DeMartino and Gary DeMartino (our childhood friends), and Mary Jane Reid Maidment (my college roommate and lifelong pal). I have taken the liberty of adding pertinent medical and historical context to each of their voices. They speak as witnesses to our family's story and to the greater story of polio, the disease.

Frankie's voice is based on both my own memories and on episodes recalled by my parents over the years. He speaks as a bright, spirited six-year-old—the age at which he died of polio. As a Heaven-dweller he becomes more articulate, a little wiser perhaps.

The life that I envision for Frankie in Heaven is derived from the religious beliefs I held as a child. For the first few years after Frankie died, much of my time was spent trying to imagine what the afterlife held in store for Frankie. My parents told me that God had called Frankie home for a very special reason. I surmised, therefore, that he must have a very important job in Heaven. I have chosen to introduce the voice of polio victim President Franklin Delano Roosevelt in the "Frankie" chapters although I knew nothing of FDR's plight at the time of Frankie's death. Who better to greet and guide my twin in Heaven than the world leader who mobilized our country to provide aid and comfort to those afflicted by the disease and find a cure or vaccine to combat the killer virus?

Today, I remain a woman blessed with the same simple faith that sustained me through the hardest of times. I am enriched by the mysterious bond that exists between twins and continue to believe that we share connections with those who have crossed over. I live in the hope that someday, no one will suffer from polio.

Our polio story began in DeWitt, New York (a suburb of Syracuse), in 1953.

PART ONE:
TOUGH TIMES

Janice—A Twin on a Mission

The worst polio epidemics in the United States took place in the 1950s. In the fall of 1953, polio struck our suburb and our grade school in particular with a vengeance: my twin brother died, two friends eventually died from complications, and I and several children in my class experienced mild to severe cases of the disease. Nineteen fifty-three was an odd polio year in Syracuse, New York, in that the virus struck both earlier and later than was typical. Nationwide, 35,592 polio cases were reported that year: 15,648 cases were classified as paralytic; 1450 deaths occurred across the country.[1]

As much as my twin's death, the death of friends, and my eventual recovery from polio continue to influence my life, until recently, I never considered writing about polio. I believed that my experience was simply a personal matter, certainly not a story that would interest anyone who didn't know me. More importantly, I thought that polio was a thing of the past—how wrong I was!

A few years ago, I learned that the World Health Organization (WHO), Rotary International (through its PolioPlus program), United Nations Children's Fund (UNICEF), the Centers for Disease Control (CDC), agencies of donor nations, governments affected by polio, development banks, private foundations, and pharmaceutical companies have spent the last two decades attempting to eradicate polio throughout the world. I was shocked to read that in 1988, when the Global Polio Eradication Initiative (GPEI) was launched, 350,000 people in 125 countries would be infected annually, in spite of the fact that the United States had been free from the "wild type" polio virus since 1979. The "wild type" refers to the polio virus that is found in nature. I spent the next several months combing books on polio, and my review of global polio eradication data continues.[2]

The relentless efforts of the Global Polio Eradication Initiative (the name given to the coalition mentioned above) have paid off. Vaccination has yielded remarkable results. In 1994, the Americas were certified polio-free, and the Western Pacific Region and the European Region were certified in 2000 and 2002 respectively. As of July 2005, over 70 percent of the world's children lived in polio-free countries. Since 1985, the worldwide incidence of polio has decreased by 99 percent. The Global Polio Eradication Initiative is the largest public health endeavor the world has ever witnessed. Yet, polio continues to kill, disfigure, and disable children and adults in several Third World countries. Polio, the disease, has been largely forgotten by the industrialized world. Polio, the virus, has not forgotten the members of our global family who remain unvaccinated.[3]

◆   ◆   ◆

What are my wishes for the book?

I want people to learn something about polio without being subjected to a dry, medical textbook. Polio is a complex disease that has always had plenty of tricks (and surprises) up its sleeve. Even for those who remember the days of polio epidemics and those of us who live with the late-term effects of the virus, there is much to learn. Moreover, not all of polio's mysteries have been unraveled.

From an historical standpoint, I want people to remember the horror of polio and to understand that the battle to find a vaccine for the crippler was fought long and hard. Without the support of a majority of American citizens giving of their time, talents, and treasures to the National Foundation for Infantile Paralysis (known today as the March of Dimes), polio epidemics could have well plagued the entire globe for several more years or decades. Likewise, foreign leaders, scientists, physicians, public health officials, and private citizens from around the world joined in the fight. Those born after the era of widespread epidemics should be aware of the efforts made by those who came before them.

I want parents to appreciate the importance of vaccinating their children against polio, especially at a time when some are questioning the value and safety of vaccination programs. For young parents, born after the age of terrifying yearly polio epidemics, it may be difficult to comprehend what the pre-polio vaccine era was like. I hope that you will consider our story when making your decisions. Current media reports, while informative, can also lead to confusion and misinformation. Therefore, please address your questions and concerns to your medical providers. The CDC and the American Academy of Pediatrics are excellent resources for parents. Additional online resource sites are included in a later chapter. We cannot afford complacency. Polio is an infectious disease without a known cure. Continued vaccine vigilance throughout the world is the only way to guarantee polio's eradication.

My goal for this book is that in addition to providing you with insight into a disease that once terrorized the entire planet, you will consider contributing to the organizations still involved in the global fight. Polio eradication will not only prevent unnecessary suffering but also will free valued resources that can then be used to tackle other diseases that continue to confound the medical community.

You might say I'm on a personal mission. I don't write as a renowned polio researcher, as an accomplished journalist, or as a well-known author. I can only speak as a child who learned to walk, run, and dance again, as a twin who mourned the death of her birth-partner long and hard, and as a rehabilitation counselor of the physically disabled.

◆   ◆   ◆

I must warn you that the next few pages are full of facts and figures, but they are important facts and figures. So, take your time—I would like you to be familiar with them before we begin the deeply personal story of the Flood family's bout with polio.

Our polio story, as I present it in coming chapters, can only be appreciated if we understand the nature and power of this devastating disease. Today, polio remains the world's greatest crippler. If I were a betting woman, I would wager that few individuals in the western world are aware that between ten to twenty million people continue to suffer from disabilities caused by the polio virus. Conditions range from slight limps and leg-length discrepancies to paralysis and dependency upon respiratory aids. Many long-term survivors have developed a condition called post-polio syndrome whose symptoms range from fatigue, muscle and joint pain, and weakness to debilitation necessitating a return to braces, wheelchairs, or ventilators. Their struggle could continue well into this century. Present-day acute patients will require long-term follow-up and care as well; their struggle has just begun.[4]

In later chapters, you'll learn about the history, cause, method of spread from person to person, symptoms, diagnosis, and treatment of polio through the "voice" of Dr. Alice (Jaros) Turek, a pediatric resident at City Hospital in 1953, when Frankie and I were patients at the facility. Dr. Turek will also discuss the classification of polio strains into virus Types I, II, and III as well as the development, differences, and historical controversies between the two types of polio vaccines (killed-virus or IPV vaccines and live-virus or OPV vaccines). For most of us, our knowledge of polio vaccines is limited to whether we (or our children) received the vaccine by shot, or drops, or serum-saturated sugar cubes. But additional explanation is necessary in order to provide you with a better understanding of the past, present, and future of polio eradication efforts.

Although the incidence of polio has been drastically reduced since the introduction of the polio vaccine some fifty years ago, setbacks continue to frustrate eradication efforts. Let's take a brief look at some of the challenges that remain and the strategies that have been developed to end the spread of the virus, once and for all. So much has been accomplished since the Global Eradication Initiative commenced in 1988 that it would be impossible to cover the entire history within these pages. Therefore, I've included an extensive bibliography that you may wish to consult. I've focused on significant current data in the hope that you will conclude, as I have, that polio eradication is within our reach. Unfortunately, the opportunities are not open-ended.

You may find it useful to return to this chapter periodically not only to compare future reports to the present situation but also to gain a better appreciation for the various factors that impact eradication efforts. Moreover, the facts and figures presented in the next few pages are far too numerous to digest in just one reading.

Present Status of Polio Eradication Efforts

As I mentioned earlier, there is no known cure for polio. Therefore, polio is a disease that can only be eradicated through prevention. In the case of the polio virus, vaccines have proven to be a highly effective eradication tool. Fortunately, recent technological advances have aided in the dissemination of effective vaccine supplies. This is especially critical since the polio vaccine is especially sensitive to temperature factors. Polio vaccine supplies are now shipped with vaccine vial monitors (VVMs) that are attached to each vial of serum. The monitors record temperature extremes during shipment; and vials that have been exposed to conditions affecting potency are discarded. This advancement is especially important when we consider the climates of areas in Africa and Asia where the virus persists. The technology has been available since 1996. In addition to vial monitors, "Vaccine Arrival Reports" are also used to insure vaccine quality. When each vaccine shipment is received, it is inspected to insure that all safety and potency requirements have been met. Before these technologies were introduced, it was more difficult to ascertain compromised vaccine supplies that could impede prevention efforts.[5]

Due to the Global Polio Eradication Initiative's ongoing massive immunization campaigns, polio remains endemic (constantly present but in low frequency) in only four countries: Nigeria, India, Pakistan, and Afghanistan—the smallest number of polio endemic countries in recorded history. But, for the past few years, there has been a disturbing increase in new wild-virus transmissions. For instance, while the July 2006 Rotary International PolioPlus Committee Statement indicated that Niger had been removed as an endemic country, it also reported that between early 2003 and mid-2006 the polio virus had spread to twenty-four countries previously declared polio-free. Fortunately, only ten of the twenty-four countries continued to report cases as of the mid-2006 report date. These countries include: Angola, Ethiopia, Indonesia, Nepal, Somalia, Yemen, Niger, Bangladesh, Democratic Republic of Congo, and Namibia. Sadly, an eleven-month vaccination boycott in Kano, Nigeria, triggered the recent outbreaks. The suspension had been initiated by local tribal leaders who, because of misinformation and distrust, believed that the polio vaccine was unsafe. [6]

While recent setbacks have occurred, the success of the global partnership is evidenced by statistics offered by the same 2006 Rotary report. Since 1988, it is estimated that the Global Eradication Initiative has prevented more than half a million cases of polio each year. The 2005 initiative inoculated over four hundred million children in forty-nine countries throughout the world using nearly 2.2 billion doses of oral polio vaccine. [7]

It would be easy to conclude that the successful history of the Global Polio Eradication Initiative coupled with the low number of new polio cases reported each year, is proof that polio no longer represents an international public health concern. But, the world cannot afford to be deceived by low yearly case count numbers. Thus, while GPEI indicates that only 1,997 new polio cases were reported in 2006, the sobering reality is that the coalition now predicts that if polio is not eradicated, more than ten million children could be paralyzed over the next thirty-plus years. As a polio survivor, this prediction sickens me. It is why I have written *Twin Voices.* [8]

Current Eradication Challenges and Responses

To tackle the lingering outbreaks that have plagued the world over the last few years, the Global Polio Eradication Initiative has launched a number of new aggressive vaccination campaigns. One such initiative was undertaken to prevent the reestablishment of polio in the Horn of Africa. The campaign was deemed especially critical following the announcement that a new case of polio had been confirmed in Mogadishu, Somalia, in 2005. In spite of intervention, as of early 2006, cases had been reported beyond Mogadishu but the total number of polio cases in the country had decreased. Prior to this outbreak, Somalia had been polio-free since 2002. The effort, made possible by a $25-million grant from the Bill & Melinda Gates Foundation and support from other donors, including the Humanitarian Department of the European Commission (ECHO), accomplished inoculation of over thirty-four million children across eight countries. [9]

In addition to massive immunization campaigns such as the one described above, monovalent vaccines (MOPV1, providing immunity to Type I polio, and MOPV3, providing immunity to Type III polio) have been developed to more effectively target endemic countries and geographic pockets where polio transmission continues. WHO recommends the use of monovalent vaccines in areas where continuing outbreaks are limited to only one virus Type (since these agents have proved more effective against the virus). The wild-virus Type II has been interrupted since 1999.[10]

The Bill & Melinda Gates Foundation provided financial support to aid in the development and use of MOPV1 in Egypt, where outbreaks had been linked to the Type I polio virus. Drug manufacturer, Sanofi Pasteur, produced millions of doses of MOPV1 vaccine for use in the Egyptian eradication effort. During its decade-long partnership to rid the continent of Africa of polio, Sanofi Pasteur has donated 120 million doses of polio vaccine. Due to the effectiveness of the monovalent vaccine, Egypt was declared polio-free in February 2006. In December 2005, the other monovalent vaccine, MOPV3, was introduced in selected districts in India to aid in outbreaks linked to the Type III polio virus. Pakistan, Angola, Eritrea, Ethiopia, Somalia, and Sudan have also benefited from the monovalent vaccines. MOPV1 and MOPV3 will continue to be used as needed. Since children in endemic and active polio transmission areas often suffer from poor nutrition and inadequate medical care, immunization programs in Africa and Asia routinely give children a Vitamin A capsule as well as the polio vaccine. Since Vitamin A deficiency can lead to blindness, increased risk of infection, and higher death rates from measles, diarrhea, and other diseases, it makes sense to provide this vitamin to prevent health complications. In addition to the enhanced effectiveness of the two monovalent vaccines and the benefits of offering children Vitamin A, rapid laboratory analysis has also proved an effective eradication tool by aiding in timely diagnosis, treatment, and vaccination intervention.[11]

An October 2006 Rotary International update indicates that all four polio endemic countries have reported new cases during the year. Because of travel between countries, individuals infected with the polio virus in India have spread the virus to unvaccinated residents in Nepal, Bangladesh, Namibia, and Angola. Sadly, a three-year-old girl from Kenya was diagnosed with the disease in October 2006. Kenya had been polio-free since 1984. Rotary responded with a sizable rapid-response grant to halt further spread of the virus.[12]

Following the boycott in regions of northern Nigeria, inoculation programs have resumed in most parts of Nigeria. Unfortunately, some areas of northern Nigeria remain responsible for over 80 percent of all 2006 worldwide reported polio cases. In five states in northern Nigeria, 40 percent of children have never been immunized in spite of numerous immunization programs. Final 2006 polio case totals in the four remaining endemic countries, as reported by the

Global Polio Eradication Initiative, include 1124 for Nigeria, 674 for India, 40 for Pakistan, and 31 for Afghanistan. One hundred twenty-eight additional cases were reported in non-endemic countries. To date, the 2007 global polio case count is encouraging, but instances of importation and spread, continued outbreaks, and extremely rare cases of circulating vaccine-derived cases attest to the need for continued vigilance.[13]

Fortunately, research demonstrates that the spread of polio in previously certified polio-free countries can be quickly stopped within six to twelve months with comprehensive immunization programs. For instance, a November 2006 UNICEF press release discussed a planned December 2006 inoculation of 5.5 million children under five years of age in the eighteen provinces of Angola to supplement the successful July and September 2006 campaigns in the country. The UNICEF report indicated that the late 2006 program would mobilize 24,950 vaccinators to guarantee its success. This comprehensive response was deemed necessary following a new circulation of the wild polio virus in June 2005. Until that outbreak, Angola had reported no polio cases since 2001. According to UNICEF, migratory patterns of Angola's residents coupled with the country's low routine vaccination rate (less than 60 percent) have hampered eradication efforts. Rotary International's July 2006 International PolioPlus Committee Statement reported another successful response—synchronized immunization programs initiated by the African Union (AU) had stopped recent outbreaks in most areas of western and central Africa. Over 25 countries were involved in the AU's recent endeavors. Due to such efforts, 2006 importation of the wild polio virus into previously polio-free countries dropped significantly from 2005 levels. However, re-infection in previously polio-free countries highlights the risk that polio continues to pose until wild-virus polio is eliminated in the remaining endemic countries.[14]

Sadly, political unrest in many parts of the world will continue to complicate eradication programs undertaken by such groups as UNICEF and Rotary International. Yet, the work of dedicated professionals and volunteers continues. Thus, for example, in 2005, the U.S. Agency for International Development immunized 97 percent of Iraqi children under five against polio. In the spring of 2006, an additional successful vaccination program was completed. Several thousand mobile vaccinators conducted the door-to-door effort with an additional campaign undertaken in November and December, in spite of dangerous conditions on the ground. The 2006 programs were launched by the Iraq Ministry of Health with organizational assistance provided by WHO and UNICEF. UNICEF also provided transportation and communication services as well as the necessary oral polio vaccine. The last recorded case of polio in Iraq was in 2000.[15]

World Health Organization Eradication Strategies

In addition to concern over wild-virus transmission in several Third World countries, some polio-free countries have reexamined the use of the Sabin live-virus polio vaccine.[16]

Between 1980 (one year after the United States had been declared polio-free from the wild-virus type) and 1996, there were six to eight Sabin vaccine-related paralytic polio cases reported in our country each year. In 1996, physicians began using a "mixed" vaccination program in which every child received two doses each of the Salk and Sabin vaccine. When polio cases persisted, the Centers for Disease Control mandated that the live-virus vaccine be discontinued. The United States returned to the killed-virus vaccine in 2000 (Dr. Turek will discuss this development in more detail in later chapters).[17]

Having missed earlier target dates, the World Health Organization has now set 2008 as its target year for global eradication. In an effort to achieve this goal, the organization is urging polio-free countries to begin phasing out the oral vaccine in favor of the killed-virus vaccine for routine immunization. This recommendation has been made, as discussed above, because polio could continue to be transmitted, in spite of eradication from the wild-virus type, via the live-virus vaccine. Incidence of vaccine-associated poliomyelitis has always been a concern, albeit such transmission is very rare. Some researchers indicate that one case of paralysis occurs in every 750,000 to one million administered live-virus vaccine doses; WHO estimates occurrence at one case per 2.5 million doses. As of October 2006, WHO indicated that only thirty nations have returned to the killed-virus vaccine; a list of these countries is included in Appendix F of this book. According to the Global Polio Eradication Initiative "FAQs on OPV Cessation," cessation can be divided into three stages: regional certification and OPV cessation preparatory phase, OPV cessation and verification phase, and post-OPV phase. OPV cessation cannot take place until wild poliovirus eradication is certified. An international stockpile of monovalent vaccines is being organized to manage any polio outbreaks, if they should occur after OPV cessation. Killed-virus vaccine and antiviral agents are also being considered for future responses. Authorities believe that there is a limited 3–5 year window, following worldwide oral polio vaccine cessation for routine immunization, in which circulating vaccine-derived polio could occur.[18]

In some Third World countries, inoculation efforts continue to be plagued by access problems, political agendas, financial constraints, and safety issues. The live-virus oral polio vaccine remains in use in these areas because mass inoculation clinics continue to be the only practical method available to offer immunity to millions of vulnerable children.

For a more thorough discussion of OPV cessation and eradication strategies, consult: http://polioeradication.org/content/fixed/opvcessation/opvc_QA.asp.

Eradication Target: 2008 and Beyond

Rotary International (the largest private sector contributor to the polio eradication effort) donated more than $500 million between 1988 and 2005. It is estimated that by the 2008 target date, Rotary's contributions will reach nearly $650 million. The efforts of Rotary volunteers around the world, acting as contributors, organizers, and vaccinators in mass inoculation clinics and National Immunization Days, can never be adequately recognized or rewarded. Countless Rotarians worldwide have joined the global fight, and hundreds of thousands of volunteers, at the local level, have assisted in immunization activities. Rotary's International PolioPlus Committee reports that 122 nations have benefited from its immunization and eradication program grants. The Bill & Melinda Gates Foundation is the second-largest private sector partner in the global eradication effort.[19]

Continued funding is imperative in order to reach the eradication target. A January 11, 2007 Global Polio Eradication Initiative Funding Update indicated that over $1.27 billion will be needed between 2007 and 2008 to accomplish goals (with a total funding gap estimated at nearly $575 million). Total needs for 2009 are estimated at just over $237 million, with a funding gap projected at $140 million.[20]

The United States leads the world in public sector donations, followed by Japan, the United Kingdom, the European Commission, Canada, the Netherlands, and Germany. A complete list of received and confirmed donor contributions, divided by public sector partners, development banks, and private sector partners in millions of dollars, can be found in Appendix K of this book.[21]

In 2004, UNICEF reported that its Supply Division procured vaccine for 40 percent of children in developing countries that year; the number of children dependent on UNICEF supplies increases each year. In 2004, over 2.1 billion doses of oral polio vaccine (OPV) were purchased by the organization in support of the global eradication initiative. The United Nations Children's Fund contracts with several pharmaceutical companies in an effort to control costs. According to UNICEF, the weighted average cost per dose of its procured polio vaccine in 2004 was between ten and twelve cents. A July 2006 Rotary International PolioPlus Committee Statement estimated current per vaccine costs at sixty cents for developing nations. As the largest global organization dedicated to helping children throughout the world, UNICEF utilizes a tiered pricing mechanism that has been well received by the pharmaceutical industry. Thus, manufacturers offer their lowest market price to the poorest countries that obtain their supplies through the UNICEF network.[22]

UNICEF reports that each year funding for procurement of polio vaccines for developing countries is acquired through more than four hundred funding mechanisms. In some instances, funding is supplied by only a few donors, but for the most part, funding is received from many sources. Obviously, the activities of UNICEF (and its donor partners) and the continued cooperation of the pharmaceutical companies that manufacture polio vaccine are critical to eradication efforts.[23]

The Advisory Committee for Polio Eradication (ACPE) acts as the technical oversight body for global polio eradication efforts. The group recommends a number of procedures to be followed in order to stop endemic and importation polio cases. Please consult Appendix I of this book for a listing of these specific recommendations. ACPE suggests that the Global Polio Eradication Initiative prepare an updated global strategic plan for 2007–2010 to provide a long term framework for eradication and post-eradication efforts. The World Health Organization will assume responsibility for vaccine stockpiles while UNICEF will assume responsibility for storage processes and procurement issues. It is imperative that all countries adhere to present and future OPV cessation guidelines.[24]

Public health officials caution that polio can be eradicated only if an adequate vaccine supply is guaranteed, funding needs continue to be met, political will is maintained, and immunization efforts receive public support. As long as one case of polio exists in the world, no country can risk the elimination of its vaccine programs. Moreover, a worldwide surveillance network would be required to certify several years of a polio-free globe before vaccination could cease. *The Last Child* (published by Bullfrog Films) is a moving documentary on eradication efforts.[25]

Many experts conclude that, unless eradication is accomplished within the near future, we could lose our last chance to realize a polio-free planet. Funding shortfalls currently threaten eradication efforts. Newly inaugurated World Health Organization Director-General, Margaret Chan, has promised to make polio eradication an important commitment, calling for candid discussions and a renewed course of action.[26]

◆   ◆   ◆

I couldn't believe what I was reading!

Maybe there was a reason to tell our story, but it needed to be a story different from the excellent scholarly works that were written in anticipation of the fiftieth anniversary of the Salk vaccine trial results. Perhaps my dual perspective, as both polio patient and surviving twin, might add to the collection of personal accounts that have been penned. Countless polio survivors have spent their lives coming to terms with the loss of physical function, but my struggle also demanded that I accept the physical loss of my twin.

My professional training, as a rehabilitation counselor, has reinforced the belief that, although the polio virus is responsible for a relatively brief acute infection, the spiritual, emotional, social, financial, vocational, and physical impact of the virus is lifelong. I had to ask, therefore, what approach told our story best—one telling the story as a "one person memoir" or one that allowed many individuals to explain their unique perspectives? Since polio does not occur in a vacuum, I decided to introduce you to many of the people who witnessed our struggle.

Writing this book has afforded me an opportunity to reconnect with childhood friends and their parents. We've all had a chance to chat about things that I don't think any of us had thought about in years. Who was in the 1954 Salk vaccine trial? Did you get the vaccine, the placebo, or were you one of the control subjects? Did your parents refuse to let you participate? Who still has their "Polio Pioneer" card and button?

None of the people you will meet in the coming pages are different from the innumerable patients, parents, siblings, extended families, friends, and medical personnel who struggled through the years of devastating polio epidemics in this country and abroad, or who continue to struggle with the horror of polio in several countries around the globe. I am writing in the hope that the world will soon put an end to all future stories, with similar casts of characters.

Janice—So, Here We Are

I'm about to introduce you to many people, not as well-crafted characters in a novel but as real men, women, and children who remain affected more than a half century later by the 1953 polio epidemic in DeWitt, New York. Frankie was a real little boy you can come to know only through the six years of memories I hold dear. My parents spoke little of their sorrow. But, you will gain a glimpse into their sadness, love, and wisdom. My father joined Frankie in 1981; Mom joined them both in 1994. You will meet several family members and friends. Each of them tells a slightly different tale, giving credibility to my basic premise that polio, like all serious diseases and injuries, affects many beyond the nuclear family. My voice is the story of a successfully rehabilitated child who learned to navigate the rocky road of grief. In contrast to the emotional recollections of my family and friends, the voices of my husband and Dr. Alice (Jaros) Turek offer medical information that has been interpreted for a lay audience. For ease of reference, the medical chapters are organized in modified outline form.

I tell our story, and the story of polio the disease, as it unfolded in real time. Thus, Frankie's life and death, my parents' struggles, the involvement of family and friends, progress made in the fight against polio, and my personal journey will be introduced, for the most part, in chronological order. The chapters are short and specific in content. They are designed to give you an opportunity to go back and easily reference topics that you found particularly interesting such as the Sabin vaccine, post-polio syndrome symptoms, twin-loss, the March of Dimes, or how polio is contracted. The book begins with Frankie telling you about his short life on Earth and concludes as he greets yet another young polio victim who has died.

Frankie—My Short Life on Earth

My name is Frank T. Flood Jr.—most people just call me Frankie. My twin sister and I were born on June 28, 1947, to Frank and Dorothy (Coolican) Flood.

We loved the stories our parents told us about how happy they were when we were born. Right after Mommy and Daddy got married, Daddy left to fight in World War II. He had to stay in Germany for a long time after the war ended, because it was his job to sign papers so that other soldiers could come home. Mommy and Daddy didn't see each other for almost three whole years, but they wrote lots of letters to each other. Mommy sent packages to Daddy, too. She said that there were many things that they couldn't eat or buy during the war because everyone had to make sure that the soldiers had enough food. It was even hard to get sugar and butter to make good cakes and cookies.

During the war, Mommy lived with our grandparents, James and Margaret Coolican, so that she wouldn't get too lonely. We always called our grandparents Bompa and Nona. Mommy always spelled our grandmother's nickname "Nona" even though the rest of the family spelled it "Nana." Our big cousin, Bonne, gave our grandparents those special names.

When the army finally let Daddy come back home, Mommy and Daddy moved into an apartment, and Daddy decided to finish law school at Syracuse University. I guess Daddy must have been very smart because he had started law school after he had studied only one year at Manhattan College. Daddy worked as a security guard at night so that he could study and save some money. Pretty soon, our parents learned that they were going to have a baby, and that's when things got very, very interesting.

Back then, they didn't have all the medical tests that you have today. So, our parents got ready for a little boy or girl to be born in late August. Daddy's parents bought a bassinette, diapers, and baby clothes. One week in late June, when Mommy went to the doctor, he told her that she had gained too much weight. She cried because she didn't want to do anything wrong. A few nights later, she went to the hospital and we were born. Jan was born at 5:45 PM, and I was born one minute later.

Mommy and Daddy were very surprised. They only had enough clothes and diapers for one baby. I bet the doctors were surprised too. Mommy said that we were just in a hurry to start having fun, and we didn't want to wait to be born until the end of the summer. We each weighed only a little over four pounds, so the doctors made us stay in the hospital for five weeks. Daddy said that that was a good idea because when we came home, we made Mommy awfully tired. Daddy even got Mommy a lady called a baby nurse to help out. I don't know why we made Mommy tired. Don't babies just sleep and eat? Daddy was so happy to have us that he often let Mommy sleep when we got hungry in the middle of the night. They both learned to hold us together and just tilt the bottles toward our mouths—that sounds very hard. They could have just fed Jan after they fed me.

At first, we shared a bassinette, and Mommy played tricks on Daddy. She would switch our blue and pink booties so that Daddy would think that I was Jan and she was me. I still laugh about that. The trick didn't last long because Daddy's parents bought another bassinette so that we would both have more room. Pretty soon, we didn't look anything alike, so Daddy could always pick me out. My eyes turned from blue to dark brown. When I finally stopped being bald, I had dark brown hair. Jan's eyes stayed blue, and she had golden blonde hair with loose curls that I loved to twirl around my fingers. It was also fun to pull her curls. I had a dimple in my chin just like Daddy's. I think it's called a cleft chin. Jan didn't have a dimpled chin, but she had a hairline called a widow's peak just like Daddy's. Later on—after we learned to talk—when grown-ups told Jan that she had beautiful blue eyes, she looked right at them and told them that she did not have blue eyes, she had brown eyes. I guess my twin wanted to look just like me.

Mommy and Daddy said that Jan always acted like a little mother to me. Whenever Mommy wheeled us down the sidewalk in our double stroller and grown-ups walked by, Jan pointed to me and said, "See, honey. See, honey." Mommy told Jan she didn't care if she was noticed—Jan just wanted everyone to notice me. I think boys who have twin sisters are very lucky, because they give us lots of extra attention. Jan and I never fought about anything, and I always got my way (now that I live in Heaven, I know that wasn't fair).

When we were two years old, we moved to a new home in DeWitt, New York. Soon after the move, Daddy decided to go into the construction business with his father and our Uncle Bob. Sometimes, when we got bigger, Daddy took us to the new homes he was building (our friend Brett often came along too). Daddy let us play in the dirt while he checked things out. He even let us ride on bulldozers. I couldn't wait to get big so that I could drive the bulldozers all by myself. Jan liked looking inside all the pretty houses, but Brett and I didn't care much about that. We just liked all the dump trucks and bulldozers.

Lots of parents in our neighborhood had children right after the war, so we always had loads of kids to play with. Brett Sagenkahn and Alan and Gary DeMartino were my best friends. Mommy decided that Jan should stop calling me "Honey," because the boys would start teasing me. So, she had a talk with Jan, and Jan started calling me Frankie right away. Sometimes, the boys in the neighborhood got mad because Jan always took my side. She told the boys that she had to take my side because I was always right—boy, did that make me proud. I was glad that there were more boys around than girls, because some of the girls didn't like to play baseball, but Jan liked to play with the boys because I think she wanted to be with me. She had a bunch of dolls, but I don't remember her making me play with them—that would have been really boring.

We didn't go to regular school until kindergarten. One of the mommies in the neighborhood, Mrs. Merel, was a teacher, and she had a fun play school that all the kids went to. She read lots of stories to us and had us practice doing different things. She had a big pile of books and magazines with pictures in them. We cut out the pictures with scissors. At first, that was hard, but after awhile I got very good using scissors. Jan used to like to wear dresses when she went to play school, and sometimes she went into Mommy's dresser and put some perfume on just like Mommy did every morning. I just wore my play clothes. I don't remember if Mrs. Merel made us take naps. Mommy made us take a nap every day. Jan and I didn't like naps, so sometimes we pretended that we were asleep and just stayed quiet so Mommy couldn't hear us. If you ask me, mommies make their kids take naps because they want to take naps themselves. I don't think that's fair.

We had a big back yard with lots of toys. We had swings, a slide, a little plastic swimming pool, and a real seesaw. One day, Jan and I twirled around so fast on the seesaw that I flew off the seat. Mommy came running outside, and she was crying. She said that she thought that I had hurt my head. Mommies can be kind of funny sometimes, because they're always afraid that their kids will get hurt. I only remember crying once, when I sat right on a bee that was on the top of the slide. Other than that one bee, I always liked bees. Mommy gave me a jar with holes poked in the top, and I tried to catch lots of bees and look at them flying around in the jar. If I really wanted to scare Jan, I'd tell her that I was going to open the jar and let all the bees out. I also liked catching lightning bugs—Jan wasn't afraid of them, because they didn't have stingers and they glowed in the dark.

One of my favorite things was to pick the pretty yellow flowers that grew on the lawn each spring. Mommy gave me a big hug and put the flowers in a glass vase. When they died, I'd just go out and pick some more. I wonder why God didn't have flowers growing in the grass all year long. Then, Mommy would have always had pretty flowers.

Way in the back, there was a huge hill that we slid down in the winter. We thought that a skating rink at the bottom of the hill would be a good idea, so Daddy, Mr. DeMartino, and Mr. Sagenkahn figured out how to make one with a long water hose that they hooked up to our house. Sledding and skating made Mommy scared, but Daddy told her not to worry. He said that kids had to be kids or something like that. Mommy made us hot cocoa when we came inside so we wouldn't feel cold anymore. I liked the marshmallow stuff she put on top the best.

Everybody rode their tricycles and wagons in the driveways. Before I died, I got a big bike with training wheels that Daddy took off when I got good at riding without falling and hurting myself. Grandma and Grandpa Flood gave us lots of toys and clothes. They even gave us play horses that we could ride in the house if we were very careful of the furniture. Jan's horse was on the front of a wagon that she sat in. My horse looked just like the Lone Ranger's horse. I was lucky to be the boy and get the cowboy kind of horse. Sometimes I'd forget that I was inside and run into a door or wall. It's a good thing Jan was never a tattletale.

Besides our regular dog pets, we had baby chickens for a few days. I got too excited and put one of the chickens in my pocket. Daddy said that could hurt the chicks. So, the next day he gave them to a farmer. At first I cried, but Daddy said that the chicks were lonely for their mommy and daddy. I didn't want the chickens to be sad and lonely, so I decided that it was OK. We didn't have cats, because Mommy told us that we didn't like cats. How could Mommy know that we didn't like cats if we never had any? We had chameleons that I put on the living room draperies so that Mommy wouldn't be able to find them. Jan and I laughed so hard when she searched and searched for them. One time we put them in an ashtray that Mommy had on a coffee table. Did you know that chameleons turn black when you put them on things that are maroon? I wonder why.

When I was four, I tripped in the front lawn and broke my arm. Dr. Kalamarides put a white cast on my arm, and Jan, Brett, Alan, Gary, and some of the other neighborhood kids drew funny pictures on it. A few of the older kids wrote their names on the cast, but most of us didn't know how to print yet. After a couple of days, I didn't like the cast anymore—it made my arm itch—so, I pushed a stick down inside the cast so I could scratch my itch. But, then I couldn't get the stick back out. I just kept adding more little sticks. When Dr. Kalamarides cut the cast off and saw all the sticks, he started to laugh.

Pretty soon, most of our friends were going to the hospital to get their tonsils out. Dr. Kopel said that if we had the operation we wouldn't get sore throats anymore. Jan and I thought that the operation sounded like a good idea, because Mommy wouldn't let us play outside when we had sore throats. Dr. Kopel also said that it would help get rid of what my big cousins, Bonne and Bobby, always called my snuffles. Daddy took us shopping before we went to the hospital, and I got Jan a beautiful bracelet that had maroon sparkly stones all around. I picked the maroon color because that was my most favorite color in the whole world. Jan gave me some new marbles. The nurses gave us lots of bananas and ice cream to eat while we were in the hospital. After we came home, Jan started bleeding from her throat. Mommy and Daddy had to take her back to see the doctor, and he did something to stop the bleeding. It made me really scared. I didn't like it when Jan got sick. I was scared that I'd start bleeding too. We had to be very quiet for a few days. Mommy said that Jan better not play with the brown-suede high heels that Mrs. Sagenkahn gave her until she was all better. Jan didn't like that because she loved to play dress-up.

Every year, Mommy took us shopping for birthday party outfits. Jan always wanted to go to two downtown lady stores, Flah's and The Addis Company, and spend lots of time looking at all the different dresses. Mommy got my clothes at a store called Wells & Coverly. If I was lucky, I didn't have to try them on. We also had to go to a shoe store called Park-Brannock's. That was kind of fun, because we had to stick our feet into a metal thing that a man put on the floor. He made us stand up, and then he pushed something up against our toes and something else on the side of one foot and told us how big our feet were getting, even though Jan's feet never seemed to get much bigger. I always got Buster Brown shoes that came in shoe boxes with pictures of Buster Brown and his dog Tige on the top. I really liked the boxes. For the last birthday I lived on Earth, Mommy bought me a short blue suit. I also got to pick out a new baseball bat. Jan got a red and white striped dress and a white bracelet with white beads all over it. We both wore our new birthday outfits when we had our picture taken, just before we started first grade.

If we were good when Mommy took us shopping (Jan was always good, but sometimes I wasn't), Mommy would take us to Schrafft's Restaurant, and Jan and I would have a peanut butter and jelly sandwich and a hot fudge sundae. Jan and I loved the little metal bowls that the sundaes came in. Mommy liked the sundaes too. Sometimes, Mommy bought a box of Schrafft's candy. When we got home, she hid the box in a secret spot in the attic off Mommy and Daddy's bedroom. We weren't allowed in the special attic.

Daddy didn't like to go with us when we got our birthday clothes, but he liked the parties. Mommy made big birthday cakes, and Daddy and our cousins, Bonne and Bobby, played games with all the kids. The kids could win prizes, but Daddy said that we shouldn't get any of the prizes because we got all the birthday presents. Our favorite games were pin-the-tail on the donkey and guessing how many pennies had been put in a big jar. The winner of the penny game got to keep all the pennies. One time, I asked Mommy to make pumpkin chiffon pie for our birthday party, but, Mommy said that pumpkin pie was only for Thanksgiving and Christmas. Mommy was the best cook in the whole world.

Daddy liked Fourth of July parties even better than birthday parties. He bought sparklers, and we got to hold them. Mommy was always afraid that we'd get burned, but Daddy made sure that we didn't. We sometimes took long car trips into Canada to buy some other things for the parties. Mommy said that Daddy shouldn't buy fireworks, but Daddy said that we should. One time, we even stayed overnight at a hotel in Niagara Falls. Jan and I loved looking at the falls, but it made us dizzy. We went on a big boat called the *Maid of the Mist* that went really close to the falls. We had to wear raincoats, and Jan and I were kind of scared.

I always got to decide what games we were going to play, like the ghost game "Spook" that Daddy played with us. Once, I tried to climb up on the fireplace mantle so that I could fly just like Superman. Mommy came in the room just as I was starting to stand on top of one of the fireplace chairs. Mommy said that I could get hurt, but I didn't see how—Superman never got hurt. Jan and I couldn't play outside for the rest of the day.

We used to love to sing *Somewhere over the Rainbow* together. We would sit on the bottom step of the staircase and sing and sing and hold hands the whole time. Sometimes we'd go into our playroom and sing along with our little red record player. Even today, I sometimes peek down from Heaven and see Jan with tears in her eyes when she hears that song. Jan thinks I'm saying hello every time she sees a rainbow. Sliding down the stairs holding hands was also lots of fun. Mommy didn't like us to do it, but sometimes we did it anyway when she was busy in the kitchen and couldn't hear or see us.

There were loads of storybooks and toys and records in our playroom. Mommy and Daddy read to us every single day. Sometimes, we made up our own stories. There were two stories that made Jan scared. One was called *Henny Penny.* Jan was afraid that the sky would really fall every time we heard the story. So, I would give her a kiss and tell her that that couldn't happen. Because I liked the story, Jan said that it was OK to have our babysitters read it to us, because I'd always take care of her. Jan was also afraid that if we played the *Peter and the Wolf* record, the wolf could come through the heating vents. Girls can be so silly. Didn't Jan know that wolves are way too big to climb through a little space? Our favorite babysitter was a boy named Ray McVey. I think he became a priest when he grew up.

Sometimes (but not very often), I was the one who was scared to do things. When Daddy taught us how to swim, I was what you would call tentative (that's one of the new big words I've learned in Heaven), but Jan just jumped in the water and never looked back. I'm glad that she was like that because it probably helped her when she got polio and had to learn to walk again.

Besides being stubborn and getting so mad sometimes that I held my breath and turned blue, I think I had only one other bad habit. It made Mommy very upset. I wanted to be just like Daddy, and even though Daddy never used some of the bad words that lots of daddies did, he did say God's name with a bad word after it. When I started talking the same way, Mommy had a big talk with me and told me that I could not use those words ever again. So, I tried to be very good, but every once in awhile, I slipped and said the words I wasn't supposed to say. When I goofed up, Mommy would take Daddy in another room and say something to him. I really don't know what mommies and daddies say to each other when the kids aren't around. Sometimes Jan and I tried to listen.

One time, we went for a family drive and some lady driver almost hit our car. I got so mad that I rolled down the car window and yelled out the bad words. Mommy told me that I should hold my temper. Then, she looked at Daddy and gave him the same look that she used when Jan and I knew we were in trouble. I don't ever remember Mommy raising her voice, but I sure remember that look.

Daddy did something different when Jan and I disobeyed. He had a special chair that he could sleep in, and when we did something naughty, we heard that chair make a noise as Daddy started to get up. We knew that Daddy was coming to talk to us, and Jan and I would start being good right away. By the way, do you know how mommies always know when you're doing something wrong, like when you try to sneak across the road? Mommy said that she had eyes in the back of her head. I looked lots of times, but I never saw any other eyes. One night, when we went to bed, I asked Jan if she ever saw Mommy's extra eyes. She never did either.

Daddy liked to take family car trips. We also took lots of Sunday drives after church. Mommy didn't like to drive the car on big roads, so Daddy did all the driving. I could hardly wait until I got big and could drive too. One of our best family vacations was a trip to the North Pole in the Adirondack Mountains. Jan still has a picture of Daddy holding our hands after we fed some of the baby animals, and there's another picture of us with Santa. I still can't believe that we got to see Santa Claus and all the elves working.

When we got back home, Jan and I decided that we were the luckiest kids in the whole world to get to see Santa. Every year, we tried to sneak downstairs on Christmas Eve and see if we could catch Santa leaving presents, but we never saw him. Seeing him at his house in the mountains was even better, because he wasn't in a hurry to deliver presents to all the families in the world. Even though Santa brought most of the toys, Daddy and Mommy took us Christmas shopping so that we could buy presents for each other. I always picked out beautiful necklaces and bracelets for Jan and she usually got me something for baseball. One of the best things about Christmas shopping was looking at the window displays at a store called Edwards. Daddy always stayed outside with us so we could watch the train set and look at all the decorations. Mommy used to go inside to get some more perfume—a lady behind a counter would take a big bottle and pour some of the smelly stuff right into Mommy's tiny bottle. One time, Jan cried because she wanted her own bottle of perfume. Mommy said that she couldn't have her own bottle until she was a teenager. I just couldn't figure out why Jan would cry over such a silly thing. Maybe girls make more sense when boys get older.

The only bad vacation I can remember was a trip to Lake Champlain. We took a big boat that was supposed to take us all around the lake, but I got so sick on the boat that the Captain pulled into a dock along the shore. The Captain must have been a daddy, because he got off the boat and went up to a house to see if the mommy who lived there had any ginger ale or crackers to make me feel better. I did start feeling better, but I decided right then and there that I wasn't going to go on any big boats ever again. Every summer before I died, Mommy and Daddy rented a camp on Skaneateles Lake. They didn't let us swim in pools, because they said we could get polio. I liked the boat we used on Skaneateles Lake a whole lot better than the one on Lake Champlain, because it was smaller. The lake wasn't very big (it was kind of long and skinny), and the waves weren't very high, so I never got sick.

◆   ◆   ◆

I was the keeper of all the money that our grandparents and aunts and uncles gave us. By the time we were five years old, we had two silver dollars and so much change that Daddy turned the change in for a new ten-dollar bill. I'll never understand why, but a few weeks before I got polio I gave Jan all the money. I'm glad that I decided to share. Would you believe that Jan still has the ten-dollar bill in her drawer? When Jan got a little older, Mommy and Daddy told her that I gave her the money because I wanted to make sure that she would never be poor. Jan believed that story, because I always told her that I would protect her from monsters and other scary stuff. Not having any money for food and toys would be very scary.

Kids can't remember things about being babies, but after I died, my parents told Jan all our baby stories over and over again so that she would have special memories. Jan also liked Mommy and Daddy to retell funny stories about all the stuff we did together when we got bigger. I think that was a good idea, because Jan really missed me. She didn't want to forget anything.

Frank—Our Life before Polio

I was the luckiest man on Earth. I had a beautiful wife, rambunctious twins, and a successful career. I fell in love with my wife when we were in the first grade at Cathedral School. We attended different high schools (Dodie went to Rosary and I went to Christian Brothers Academy, but Dodie remained the only girl for me). With her porcelain white skin, dark brown hair, ice blue eyes, and features and figure that could have landed her in the movies, she had plenty of suitors, but I had an important advantage over the other guys. You see, my father had many business ventures; among them were several gas stations. Some of the girls around town discovered that their money went a lot farther at one of the Flood gas stations—I'm not sure how many of the girls ever figured out what I was up to, but I was regularly undercharging attractive females. Fortunately, Dad was an understanding man who must have observed how I looked at Dodie every time she and her friends pulled in for gas. I suppose he reasoned that losing a little money was worth it if his son won the heart of the beautiful Dorothy June Coolican. At the time, I thought my special gas price for Dodie and her friends was a pretty clever way to get to see the girl of my dreams long before I ever got up the nerve to ask her out. Although I was persistent (and according to Dorothy quite handsome), I was no Don Juan. Special gas prices provided the edge I needed to slowly work my charm.

We were married in April 1943 and honeymooned in Niagara Falls. Within days, I left for active military duty and training at Fort Benning, Georgia. Before I shipped out after training, my beautiful bride and one of her friends (whose husband was stationed at the same army post) drove to Georgia for a visit. My father loaded up the car (the backseat as well as the trunk) with numerous cans of gasoline. Looking back, that could have had disastrous consequences. But, at the time, it was the only way that the girls could have made the trip. Gasoline was strictly rationed during the war years.

For the next few years, I dreamed of returning to my bride. I had started out in the infantry as a second lieutenant in Patton's Third Army, but a bout with a serious stomach illness while I was stationed in France and a reevaluation of my aptitudes and law school background led the army to determine that I was probably better suited as an MP and, eventually, as an officer in the Office of the Adjutant General. En route to Germany, a few of us stopped long enough in a Belgian town to purchase gifts for our girls back home. I chose a beige dresser scarf of linen and lace, placed it in my duffel, and presented it to Dodie when I reached the New York Central Train Station in Syracuse in 1946 (the scarf is in safekeeping in Janice's sideboard to this day). The Allied Forces celebrated V-E Day on May 8, 1945, but I remained in Europe to help process my fellow soldiers back to the States. The Adjutant General Corps coordinated the discharge of more than six million soldiers at a rate of a half million per month. Finally, after months of paperwork, I was sent home—and, it didn't get any better than that.[1]

Most soldiers returned to the States thinking that we had seen it all. Nothing could ever be as bad as war, and no one was more ready to get on with the business of living than Frank Flood. It had been difficult to interrupt my studies at Syracuse University but so many of the guys were in the same boat. We all hit the books and began the countdown to law school graduation. Dodie had worked at Niagara Hudson Power Corporation (today's Niagara Mohawk) during my time overseas. Fortunately, the combination of her continued salary, some extra cash that I earned as a night security guard, the GI bill, and an academic scholarship that resumed upon my return, allowed me to pursue the study of law.

The postwar years seemed to hold so much promise. It must be hard for the young of today to envision a world without DVDs, iPods, laptops, and cell phones. Would you believe that until I returned from France and Germany, I knew nothing of a thing called a television set? After enduring the Depression and a long, bloody war, the economic boom of the 1950s offered men of my era the hope of caring for our growing families in comfort. We all wanted to forget the carnage that we had seen in Europe and the Pacific—the slaughter that our loved ones prayed each day would never touch us. Dodie and I were anxious to start a family, and I wanted Dodie to settle in as a happy, suburban housewife. The war had stolen precious years from our young lives.

When the twins were born (two months early) while I was still in law school, I began to rethink my career options. Dorothy and I made plans to move to Dewitt, an eastern suburb of Syracuse. During the Depression, my family had moved from their home in the city to a white frame colonial on East Genesee Street. In semi-retirement, my parents had purchased a nearby two-family home to generate additional income. Syracuse was expanding in all directions following the return of the GIs. My father's construction company was busy building homes to accommodate the explosion of young couples and their children. Dewitt had an excellent school district, safe neighborhoods, and lots of kids for Frank and Kitty Kat (my nickname for Janice) to play with. The area was close to my parents and to several of my father's construction projects. Before I forget to mention it, I had one other nickname for Jan. Frankie never required as much sleep as my little girl did. If Jan stayed up past her bedtime, her sunny disposition would suddenly change. I therefore dubbed her alter ego, Witch Kat.

Soon after the move to DeWitt, I decided to forego the practice of law—at least for a while. At the time, our construction business provided my family with a far better income than could be made in the early years of law practice. I loved the freedom that the construction business offered. To this day, I hate sitting behind a desk.

God, how I loved our little ones—I had never seen babies with such tiny feet, toes, fingers, and hands. They were so small when they first came home from the hospital that they looked like they would break if I held them too tightly. It took them five weeks to make it to the magic five pounds required for hospital discharge—each one of them fit neatly into the palm of my hand. Within no time, they outgrew both their bassinettes and newborn attire.

When the twins were two years old, we packed our "gruesome twosome" into the backseat of our Olds sedan and headed for our new home in the suburbs. The parents in our neighborhood delighted in the young ones' antics. As professionals or business owners, we were proud that our livelihoods allowed our wives to stay home and take care of our growing families. We didn't talk of the War. I still don't.

A nearby vacant lot acted as a ready-made baseball diamond. The kids played hard during the day and then plopped into bed totally exhausted each night. Frankie and Jan both shared my passion for baseball. Even though Jan loved the beautiful dresses and party shoes that Dodie always bought for her, she was adept at keeping up with the boys (she had a pretty decent arm). I loved being a father, whether that meant tending to a cut finger, reading bedtime stories, or giving baths. Even changing diapers was OK with me. I had no sisters, and while we were growing up, my mother made certain that my brother Bob and I became familiar with household chores.

My specialty was playing games with the kids, any kind of game. We made up one called "Spook." Needless to say, I was chosen to be the silly, ghost-like figure. The kids always found me somewhere in the house or yard, making them the hero and heroine who continually saved the planet from the ghostly figure.

I made up funny word games (some real words, some nonsense words). Frankie let out a bellyache kind of laugh at the sound of long, new words. Jan liked the nonsense words even better than the real words. As an adult, she's still famous for making up words. Every once in awhile her husband, Dave, has to remind her, "Jan, I don't think that's a word."

Frankie and Jan enjoyed creating special concoctions just for me. They'd go out to the kitchen (you could always hear them giggling) and mix mustard and milk and pepper and God only knows what else and present the liquid to me in a special little glass. They both stood there, pretending that they had just created a delicious beverage. Their little eyes bulged out when I downed the awful mixture and pretended that it was wonderful. They turned to each other, bewildered, and said something to each other in that secret way of theirs while I'd run to another room in the house to get rid of the awful stuff.

On Friday or Saturday nights, we often put the kids into their pajamas and headed for the nearby drive-in on Erie Boulevard. After eating popcorn and a hot dog, Janice and Frankie were usually fast asleep within minutes of viewing the last cartoon. Once the kids had dozed off, Dodie and I settled in to a movie starring one of our Hollywood heroes.

Sunday afternoons usually found Dodie in the kitchen, preparing her luscious roast beef dinners. My parents, my maiden Aunt Rose, and my father's sister, Margie McCarthy, and her husband, Michael, were all frequent guests at our weekend table. Quite often, we invited our neighbors, the DeMartinos, to join our weekend feast. If Dodie didn't have a roast beef dinner planned, the DeMartinos sometimes invited the four of us to one of their famous spaghetti suppers. Louise's sauce was fantastic. On Sunday evenings, we usually continued the festivities with get-togethers at the home of Dodie's parents.

◆   ◆   ◆

Life in the early 1950s was pretty simple by today's standards. We had Korea and the Cold War to worry about (the army actually called me up during the Korean War but granted me a deferral because of my family responsibilities), but we lived our lives day to day with the belief that we could protect our families from just about anything. After all, we had quite literally dodged more than our fair share of bullets. The kids were glued to *Howdy Doody* and *The Lone Ranger,* while the adults tuned into *I Love Lucy.* Yet, in the back of our minds, there was always one "bullet" we continued to fear.

Polio epidemics had long ago become a yearly summer occurrence, but the epidemics were getting worse. The year before the kids got sick, the country endured the deadliest epidemic in United States history. We were all terrified because we didn't know how to protect our families. I don't know any parent who could pass a March of Dimes poster without experiencing a devastating rush of fear. In 1949, the National Foundation commissioned several famous artists to create educational posters about polio, and we adhered to their general public health warnings: avoid large gatherings, never let your children swim in public pools, never use public water fountains, avoid public bathrooms, wash your hands frequently, take your children to pediatricians and other medical specialists, and keep spotless homes. We even knew couples who were afraid to take their children to church on Sundays during the warm summer months.[2]

Although we'd eventually get our own place on Skaneateles Lake, we certainly weren't ready for that kind of investment when the kids were little. So, from the time the twins were three, Dodie and I rented a cottage on the lake each summer (I must admit that I will be forever partial to central New York's beautiful Finger Lakes Region). We wanted Frankie and Jan to be able to enjoy swimming and boating without fear of contracting polio from contaminated water in a city swimming pool. We were naïve enough to believe that our nice schools, nice churches, and nice neighborhoods—might, just might—keep our families safe.

I wish I could make the young parents of today understand what it was like before the polio vaccine was developed. Each summer, parents lived in absolute terror. Polio was unpredictable. The public health officials told us what to avoid, but often, that didn't make any difference. One year, a significant polio epidemic would strike a particular community; the next year, the area would experience only a few cases. No one could explain why. Polio struck whoever, wherever, whenever. Every year, the number of polio cases increased.

The summer of 1953 came and went, and as autumn turned the trees brilliant shades of crimson and gold, we all breathed a sigh of relief. After all, polio was a summer thing, not a fall or winter nightmare.

◆   ◆   ◆

I hear that our old house looks better than ever. The weeping willows that my Kitty Kat always loved have grown ever more majestic. The present owners have replaced some of the brick with cedar siding and ivy and have added a second floor rear deck off the master bedroom. I wonder if they know that we lost Frankie in the 1953 polio epidemic or if they realize that our dog, Mittz the First, is buried in the backyard. Is the playhouse still used by children or grandchildren? Janice loved that little house, complete with its kid-size bunk beds and pink floor tile.

Frankie—My Last Days on Earth

In September, we started first grade at Moses DeWitt School, but our class was moved to the basement of Holy Cross Church because there were too many first graders. Both Jan and I forgot about the church classroom until she talked to Brett while she was writing this book. Now, it's all coming back to me. The classroom was really dark and kind of spooky. Brett and I hated that old room. Our teacher, Mrs. MacDougall, was a very nice lady with dark hair. Before getting on the bus to come home each afternoon, Jan used to line us all up (Brett, Alan, and me) to make sure that we had our jackets on. When we got home, we changed our clothes and played outside until dinner. We had a nice round maple table with two chairs that Mommy placed in front of the TV set as a special treat when we were going to eat dinner before Daddy came home. In those days they didn't have homework in first grade so we got to play a little more before taking our baths, saying our prayers, and reading our bedtime stories. I don't think that little kids should have homework.

Jan and I shared a bedroom, but Mommy and Daddy told us that we were getting too old and that very soon we would have to have our own bedrooms. We didn't like the idea. Jan always made me feel safe, and I know I made her feel safe too. I still don't know why parents have to make so many rules.

All the kids in the neighborhood were getting ready for Halloween—it was such a fun night. There was only one family that turned all the lights off and pretended they weren't home. That was really mean. Some of the big boys used to sneak up, late at night, and put eggs and soap all over the windows of that house. I thought it might be fun to do that when I got bigger, but the idea kind of scared me. Everyone gave us chocolate candy bars, apples, or money. I liked candy the best, and every year I ate too many candy bars and got sick.

The boys liked to dress up as cowboys and pirates and monsters, but Jan and the other girls always wanted to dress up like princesses or something ugly like that. With our masks on, lots of parents didn't know who we were. I can't remember what costumes we had picked out for that last Halloween.

I started getting the sniffles at the beginning of Halloween week, so Mommy kept me home from school. Jan wanted to stay home too, but Daddy said that she couldn't miss school unless she was sick. Jan and I hoped that she would catch my cold so that we could play together. On Friday, I got real hot, and Mommy said that I had a fever. Then, all of a sudden, I had trouble breathing. I don't remember anything after that until I ended up here in Heaven two days later.

Dorothy—Our Polio Nightmare

We tried so hard to do everything right. In the end it didn't matter. Polio found us anyway.

How could your little boy be running and jumping one day and be dead less than a week later?

I kept Frankie home from school that week. He had the sniffles, and I was just trying to prevent a full-blown chest cold. But, on Friday afternoon, Frankie started having trouble breathing. It came on so suddenly. I can't remember if the poor little guy called out to me or whether I just went into the bedroom to check on him. I made a frantic call to our pediatrician, Dr. Kopel, who instructed us to rush Frankie to City Hospital—not to even wait for an ambulance. I was terrified, but I never imagined that by the end of the weekend we would be making funeral arrangements for our beautiful brown-eyed child—a little boy with lush, long eyelashes, who could be full of the dickens one minute and so sweet the next. All I could think of was pneumonia. The thought of polio never crossed my mind—after all, it was fall and getting colder. Neither Frank nor I had ever heard of anyone contracting polio so late in the year.

I don't remember who we called to stay with Janice. I can still see her little face peeking out one of the dining room windows watching our car drive away. What did she understand? Was she too young to be afraid? Did she sense how sick Frankie was?

I have absolutely no recollection of our drive to the hospital or of Frankie's condition during the ride. I'm thankful that I don't remember every detail of that horrible day, or of the days that followed. It's so hard for me to talk about. Over the years, I tried to bury as much as possible. I was always afraid that if I allowed myself to relive our nightmare, I'd collapse and never recover.

Once the hospital staff examined Frankie, they told us that he required a spinal tap. The doctors explained that Frankie had contracted either polio or spinal meningitis; they could not make a definitive diagnosis until they examined the spinal fluid. What a choice—could one of those diseases possibly be less serious than the other? Which disease should I pray that Frankie would have?

◆   ◆   ◆

In those early hours, when we still had hope, I found myself clinging to those precious, everyday memories that we all take for granted. I had to believe that everything would be OK, that Frankie would be home in a few days.

Frankie and Janice had never ceased to surprise us, beginning, of course, with their premature births. Oh, how frightened I was as a new mother! I wondered why God had chosen to place two tiny, little miracles in my care. I was overwhelmed, exhausted, and terrified. An experienced mother knows that she makes mistakes but comforts herself with the realization that she always tries her best. However, a young, first-time mom is determined to be perfect—any mistake or misstep is unacceptable. I couldn't believe how tired two five-pound babies could make me. I think I lost at least ten or fifteen pounds during those first few months. The gaunt look was not the "in" look in the 1950s, and I was gaunt.

Within a few months, Frankie and Jan's little personalities began to emerge. Having boy-girl fraternal twins provided a unique opportunity to observe some of the innate differences between the sexes. Little boys and little girls are different from day one. I passed the late hours of that first night in the hospital by recalling some of those wonderful differences.

One of my favorite pictures is of the twins when they were about six months old. Frankie has an all-boy pose with hands clasped; he looks like his tummy is full. He's busy trying to figure out what that object is that the man is holding in his hand, and he's not quite sure he likes what's going on. Jan's pose is all-girl. She's holding her party dress with her hand, and her eyes are open wide with excitement. She seems to be saying, "Hey, I like this photo op thing."

During the Christmas season of 1949, the *Syracuse Herald American* printed a photo of Janice and Frankie. Although they were only two years old at the time, Jan is busy in the picture being a little mother to her brother, who is more than pleased to have his sister feeding him. His eyes are closed as if he could not possibly be happier. Life doesn't get any better than when your twin is pampering you. This is how I liked to picture my little ones—healthy, happy, together.

Our children were as different as night and day, yet, there was a special bond between them. There really is something different about twins. There was no sibling rivalry, no normal kid squabbles. All I ever saw between them was love and delight. As far as Jan was concerned, Frankie could do no wrong. They had their own brand of communication when they were little ones with "words" and gestures that only they were privy to. Although they both enjoyed playing with their friends, they were just as content to be a twosome. Like all mothers, I knew it was trouble when I couldn't hear them playing. Jan was definitely the more outgoing of the two, but Frankie was the boss.

◆   ◆   ◆

I desperately wanted to take Frankie home from the hospital that October. Jan needed her soul mate.

The doctors placed Frankie in an iron lung, and believe it or not, I still told myself that the doctors would be able to help him. If Frank was less hopeful, he didn't let on. Early Saturday morning, the doctors confirmed that Frankie had bulbar polio—the most lethal form of the disease. How can your whole world change in less than a day? We had heard enough about polio over the years to know that children confined to iron lungs did not always make it. But, when it's your child in an iron lung, you hope, you pray, you know that your child will beat the odds.

In the 1950s, hospitalized polio patients who were unable to breathe on their own were confined to iron lungs. The iron lung was a terrifying-looking machine. My beautiful little boy's body was completely encased in a sealed metal tube with only his head protruding from the cylinder. The machine made a haunting, hissing sound as it did the work of Frankie's lungs. The nurses explained that by changing the air pressure in the cylinder, air was forced in and out of the lungs. The machine thus compensated for Frankie's paralyzed muscles.

We were allowed to visit Frankie periodically. We watched that iron lung do what normal human lungs are supposed to do and prayed that our little boy felt no fear or pain. His fever was so high that he just slept. We couldn't rouse him at all. He was so hot. I wanted to take Frankie in my arms but I couldn't. The iron lung held his body in its grip. His head rested on a metal board and pillow; the nurses used holes on each side of the machine to reach in and care for his needs. When we were allowed to see him we told him how much we loved him. I didn't want Frankie to sense my fear though I doubt if he even knew we were there. Frank talked to him about baseball and the ghost game that he loved to play with Janice. For the most part, our son remained alone with the doctors and nurses who worked desperately to save his life.

Parents are supposed to keep their children safe. There was no way that we could shield Frankie from the wrath of the disease. It could do to him whatever it chose to, and we were helpless to intervene, other than to make sure that he received the best medical care possible.

Over the years, I've been told by several physicians and nurses that there is a dimension, somewhere between this life and the next, where many critically ill patients are suspended in a state free from physical and emotional pain. I still pray that our inability to wake Frankie was an indication that he was truly in that peaceful place between Heaven and Earth. He was so sick. I have to believe that he never knew what hit him.

◆   ◆   ◆

The staff questioned us about our other children. Frank told them that we had recently learned that I was pregnant and that Frankie's twin sister was at home. The doctors indicated that there was a high probability that Janice would contract the virus as well. We were numb. A few days ago, we had beautiful twins getting ready for Halloween and another child on the way. Now, we were faced with the possibility that both of our children could die or be disabled for life. I was also worried about the baby I was carrying.

The doctors explained that a new treatment, gamma globulin injections, had been used successfully since 1951. Gamma globulin was a mixture of antibodies obtained from human blood. Sometimes the injections could prevent the disease, and if not, the injections might make the polio case less severe (Dr. Turek will discuss the use of gamma globulin in her chapter, Polio the Disease). It was worth a try. Immediately, we were on our way to pick up Janice and return her to the hospital for multiple shots in both legs and arms, as well as the standard shot in the buttock. They told us that the serum was expensive and in very short supply, but in spite of that, the doctors wanted to give Jan a much higher dose than was normally prescribed because of the severity of Frankie's case.

Frank and I were grateful that the doctors were willing to try anything to spare our daughter from her twin's fate! The shots were painful, but Jan didn't complain. The poor little thing was so weakened by the shots that the nurses had to put her in a wheelchair and push her back to our car. We took Janice back to Frank's mother's home, and we returned to the hospital to continue our vigil.

◆   ◆   ◆

By Sunday, November 1 (All Saints' Day in our faith), Frankie's condition had deteriorated. That evening, the doctors determined that an emergency *tracheostomy* was the only thing that might save Frankie's life. Because he couldn't swallow or cough on his own, the staff was having trouble keeping his airway clear of secretions. The surgeons explained that they wanted to create an artificial airway by cutting a hole in Frankie's trachea. Then, they'd insert a tube that would protrude from his neck. The tube would allow the nurses and doctors to remove the secretions more easily with a special suction device. Frank and I gave permission for the operation without even bothering to ask any questions. We would have agreed to anything.

As the doctors moved Frankie to the operating suite, they allowed Frank to accompany them. I don't know if Frank asked if he could embrace our little boy or if the staff sensed that father and son needed to be close. The doctors must have known that Frankie's situation was hopeless.

Frankie died, with his father's arms cradling him, before the surgery could be performed. My husband needed that opportunity to perform that last fatherly gesture. I can't remember who told me that Frankie had died or how the news was broken to me—it's best that I can't recall. What terrible words to play over and over again in my mind.

The doctors asked if we would allow an autopsy. We readily agreed, hoping that the medical community could learn something that would help other children. The next morning, I woke up with a crop of white hair that had mysteriously replaced a portion of my dark brown bangs. They say that shock can do that to a person. A few days later, I lost the baby I was carrying.

Frank was never able to talk of Frankie's death, nor was he ever able to cry. Can any parent ever get over watching his child take his last breath? The memory of our son's final moments haunted my husband until his own death. During Frank's last hospitalization in March, 1981, it became apparent that his medical condition was rapidly deteriorating. When my husband knew that he would soon be reunited with Frankie, he finally felt free to cry tears that had been held back for so long. I think he welcomed death. At last, he'd be with his only son. Frank had waited nearly thirty years to see that beautiful little face again.

◆　　　◆　　　◆

It took me many years to get beyond the guilt. I kept asking myself if I had only done something different, would Frankie have lived, would Janice have been spared? Polio didn't care if I kept an immaculate home and immaculate children. Polio just wanted more victims. It has always wanted more victims.

Alice (Jaros) Turek, MD, MPH—Polio the Disease

During World War II, I enlisted in the Women's Army Corps. I trained first as a cook and baker, but I eventually became a message decoder. Official communications were typically encoded to confuse anyone who might intercept the message. It was my job to replace code words with the correct information so that our superiors could read the intended message. I found the work interesting and rewarding, but my work was curtailed when I contracted a severe case of malaria that necessitated a long recuperation.

Following my discharge from the service, I completed my undergraduate work at Syracuse University. After a hard-fought battle with administrators, who felt that women did not belong in medicine, I entered medical school on the GI bill. I was one of five women in the Class of 1951 at SUNY Upstate College of Medicine at Syracuse. I completed my internship and first year of pediatric residency in Pittsburgh, Pennsylvania, but wishing to complete my studies in my hometown, I returned to Syracuse for my second year of specialty training.

I chose pediatrics as my specialty area because, for the most part, it's a happy field, where we can almost always make a difference. As a rule, we see little ones with colds and cuts and bruises who ultimately become teenagers and nag their parents to take them to a doctor who doesn't have cartoon characters on the wall. Occasionally, we care for children with serious illnesses, but for the most part, they recover. Yearly polio epidemics were one of the few things that could strike instant fear in the hearts of the most experienced pediatricians.

I spent my internship and first year of residency in the city where Jonas Salk was conducting his polio research. We were occasionally permitted to hear seminars conducted by Salk and his team. Although Dr. Karl Landsteiner and Dr. E. Popper had discovered that polio was caused by a virus in 1908, polio prevention remained elusive until the Salk vaccine was introduced in the mid 1950s. It is estimated that from 1915 to 1950 there were 368,000 cases of polio in the United States with 49,300 deaths. The period between 1951 and 1954 added an additional 160,333 cases with 7,514 deaths.[1]

In 1950 (the year before I graduated from medical school), City Hospital in Syracuse reported its highest number of polio cases, with 328 admissions and five deaths. At the time, all central New York patients suffering from communicable diseases were treated at this facility. Throughout the country, newspapers provided daily counts of reported polio cases in their circulation areas. The papers also frequently published human-interest stories, documenting the trials and triumphs of polio patients. Fearing that crowds were dangerous sources of infection, pregnant women, who seemed to be especially susceptible to the virus, remained house-bound as much as possible. Each spring and summer, parents prayed that the polio virus would spare their youngsters. It was a terrible time.[2]

◆   ◆   ◆

When, as a second year resident, I walked into City Hospital on the morning of November 1, 1953, I knew that I would be making rounds on several children desperately ill with polio. During rounds, I learned that the twin of one of our critically ill polio patients had come to the hospital on Halloween morning to receive gamma globulin injections. Because of the severity of her twin's case, my colleagues had opted to inject the child with multiple doses of the serum. Fortunately, she had not been admitted overnight. Her name was Janice Flood.

By 1953, there was hope for a vaccine, but gamma globulin was still the best protection we could offer. As mentioned in an earlier chapter, gamma globulin is a mixture of antibodies derived from human blood. For some time, physicians had observed that the serum was useful, if administered during the incubation phase, in such diseases as measles and viral hepatitis. Field trials conducted in Utah, Texas, and Iowa in 1951 and 1952, under the direction of Dr. William McDowell Hammon, indicated that gamma globulin produced a short-term immunity to the polio virus. In the summer of 1953, the National Foundation sponsored a mass gamma globulin inoculation program in which several thousand children received the intramuscular shot. It was believed that it was best to receive the inoculation during the summer, in the middle of polio season.[3]

The local medical society bulletin kept us abreast of current gamma globulin supplies. An article in the February 1953 *Bulletin of the Onondaga County Medical Society* predicted that two million more pints of blood would have to be collected in the United States during the first half of 1953 than had been collected in the previous six months in order to process an ample supply of the antibodies for the year's coming polio season. In the May 1953 issue of the *Bulletin*, Dr. A.C. Silverman discussed the problem of gamma globulin supplies in his "Report from Communicable Disease Bureau." In 1953, there would be enough gamma globulin to inject one million children under the age of fifteen—certainly an inadequate supply to service the potential needs of all of our country's children. Area physicians were urged to donate blood and encourage others to do so as well. Gamma globulin was a precious commodity.[4]

Ultimately, the passive (or short-term) immunity attributed to gamma globulin was proven to have inconsistent results. It was difficult to determine when the gamma globulin shot should be administered and to whom. Likewise, it became evident that effective use of the serum required that health officials be able to predict epidemics—surely an impossible task given what we knew of the virus' mercurial properties. A study sponsored by the National Foundation and the National Research Council proved disappointing when gamma globulin was given to family of polio patients. Virologist Thomas Rivers had argued against the study since it could be assumed that family members would all be infected, even if they remained asymptomatic. Within a few years, the use of gamma globulin had been abandoned. But, regardless of the disappointing conclusions of some studies, I cannot help but believe that the multiple gamma globulin injections given to a six-year-old child named Janice Flood, may have saved her life.[5]

We desperately needed a vaccine to prevent the disease. Our prayers would be answered none too soon. I still shudder when I recall the early days of my career. In spite of the revolutionary therapeutic methods (attributed to an Australian nurse named Sister Kenny) that had been embraced by the medical staff at City Hospital in the 1940s, I was well aware that many of my patients would endure a lifetime of disability. Every day, these young children pulled on my heartstrings. The Salk polio vaccine (licensed in 1955) and the Sabin polio vaccine (licensed between 1961 and 1963) gave us tools to prevent the disease, but it would be another sixteen years before the United States would be declared polio-free of the wild polio virus. More than fifty years after earning my medical degree, public health intervention remains the world's only means to prevent polio. And, as of 2007, we have not eradicated polio.

◆   ◆   ◆

Before continuing my role in this story, it may be as good a time as any to give you a concise medical primer on polio. I'll discuss what causes polio, how polio is spread from person to person, how it is diagnosed, and what is meant by the terms "abortive polio" and "true polio." I'll also include recovery and mortality statistics and provide information on the history and study of polio epidemics in our country as well as some interesting facts related to polio's idiosyncrasies. The development and evolution of polio vaccines as well as treatment of polio patients will be discussed in later chapters.

At first reading, you may find some of the medical information confusing. Polio is a mysterious, insidious disease that continues to confound the medical community. Moreover, it is a disease that is poorly understood by the lay community. Thus, my intention in this section is not only to educate you regarding the disease but also to dispel misconceptions that many people who lived through the epidemic years still hold. Younger generations often know nothing of the disease, other than that they received vaccination against polio when they were children. I always marvel when I mention polio in conversation and a young person responds with a blank stare.

Remember that by the time you have finished reading this chapter, another child in an African or Asian village may have been diagnosed with the crippler.

What Causes Polio

Polio is a highly infectious disease caused by a virus. A virus is a simple life form with two parts, a protein coat and DNA. Far too small to be seen by the naked eye without the aid of an electron microscope, a virus is about five thousand times smaller than the width of a human hair. In order to reproduce, the virus needs to attach itself to a host cell. When the virus gets near a susceptible cell, it attaches to the cell and injects its DNA into the cell. The viral DNA uses the cell to produce more viral DNA and eventually overtakes the cell, causing it to burst and die. The second part of the virus is its protein coat. The protein coat surrounds the DNA and also adheres to the vulnerable cell. Small variations in the protein coat react slightly differently with the human immune system. The three known polio virus Types (designated Types I, II, and III) are distinguished by the protein coat variations. Each type produces the disease poliomyelitis, with each type responsible for both the mild and severe forms of the disease. Statistically, Type I is the most likely to cause epidemics and paralysis of the limbs. Type II is usually a milder virus but possesses the capacity to paralyze or kill as well. The rarest polio virus, Type III, is the most likely to lead to bulbar polio.[6]

One of the cruelest characteristics of poliomyelitis is that it prefers children; historically, the disease was referred to as "infantile paralysis." Older children and adults are not always spared; sadly, incidence of paralytic polio increases with age.[7]

How Polio Spreads from Person to Person

Polio usually spreads from person to person via what physicians describe as the fecal-oral route. The virus is generally transmitted from person to person because of inadequate personal hygiene practices (such as inadequate hand washing). If, for example, an infected person does not wash his hands thoroughly after using bathroom facilities, some viral material will remain on his hands or other surfaces. The virus can then be transmitted to another person who directly touches the viral matter and inadvertently transfers the material to his mouth. Less frequently, the virus can be transmitted via the oral-oral route. Rare outbreaks can also occur from contact with contaminated food or water. The likelihood of viral transmission among susceptible children in the same household is nearly 100 percent, and greater than 90 percent among susceptible adults in a household with an infected person.[8]

The poliovirus is most contagious just before and after onset of the clinical illness. The virus remains in the throat for about one to two weeks and is excreted in the feces for several weeks. Patients can remain contagious as long as fecal excretion persists. Onset of first symptoms normally occurs within nine to twelve days after contact (with a range of five to thirty-five days). Onset of paralysis or profound weakness in paralytic poliomyelitis normally occurs within eleven to seventeen days after exposure (with a range of eight to thirty-six days). Some experts report slight variation in incubation and onset ranges.[9]

Diagnosis

Early symptoms of polio include fever, fatigue, headache, vomiting, stiff neck, and limb pain. Paralysis and death can occur within a very short period of time.[10]

When Frankie and Janice contracted the disease in the 1950s, diagnosis of poliomyelitis was confirmed by a spinal tap, which was used to differentiate polio from meningitis (a disease with many similar symptoms). The test was performed by inserting a three-inch needle into the spinal column and withdrawing spinal fluid. The spinal fluid was then analyzed by the pathology department. Today, diagnosis is made by obtaining viral culture of stool and throat swab specimens. Based on the circumstances, additional testing may be required to determine if the infection is of a wild or vaccine-induced type.[11]

"Abortive Polio"

In 95 percent of people, polio causes no symptoms. Some individuals experience a low-grade fever and sore throat or symptoms similar to the intestinal flu. With such cases, the disease does not progress beyond this malaise and recovery occurs within twenty-four to seventy-two hours. Physicians often call this minor illness "abortive polio."[12]

"True Polio"

In a very small percentage of people (less than 3 to 4 percent), the virus enters the bloodstream and specifically attacks motor neuron cells in the spinal cord, in the base of the brain, or in both areas. Practitioners often refer to these cases as "true polio." The virus most frequently attacks cells that control movement. When these cells die, a person can no longer move the muscles that were controlled by the cells. This loss of nerve function produces paralysis or profound weakness of muscles that had been normal. It is still not known why the virus favors motor neurons over other types of cells, though theories do exist. Patients do not lose sensation in the affected muscles.[13]

If the virus attacks only the muscles that control arm and leg movement, the patient suffers from paralysis or weakness in the limbs. If the virus attacks nerve cells (high up in the spinal cord near the brain) that control the chest muscles that expand and contract the lungs, the person is no longer able to breathe on his own. We refer to this type as bulbar polio because the area of the spinal cord (medulla) that has been affected resembles a bulb. In the acute stage of bulbar polio, unless a sufficient artificial means of breathing and eliminating secretions is established by iron lung (or modern respiratory equipment), *tracheostomy,*or both, the patient may die. Fortunately, some patients with bulbar polio are eventually able to breathe on their own. Thus, poliomyelitis can affect muscles that control movement in the extremities alone, affect muscles that control breathing, or in some cases cause complete paralysis from the neck down (bulbospinal polio). Before 1951, statistics kept by local and state public health officials did not break down case counts into paralytic and non-paralytic polio categories.[14]

Recovery Statistics

Contrary to popular belief, fewer than 25 percent of patients with paralytic polio suffer severe permanent disability. In fact, more than 50 percent recover with no residual paralysis. The greatest return of muscle function takes place within the first six to nine months after diagnosis, but improvement can continue for as long as two years. Death from polio occurs in 5 to 10 percent of cases but may increase significantly in individuals who contract the bulbar form of the disease. Young adults (between twenty and forty years) are the group most likely to die. I always reminded myself of these general recovery statistics when making medical rounds each morning, yet it was sometimes impossible to console a frantic parent or a fearful patient.[15]

Treatment

The surgical and non-surgical treatment of polio patients will be discussed in future chapters, but I would like to briefly mention advancements in the care of bulbar patients.

If there is any machine that individuals old enough to remember epidemics associate with polio, it is the iron lung. As you have already read, neither the iron lung nor the general status of medicine in the 1950s could save six-year-old Frankie Flood. At the same time, without the iron lung, many patients would not be alive today.

Thankfully, medical advances, such as chest respirators, have greatly improved the quality of life in recent decades for patients who remain dependent upon respiratory aids. But, the iron lung was the only treatment available for patients unable to breath on their own during the epidemic years. As the incidence of polio decreased and new technologies emerged, the need for iron lungs decreased. The iron lung was only in limited production by its manufacturer, the Emerson Company, during the 1960s. No new iron lungs have been made since 1970.[16]

Nonetheless, a small number of polio patients continued to use iron lungs as late as 2004. The March of Dimes honored its commitment to these patients, providing financial assistance for the maintenance of the equipment. In 2003, the maintenance company advised the March of Dimes that it could no longer provide replacement parts and repair services. Since then, the March of Dimes (in partnership with Post-Polio Health International) has provided support to patients reluctant to make a transition to newer equipment.[17]

Since a meaningful discussion of patient care needs and equipment maintenance for patients using chest respirators, the earlier iron lungs, and rocking beds (used during the epidemic years to wean some patients off iron lungs) is beyond the scope of this book, readers should consult John R. Paul's, *A History of Poliomyelitis*, for an excellent historical review. For current information regarding respiratory patient care needs, consult Post-Polio Health International (PHI) and its affiliate, International Ventilator Users Network (see Appendix B for contact information).

Breath: Life in the Rhythm of an Iron Lung by Martha Mason is an excellent story of one woman's experience within an iron lung. PHI also offers an extensive bibliography.

History of Polio Epidemics

Although polio has plagued mankind since ancient times, the disease was, for the most part, a relatively minor illness until the twentieth century. Probably most people contracted the virus within the first few years of life, but in such a mild form that the symptoms were limited to a flu-like affliction. The earliest recorded studies of serious polio outbreaks were in the mid 1800s. In Worksop, England, a small epidemic was reported in 1835; a similar event had been recorded around the same time on the island of St. Helena. The first recorded outbreak in the United States occurred in Louisiana in 1841. In the 1860s, more significant outbreaks were reported in Scandinavia; it was at this point, that some physicians began to question whether the disease was contagious in nature. In 1894, an epidemic broke out in Vermont; 132 cases were recorded. Fortunately, the doctor made note of pertinent medical factors (50 patients were paralyzed, 18 people died, 84 patients were under six years of age, and boys were more susceptible than girls).[18]

From 1916 onward, the United States suffered yearly epidemics; one of the worst in history began in New York City in 1916. Twenty-seven thousand three sixty-three cases were ultimately reported and 6,000 people died. The average age for polio victims in the 1916 epidemic ranged from infancy to age four.[19]

The June to October 1916 epidemic was studied in great detail. Every pediatric resident of my era was familiar with the outbreak and its "mysterious" characteristics. The earliest cases had been identified in a poor, immigrant area of Brooklyn, New York, called "Pigtown." In an effort to prevent spread, "Pigtown" was sanitized—streets were cleaned, trash was removed, stray animals were removed and killed. Selective quarantines were employed. By the end of June, patients were ordered to remain in isolation for eight weeks, and all those unable to comply with strict quarantine regulations were hospitalized. So desperate were parents that they were willing to try almost anything to prevent or cure the disease. Many well-off families sent their children out of the metropolitan area to escape the growing epidemic.[20]

By July, the outbreak had worsened, prompting officials to forbid children sixteen years old and younger to leave New York City unless parents presented a certificate attesting that their home was free from polio. The ban was in effect from July 18 until October 3. A national conference was held in Washington DC in August to review the ban, which it upheld. Many surrounding communities reacted by posting armed police at their boundaries to turn away nonresidents.[21]

Yet, the epidemic continued to spread. By August, cases were reported in New Jersey, Connecticut, Pennsylvania, and upstate New York. By the end of October, twenty-six states had reported cases. Although the country was primarily focused on the war in Europe, health officials took note of some disturbing patterns. Why hadn't quarantine and sanitation methods worked? Why had affluent urban communities been hit with equal or greater vengeance? Why had rural areas been hit? Polio was not a disease that could be conveniently attributed to the filth that permeated the slums in 1916 or to the cooks and housekeepers that traveled each day to the homes of their well-off employers. These same observations had been made after the 1894 epidemic. [22]

As the twentieth century progressed, the general public and the medical community braced themselves each year for what they called "polio weather"— hot, sticky summer and early autumn days that in the era before widespread air-conditioning made everyone want to take a good dip in a pool. Drastic measures, including the spraying of areas with toxic chemicals such as DDT, were sometimes employed. In the case of serious outbreaks, communities attempted targeted quarantines. Businesses, schools, and churches were sometimes ordered closed as well. Yet, nothing seemed to work. Polio owned the summer. [23]

Both the average age of patients and the incidence of polio cases per hundred thousand people increased dramatically in the United States as the decades went on. By 1940, the average age of victims was between five and nine years of age. In the 1920s and 1930s, the incidence of polio cases was only four per hundred thousand people, but by 1950, the number of cases had increased to twenty-five per hundred thousand. The 1952 epidemic, the worst in U.S. history, reported 57,879 cases with 3,145 deaths. An estimated six hundred thousand cases were reported worldwide in 1952. If you reexamine the statistics that I quoted earlier in this chapter, you will correctly conclude that an alarming increase in the number of reported polio cases occurred in the United States between 1951 and 1954. 368,000 cases had been reported in the years between 1915 and 1950. Yet, nearly half that total had been reported in the short span between 1951 and 1954. The medical community was both puzzled and alarmed. [24]

A Syracuse *City Hospital Report* for 1952 reported that, according to the National Polio Foundation, fourteen hospitals throughout the United States cared for 80 percent of the patients during our country's epidemics, and that City Hospital in Syracuse was one of the fourteen. Now, I knew why I was always so tired. [25]

Polio's Idiosyncrasies—Some Answers, More Questions

Twentieth-century epidemiologic data eventually determined that polio infection occurred throughout the year in areas where sanitation and hygiene were poor—but, as previously mentioned, as a mild, flu-like illness. Ironically, indoor plumbing, improvement in sanitary conditions (especially in urban areas serviced by modern sewer systems), and a move toward clean, single-family dwellings, allowed the once innocuous disease to become an efficient killer and crippler. We had become victims of our own prosperity and innovation. The explanation for this idiosyncrasy lies in our better understanding of the human immune system. Doctors learned that children less frequently exposed to infectious disease (because of their protected, sanitary environments), were made more vulnerable to the ravages of polio—their young immune systems were simply overwhelmed. Affluent older children and adults became susceptible to the virus, having had little or no early exposure to the virus. While it may seem counterintuitive, we had learned that some exposure to infectious agents helped to fine-tune the immune system.[26]

The United States was hit harder than any other western nation, but no country was spared. Seytre and Shaffer, in their *The Death of a Disease,* report that Canada's per capita rate of infection actually exceeded U.S. rates during its country's worst epidemic years. For instance, the Canadian rate for its worst epidemic year, 1953, was sixty per hundred thousand population, as opposed to the thirty-seven per hundred thousand rate reported in the 1952 United States' epidemic. According to a 1952 report from A. Clement Silverman, Director of Communicable Diseases in Onondaga County, New York, polio outbreaks were described as epidemic when the number of confirmed cases exceeded one case per five thousand people.[27]

Due to the capricious nature of polio, a country's total number of cases could reach epidemic proportions, but it did not necessarily follow that all regions, within the country, experienced a high number of cases. The reverse was also true.

We learned that children who had their tonsils removed were made more susceptible to polio because tonsillitis often required treatments that prevented propagation of the virus in the throat. This is an especially provocative fact when one considers that during the 1950s, surgeons routinely removed tonsils in children who had suffered only a few bouts of tonsillitis. Just ask older baby-boomers if they have their tonsils; many will respond that their tonsils were removed before they entered kindergarten.[28]

While several questions had been answered, polio continued to baffle scientists. For some unknown reason, boys were more susceptible to paralysis than girls. Pregnant women were also especially vulnerable. Equally puzzling was the variability in incidence and area from year to year. For instance, while 1952 was the worst polio epidemic year in the United States, 1950 yielded many more polio cases in Syracuse than did 1952. What was going on in Syracuse in 1950 that was not going on in 1952? Questions like this will probably never be resolved.[29]

The polio outbreak that struck DeWitt, New York, in 1953 fit the above profile except that, normally, polio is a late spring and summer to early autumn event. The 1953 polio season in Onondaga County began earlier and persisted into the late fall. During the first three months of 1953, City Hospital treated three polio patients, and a six-year-old girl succumbed in May. According to data compiled by the U.S. National Oceanic and Atmospheric Administration, October 1953 was quite cool for the most part, and 6.1 inches of snow fell on November 7—not exactly the sultry weather we had come to associate with polio.[30]

◆   ◆   ◆

Late in the evening on November 1, 1953, I was summoned to the operating suite at City Hospital. A little boy I had cared for struggled for his life.

At 10:25 PM, I signed New York State Certificate of Death Registration Number 2348. I certified that Frank T. Flood, Jr. (age 6 years, 4 months, and 3 days) succumbed to bulbar poliomyelitis after 61 hours. I stipulated that I had attended him on 11/1/1953.[31]

Frankie—Heaven

Sometimes I hear people say that they flew through a long, bright tunnel on their way to Heaven. Many kids even talk about a beautiful golden light that greeted them. I don't remember anything like that, but it sounds like it would have been fun, kind of like going on a really fast roller coaster that makes your head spin and your eyes cross. I just remember being sick with a cold and fever and having trouble breathing—then, all of a sudden, lots of people were saying hello to me. I saw Grandpa Flood and our neighbor Christy. Christy died from a brain tumor when Jan and I were four years old.

I saw a little girl who smiled at me. I liked her right away because she wasn't a grown-up. I told her that I didn't know where I was and that I wanted to go home to be with Mommy, Daddy, Jan, and my friends Brett, Alan, and Gary. I didn't want to miss "Trick or Treat" time on Halloween night. She smiled and told me that I was in Heaven and that Halloween was already over. She said God had called me home for a very special reason. I didn't know what that meant. I just wanted some Halloween candy.

When Grandpa and Christy died, Mommy and Daddy had explained that when people die they go to Heaven to be with God. If I was in Heaven, did that mean that I was dead too? How did I get dead?

All the people I met that first day were very nice to me. Daddy had told me that everyone in Heaven would be nice because you have to be very good to get here. I bet giving Jan all our money just before I died helped me get into Heaven.

I met a big, smiling man who looked a lot like my Grandfather Flood but even older. He told me that his name was Franklin Delano Roosevelt. He had been the President of the United States and had had polio just like me. Until then, I didn't know that that's what made me die. I didn't know too much about polio. Mommy and Daddy always said we couldn't swim in pools because we could get polio. They made us wash our hands about a hundred times a day. But, I got polio anyway. Mr. Roosevelt said that he had started the National Foundation for Infantile Paralysis—what a long, funny name. He said that he wanted polio to stop making people sick. He also told me that all the people who greeted me, except for Grandpa and Christy, had had polio too.

Mr. Roosevelt explained that my first official job in Heaven would be to greet children who died of polio. I still have the same job. He said that the girl who met me a little earlier would show me what to do. She was six years old, just like me, and she died of polio in the same hospital I did on May 11, 1953. God thought that it might make me feel better if I stayed with someone from Syracuse, because we could talk about lots of things like our schools and baseball. I asked her if her daddy ever took her to the diner on Erie Boulevard that Daddy used to take Jan and me to. I sure could go for some of their special pancakes right now. Daddy used to order silver dollar pancakes for us. Isn't that a silly name for pancakes? They weren't big like Mommy's pancakes—they looked about the same size as the silver dollars that I had given to Jan before I died.[1]

I wonder if God whispers things in little kids' ears when He knows that they're going to die. Do you think he told me to give Jan the money, because I never liked sharing as much as Jan did? One time, she got this idea to give all of our old toys to the poor children. We got them together, and Daddy and Mommy drove us to some place to give them away. I cried all the way home because I wanted my toys back. I was pretty mad at the poor children. I think it was one of those times when I held my breath and turned blue. Mommy didn't like it when I did that. Jan used to laugh because she thought I was funny.

The Syracuse girl took me by the hand, and said that another boy was on his way to Heaven. I didn't know how she knew that. I hadn't seen any TV sets with the news on, and I had not heard any phones ring. She took me to the Greeting Area and told me what to do.

Well … now you know what it was like when I first got to Heaven.

Pretty soon, I started to learn lots of good things about Heaven. When I was still on Earth, I had trouble saying the letter "R." So, when I said my name it sounded more like "Fwankie" than Frankie. Now, I can say Frankie really well. All of my Heaven-friends can say their "R's" better too. Mommy was so surprised when she came to Heaven and heard me talk.

Up here, I don't have to practice reading, coloring, or doing cursive writing. Just before I died, Jan and I started trying to figure out how to do cursive writing even though our teacher, Mrs. MacDougall, only had us print. During that thing grown-ups call a wake, I looked down from Heaven and saw Jan trying to write her name in cursive in a special book that people signed when they came to our house. She was having lots of trouble making all the curly lines, but I guess she wanted to write like all the big people and our cousins Bonne and Bobby.

In Heaven, I just know how to do stuff—even stay inside the lines when I color. Kids don't have to go to school here either. Everybody is very smart. We all know things that we never learned in school. The library in Heaven is lots bigger than the one at Moses DeWitt. I can read a whole big book in about one second. I can even read books in French and Spanish and in languages I never heard of until I got to Heaven. There are kids from all over the world here. That's one of the things I like best about Heaven. When my friends talk to me in their language, I can understand what they're saying. Isn't that great? I think God spent lots of time making Heaven a nice place to live.

Even though we're smarter, God doesn't make us grow up if we don't want to. Personally, I like staying six. I don't think I'd be as good a greeter to little kids who died from polio if I was old. When I first came to Heaven, I bet I greeted over fifty boys and girls every single day. That might not seem like many to you, but there were thousands of kids and grown-ups who had my same job.

It was hard for me to see how sad Mommy, Daddy, Jan, and all my family and friends were after I died. God told me that I had to give my Earth family time to understand. At first, Jan worried that I might not be happy in Heaven. I kept whispering that I was OK. It took awhile for Jan to decide that Heaven was a great place for me to live. I hated to see her cry. I'm so glad that God lets us watch over our Earth families. I don't know why so many people have trouble believing that. I'm glad that Jan believes—I guess it's easier to believe when you're a twin.

Lots of polio greeters have asked for another job because they haven't been that busy lately, but I've been greeting more kids the last few years. That makes me very sad. Sometimes I talk to President Roosevelt about what's going on down on Earth. Maybe, someday, I'll ask God if I can have another job and get taller and have a deep voice just like Daddy's. But, I won't quit my job until polio stops making people sick.

Frank—How to Tell Janice?

I have no idea how Dodie and I made it home from the hospital that Sunday night.

The next morning, we had to make funeral arrangements for Frankie and tell Janice that she'd never see her twin brother again. Dodie and I had decided that, if at all possible, we wanted the wake in our home. We contacted Schumacher-Whelan Funeral Home and asked for their help in discussing the request with the Onondaga County Health Department. We knew that the Whelans would do everything possible to help us. The Coolicans and Whelans were related by both blood and profession—the Whelans owned an undertaking business and the Coolicans were in the hearse business. Fortunately, our request was granted; I don't know what we would have done if the Health Department had refused. We had to have Frankie home for a few more days. Dodie and I just couldn't let go, not yet.

After leaving the funeral parlor, we drove to Dodie's parents' home and then on to tell Jan that Frankie had died. How do you tell your child that her twin is dead? We were so afraid that she would never be able to get over Frankie's death. We didn't know how to help her. We didn't know if any of us would ever learn to cope.

Jan had been staying at my mother's home since Frankie was admitted to the hospital. We decided to bring her a little red mesh bag full of chocolate money covered in gold foil and braced ourselves for the meeting. I don't know whatever possessed us to bring Jan candy. She met us at the vestibule and asked how Frankie was. We looked at her—and lied. We couldn't bear to tell her. But remarkably, Jan returned our gaze and said the words that we lacked the courage to utter, "No, Frankie is not OK. Frankie is dead."

How did she know? Did she see the devastation in our eyes? Or, was the twin bond so strong that she could sense the loss of her beloved brother?

Since that day, Janice has continued to possess a sixth sense or what some refer to as second sight. Through dreams and a heightened sensitivity, she is often aware that someone will become ill or die long before the episode or event occurs. When Jan was a teenager, a relative suggested that we consider having her studied at a major university that was conducting paranormal research. We broached the subject with Jan who decided against the idea, simply stating, "Why would I want to do that? It's just Frankie's gift to me. He doesn't want me to ever be shocked by sadness." Who am I to question the bond between twins?

◆   ◆   ◆

Before Frankie died, I didn't think anything could be worse than war. But, the horror of war was nothing compared to the emptiness that I felt when we lost Frankie. I spent the rest of my life trying to push the memory of Frankie's last moments from my mind. You never really can, you know. Men of my generation didn't cry. Maybe I was afraid that if I ever started to cry, I'd never stop. I wanted to be strong for Dodie and Janice. I wanted to make it better for them. But you can't make it go away, can you? It only gets a little easier to accept. Some days are easier than others.

Dorothy—Decisions

Today, bookstores contain volumes on how to deal with death, and there are even texts dedicated exclusively to explaining death to children. In 1953, we had no such guides, only our parental instincts to go on. Both Frankie and Janice were precocious children, and as different as their personalities were, they were bonded in such a special way—a twin way. So, when Janice insisted that she be included in every aspect of the wake and funeral, Frank and I knew that we had to honor her wishes. In many respects, she was old beyond her years, having experienced the death of her paternal grandfather, a young neighbor, and her first dog by age four. We also knew that she was far too stubborn to be denied this time with her brother.

At the time Frankie died, our society was moving away from the ritual of home wakes. More and more wakes were held in funeral parlors. But we needed Frankie to be at home—if only for a few more days. Our worlds had been turned upside down in less than three days. We were unprepared to physically let go of our little boy, but more importantly, perhaps, our living room offered a space where all three of us could spend private time with Frankie.

I cannot put into words what it was like to watch that hearse pull into our driveway and bring Frankie's small casket through the front door of our home. The casket was placed in a part of our living room that had always been reserved for our Christmas tree. The little guy who had always been so full of life was so still—no more giggles, no more "Spook" games, no more Superman antics, no more cowboy horse, no more chameleons placed on draperies. Although Frank and I were afraid that Janice could be traumatized by the week's events, we were equally afraid that, if we denied her wishes, her trauma and resentment could last a lifetime. There was no way that we could prevent her heartache or our own. Having consulted the writings of many experts over the years, Frank and I remain convinced that we did the right thing. Even as a young girl, Janice expressed gratitude that Frankie was waked at home and that she was allowed to spend some private time with her twin. Our daughter will recall the next chapter in our journey—I have no memory of the casket being removed on the morning of the funeral and burial.

◆   ◆   ◆

After Frankie died, we didn't change our living room Christmas tree spot. As much as we had endured the worst of times in that spot, we had wonderful memories of Christmas mornings. Some people might wonder why we stayed in the home, whether it would be too hard to live where Frankie's casket had been placed. You know, this may seem odd, but I actually became more attached to our home. A few years later, Frank suggested that we move into one of his model homes. It was a lovely place, but I refused to leave the home where our little boy had lived and laughed and where I had touched him for the very last time. Frank suggested moving a few more times over the years. He tried constantly to find a way to ease my sadness, but my husband had trouble understanding that sometimes I just had to cry—that it helped me. Oh, how I hope that my insistence on staying in our home didn't add to Frank's burden. That thought never crossed my mind at the time. I just couldn't leave Frankie's home.

Janice—Frankie's Wake

On Monday morning, my parents met me at my grandmother's home. Although they anticipated having to tell me that Frankie had died, I already sensed his death. Neither my parents nor I have ever been able to explain my foreknowledge. It's just one of those things that can't be explained. I returned to our home with my parents—I was adamant that I be allowed to participate in the wake, funeral, and burial. I had never been away from Frankie, and I was not about to be separated from him while he remained in our house. The wake was held on Monday and Tuesday evening.

◆   ◆   ◆

One memory has always troubled me. I remember Dad putting chains on his car's tires (1953 was before the era of snow tires). Since it was early November, even a little early for a snowfall in Syracuse, I wondered if my memories were confused. As I began compiling research for this book, and therefore trying to recall events from long ago, I decided that I had to find out if this tire-chain memory made any sense. I called the National Oceanic and Atmospheric Administration of the Department of Commerce and requested forecasts and precipitation levels for October and November 1953. Sure enough, the recorded temperatures and precipitation levels indicated that 6.1 inches of snow fell on November 7. Just as I had recalled, my father had put chains on the car tires. He had to make sure that no amount of snow would keep his family from attending the funeral Mass or prevent another emergency trip to City Hospital. My parents had been warned there was a high probability that I would develop polio in spite of the multiple gamma globulin injections.[1]

◆   ◆   ◆

My memories of the wake are still very vivid. I remember seeing my entire extended family, as well as many neighbors and family friends. Aunt Louise

DeMartino (you'll meet her in the next chapter) brought some of her wonderful spaghetti. She handed it to me in a big pot as she arrived for the first night of calling hours. As far as I was concerned, she and mom made the best spaghetti sauce in the whole world (and Mrs. Sagenkahn made the best fudge cake). My Aunt Pat, who would soon marry my Uncle Bud Coolican, took me upstairs every so often to read to me. We also did some coloring on the dining room table.

Frankie was waked in our living room. His casket was placed in front of the French doors that separated the room from a screened porch. Frankie was dressed in a navy blue suit with his head facing west. I remember looking at all the flowers arranged around the room and being affected by their overwhelming fragrance. Many years later, I discovered that a particular perfume (I can't recall the name) so perfectly mimicked the smell of the room that one whiff could send my mind instantly back to those two days. I was especially proud of the basket of flowers sent by our class at Moses DeWitt. I placed it in front of the casket right next to the flowers from Mom, Dad, and me. The "Memory Book" recorded that seventy-five floral arrangements were banked about the casket and fireplace wall. All of our first cousins who were alive at the time—Bonne, Bob, Russ, Chris, Jim, Bob, and Mary—sent bouquets.[2]

When calling hours ended each night, my parents allowed me to have some private time with Frankie. I'm so thankful that my parents understood my needs. It must have broken their hearts to watch me, but there were things that I had to do. Although I had experienced death, and understood as best as any child could that death meant that I would never be able to see Frankie again, my concept of Heaven contained many earthly elements. Frankie loved baseball. In fact, he lived and breathed baseball. So, I got his baseball, bat, mitt, and cap and tucked them under his little body. I remember wanting Frankie to have everything that he might need in Heaven—that meant his baseball equipment had to go with him. I also remember needing to touch him and kiss him good-bye. He was cold and felt like wood.

All the adults signed their name in the Memory Book. Though I have no independent memory of signing my name in the book, its pages indicate that I was a very busy twin. I signed my name five different times. Frankie and I had been practicing what we called "curly writing." Did I want to make sure that Frankie knew I was there? Did I just want to act like all the adults? Each night, I ended my private visit by sitting on the living room sofa and just staring at Frankie for a few minutes. I can still picture him in that casket.[3]

Reflection:

I have recalled Frankie's wake so many times over the years. But, in spite of my vivid memories, I can't "call up" what I felt during those first few days. I had some intellectual grasp of death but certainly not any emotional understanding of all that would consume me over coming months and years. Losing Frankie meant something very different from losing our first dog or our paternal grandfather. I could not have possibly anticipated the consequences of such loss. I was just too young and innocent. Perhaps the only way that I was able to remember those days forever (days that I had to remember because they would be the last days I would see Frankie's face or touch his skin) was to "detach" myself emotionally from the situation. Or, was I just numb?

Many people have expressed sadness that my memories of the wake are so vivid. I'm thankful. I would never have memories of Frankie as a teenager, college graduate, groom, parent, or uncle. It has thus been very important to me to hold onto any and all memories, even the saddest ones. Priceless photos, a few precious keepsakes, and memories are what I have of Frankie. All memories other than those of his illness and death are of happy times we shared together.

A few years before Mom died, she gave me the Memory Book supplied by Schumacher-Whelan Funeral Home that recorded not only the friends and family who came to the wake, but also the time and place of the funeral Mass and interment, the flowers and Mass cards received, and the gifts of food that were brought to our family. Going from page to page, I was struck by the enormous love shown by so many. After reading recent books on polio, I am all the more touched that a few hundred people abandoned their own fears and came to offer words of comfort in spite of the fact that in those days most polio survivors and their families were shunned out of fear of contagion. Over the years, Mom mentioned many times that she and Dad were so thankful that no one who came to the house contracted polio. They also believed that the health department would have denied permission for the at-home wake if it had been deemed a dangerous situation.

Of late, I've noticed something else about the book from the funeral home. When Mom presented it to me, she had completed the page that recorded the details of Frankie's funeral Mass and burial but she had left the "In Memory of____" page blank. I completed the page in my own hand. Was Frankie's death less real to her if she left that first page blank? Sometimes what we forget to do, or choose not to do, speaks volumes. I've had many years to reflect upon Frankie's book but I had never made note of the possible significance of this detail. What my parents did during those tragic days continues to speak to me today. [4]

Mrs. Louise DeMartino—United We Stand

Jan has always called me Aunt Louise, even though she's never referred to her actual blood relatives as aunt or uncle. As far as Jan was concerned, I was her Aunt Louise and my husband was her Uncle Larry. I think it was her way of letting us know that she considered us to be very special people.

Our home was just a few doors down from Frank and DJ's (that's short for Dorothy June, Jan's mother). Our sons, Alan and Gary, were among Frankie's and Jan's closest friends, and the adult DeMartinos and Floods became great friends as well. We had a close neighborhood, where mothers watched out for all of the children and where parents enjoyed a few hours of adult company once the kids were tucked into bed. Many of the moms got together while the kids napped.

When I was just three-years-old, my older brother died of polio. I was too young to have any memories of his death, but my mother never fully recovered. Therefore, I grew up appreciating that polio was a disease to be feared. Yet, like most young parents, I lived with the belief that somehow polio would never hurt my children—or neighborhood children that we had come to love. In the early 1950s, our country was in the midst of the worst polio epidemics to ever hit the United States. We all hoped and prayed that by adhering to all the public health warnings and recommendations, we would be spared.

On that awful Friday night, LJ (my husband's nickname) and I learned that Frankie had been taken to the hospital. He had had a cold for a few days, but there was nothing unusual about that. During the first few years of school, kids pick up every imaginable bug. Some time in the afternoon, Frankie started having trouble breathing. Though we were worried, we still didn't think about polio. Summer had passed, and the kids were getting ready for Halloween. Didn't polio just occur when it was hot and sticky? It was getting quite chilly. I was worried that Alan and Gary might have to wear coats over their Halloween costumes.

Two days later, Frankie died, and our safe little world collapsed. Within just a few days, *eight first graders* had been diagnosed with the disease. I wish

I could remember if Frankie and Jan were the first children to be hospitalized. Everything happened so fast. I can recall the names of three children (other than Frankie and Jan) who were hospitalized—a little boy named Graham and two pretty little sisters named Patty and Cheryl. I have no recollection of how many residents of DeWitt were eventually diagnosed with polio. I was numb.

◆   ◆   ◆

When Jan recently called me and asked if I would lend my voice to this story, I was shocked to learn that her research indicated that many polio patients and their families were shunned by their neighbors and friends. We were all terrified of polio. Who wasn't? Yet, we knew that Frank, DJ, and Jan needed us then and would need us in coming months. That's all we thought about. I'm proud to have been part of a community that supported the Floods in spite of our fear.

Throughout the neighborhood, the women prepared for Frankie's wake—cooking, ordering floral arrangements, picking up Mass cards, and engaging babysitters. Viv Maloney made a casserole; Peg Feldmeier baked cookies; Jane Rymell prepared a salad; and I made the DeMartino house specialty, my sauce and meatballs. Viv and Bob Maloney, the Floods' next-door-neighbors, made certain that all the neighborhood knew of Frankie's death. We all felt a need to do something, anything.[1]

Flood and Coolican friends and family from all over the Syracuse area came to the two days of calling hours. Our normally quiet street was bustling with neighbors, all walking to the Flood house to pay their respects. The kids' first grade teacher, Mrs. Jean MacDougall, came to the wake. The faculty of the school sent a floral arrangement. Many of our neighbors sent bouquets as well. I had never seen so many baskets and vases of red and white roses encircling a casket. Even Frankie and Jan's pediatrician, Dr. William O. Kopel, attended the wake.[2]

Looking back, I'm thankful that Frankie was able to be waked at home. Before he became ill on that Friday, Frank and Dorothy had no way of knowing that their little boy would never run or play in the house again. They needed to remain his mommy and daddy, if only for a few more days. For our friends, that meant keeping Frankie at home rather than visiting him in a funeral parlor at specified hours. It was the old-fashioned way.

◆   ◆   ◆

A few days after Frankie's death, the Onondaga County Health Department contacted us. I don't know how many other families were called, though I understand from conversations with Jan that the Sagenkahn's home was placed under quarantine. We were asked to provide stool samples to determine if the virus was in any of our systems. This was important information to gather, since individuals with the virus were capable of spreading the disease, even if they never exhibited symptoms themselves. Fortunately, our samples were all negative, but we had some very tense moments awaiting the pathology reports.

LJ and I never told Frank and Dorothy about the health department's order. We were afraid that it would make them feel guilty. It wasn't until recently, when Jan and I were talking about the book, that I divulged the request. Our son Alan and several neighborhood children were in Frankie and Jan's class. I think there were about twenty-four in their classroom. As a precaution, seventy-four Moses DeWitt School first graders received the gamma globulin injection. Jan never knew about the other children receiving gamma globulin injections until she began research for this book and read the newspaper articles DJ had saved for her.[3]

Over the years, many people have asked why polio struck so many children in one classroom—one-third of the students in all. We'll never know the answer to that question. Jan agrees that there is no sense tying up her mind with speculation.

◆   ◆   ◆

I just thought of something you might find interesting. In the opening chapters of the book, both Frank and Frankie mentioned that, at the end of WWII, Frank remained in Europe for several months. He was busy processing his fellow soldiers back to the States. Many years after Frankie died, our son Alan found my husband's army discharge orders. Guess who had signed for Larry's return to Syracuse?—none other than a young army officer who would become our neighbor and close friend, Frank T. Flood.

◆   ◆   ◆

Some fifty years after polio hit our street, I can still call up sad memories of that terrible time. LJ and I learned to respect Frank and Dorothy's needs. For the rest of his life, Frank stopped by our house to "check in." I think he felt comfortable knowing that he was in the company of friends who had experienced the horror with him. Dorothy coped by closing herself off from most people. We were fortunate to be among the few friends with whom she felt comfortable to speak (though only occasionally) of Frankie. The death of a child changes parents, forever. Even after Frank and DJ died, Jan stayed in touch. I'm still her Aunt Louise.

Janice—Funeral, Burial, a Headache

The funeral took place on November 4, 1953, at Holy Cross Church, the same church in which my husband and I would be married many years later. Our pastor Father Ritchie, Father McCabe, and Father Shannon (a close friend of my father's) officiated at the 9:00-AM "Mass of the Angels." I recall walking into the church between my parents and immediately noting the white vestments worn by the priests. My parents explained that the priests wore white because they knew that Frankie was in Heaven.

I remember nothing else until we reached the family plot area, Section 13, at St. Agnes Cemetery. A deep hole had been dug with Frankie's coffin anchored by metal bars. Flowers were placed all around. All of a sudden, men started lowering the coffin into the ground—that act was so final. I hate the memory of Frankie's coffin being lowered into the ground though, over time, that memory helped me to accept the finality of his death. Apparently, the practice of lowering the coffin while the family was still present soon became less common.

After the burial, we went to Nona and Bompa Coolican's home. I don't remember much, other than sitting on Bonne's and Bob's laps. Around dinnertime, I began feeling sick. I told my parents that I had a very bad headache, so they decided to take me home. The next thing I remember is reclining on our living room sofa while my parents awaited a visit from the doctor. Dr. Kopel was away (later on, my parents told me that he was so traumatized by Frankie's death that he had to take a few days off). Dr. Alsever, another area pediatrician, came to the house. He approached and asked me to touch my chin to my chest. I couldn't do it.

The doctor took my parents behind a chair near the fireplace. He told my parents that he thought that I had polio—I remember listening really hard and hearing that word. I don't recall being scared that I would die even though I knew that Frankie had died of polio. Was I too young to understand the consequences of my diagnosis or was I just too sick to do much thinking about anything? I have no recollection of our trip to the hospital.

My next memory is of lying in a hospital bed at City Hospital with a doctor holding a very long needle. It may have even been Dr. Alice (Jaros) Turek by my bedside; how I wish I had access to my old medical records. Although I now know that the needle used to perform the diagnostic spinal tap was only a few inches long, it looked about ten feet long to me! I might not have been scared about having polio at that very instant but I was certainly terrified of that needle. The doctor turned me on my stomach, had me pull my legs up, and stuck the needle deep into my back. It really hurt. That's all I remember for several days.

Frank and Dorothy—Not Again

Our nightmare wouldn't end. Jan remained in a deep sleep for three or four days. The doctors couldn't tell us whether she would live or die. During that period, Jan's fever remained very high. Her front baby teeth became marked with white spots. Our family dentist later told us that they were "fever marks." We prayed that Jan's life would be spared. She had to survive—we couldn't lose them both.

We sat in the hospital hour after hour, waiting for a good sign or a hopeful word. The memories and photos that had comforted us during the early hours of Frankie's hospitalization were of no consolation now. We couldn't picture Janice without Frankie. There had never been a Janice without a Frankie in our lives. It just dawned on us that we hadn't taken many pictures of Frankie or Janice alone—they were always a twosome. We only remember one photo of Frankie without Jan. It was taken at the camp on Skaneateles Lake, just a few short months before he died. Frankie looked very sad.

That photo has always troubled our daughter. Many years after Frankie died, Jan asked us if we thought that Frankie knew that he was going to die. She wondered if that's why he looked so sad in the picture. We didn't know what to say to her, but she was right. Frankie did look very sad.

◆　　　◆　　　◆

Today, one of the walls in Janice's family room is referred to as the "family wall." Jan developed the family wall concept after both of us had died. Other than the infant photos that graced a bedroom dresser, we did not display many family photos after Frankie died. That always bothered Jan, but she respected our wishes, fearing that the photos made us sad. But, after our deaths, Jan decided that she wanted photos displayed. She needed to be connected with her past as well as with her present and future.

Over the years, Jan, Dave, and our grandson Kevin have filled the wall with montage frames capturing the lives of both families going back to great-great-great-grandparents and family pets. Needless to say, there are many photos of

Frankie and Janice. Even though Jan hates that one photo of Frankie, she decided to display it. She still wonders if Frankie had a premonition about his death.

◆   ◆   ◆

A few days after Jan was admitted to the hospital, we were contacted by a representative of the March of Dimes; we believe her name was Mrs. McCarthy. She explained that it was her responsibility to check with City Hospital to receive a list of daily polio admissions. In turn, she would call the affected families and offer aid. City Hospital records for 1952 (1953 records are unavailable) indicate that of the $120,928.27 received for care that year, the local chapter of the March of Dimes contributed $21,598.79. Compared with other diseases treated at the facility, polio care was very expensive due to the cost of such equipment as iron lungs and whirlpool therapy tubs. Average daily costs at the hospital were under $20 per day.[1]

Fortunately, we did not require financial assistance but we were very grateful for the kind words and prayers. That initial contact established a bond with the organization that persists to this day. During the 1950s, we were very involved in the yearly Mothers March. Although a vaccine or cure came too late for our twins, we wanted polio's reign to be over. We knew we had to do our part. Janice remains a volunteer for the annual Mother's March that now benefits premature babies and those born with congenital problems.

Soon after Frankie's death (while Janice remained hospitalized), we were called by the health department and told to burn all of Frankie and Jan's clothes as well as the toys and dolls that belonged to both of the kids. First, we had to bury our child. Now, we were forced to eliminate nearly all traces of his existence. Frank and I were devastated.

We were permitted to save photos and a few other objects—the twins' sterling juice cups, the money that Frankie had given to Janice, and a Swiss Army knife that we were saving until Frankie became a Boy Scout. We had to sacrifice the bracelet that Frankie had given Janice when the kids had their tonsils removed. Jan was especially sad when she learned that the bracelet had been destroyed. Although Jan had once loved her doll collection, she never asked for a doll again. That phase in her young life ended with the 1953 polio epidemic. When Janice recovered, we presented her with the remaining priceless keepsakes.

Today, the silver juice cups occupy a place of honor in Jan's dining room oak cabinet that once belonged to our old family friend, Marna Martin, who was a polio victim from the 1920s. The Swiss Army knife and the ten-dollar bill are safely stored in a dresser. Jan gave the silver dollars to our grandson Kevin when he left for college; he keeps one of them at home. Jan still wonders whether Frankie knew that he was about to die. Handing over two silver dollars and a ten-dollar bill just a few weeks before he died was so out of character for her twin. Our daughter remains adamant that Frankie watches over her family.

Janice—City Hospital, Therapy

My memories of City Hospital are sketchy. I can't recall the first several days in the hospital—as an adult I've found this fact comforting. Maybe there really is a place between Heaven and Earth that shields gravely ill people from fear and pain.

My first recollection is of looking at a glass window (or was it a door with a window in it?) at one end of the room and hearing a baby cough incessantly from the other side. A nurse told me that the little baby had whooping cough. I didn't know what whooping cough was, but even at my age, I knew that that baby was terribly ill. In fact, I remember being much more concerned about that baby than I was about my own condition. When I got a little older, my mother told me that she had had whooping cough as a nine-year-old. I've always wondered if the baby died.

I don't remember my parents visiting me. But, I do recall having my bed pushed over to a window so that I could see my parents and our dog, Mittz the Second, on the grass lawn below. The hospital is only three stories high, and yet, in my mind's eye, when I "look" out the window my parents seem very far away. Based on reports from other hospitalized polio patients, I would imagine that my parents might have had limited visitation rights. Or perhaps, we communicated through that glass window? I guess I'll never know for sure; I've been unable to locate City Hospital isolation procedures from that era.

Many polio survivors describe painful hot-pack treatments and limb-stretching exercises advocated by an Australian nurse named Sister Kenny, or of pre-Kenny treatments that included prolonged casting, splinting, and bed-rest protocols. Immobilization became especially popular in the 1930s. Fortunately, during the 1940s, four physicians at City Hospital received instruction from Sister Kenny at the University of Minnesota. I am certain that my physical care, influenced by Kenny's proactive treatment model, greatly impacted my recovery. Every effort was made to get me moving as soon as possible.[1]

From what my parents told me of my early hospitalization, bed rest was required to manage my high fever. Neither my parents nor my doctors were certain that I would survive. Once my fever broke, the hard work began—physical therapy. My hospital memories revolve almost exclusively around daily whirlpool therapy treatments. Fortunately, I never required bracing or surgery, but many patients endured such intervention. Based on Kenny methods, although bracing of polio patients was often necessary to prevent or minimize deformity and provide stability, such techniques had to be counterbalanced with exercise to prevent stiffness and to restore as much normal range and flexibility as possible. The Sister Kenny method used hot packs to relax muscle spasms suffered by many polio patients. I'm very fortunate to have no memory of such spasms (or of the dreaded hot packs). It appears unlikely that I could have endured spasms and hot packs without any memory of either. I don't know why I was spared, unless early exercise in the whirlpool area helped to prevent that complication. As for bedside massage, I probably benefited from such early intervention but I have no memory of nurses or therapists exercising my limbs in my hospital room either before or after I began whirlpool therapy.[2]

John R. Paul's, *A History of Poliomyelitis,* indicates that Sister Kenny was a controversial figure in the United States, in part, because she locked horns with members of the medical establishment. But, she had significant influence on the aftercare of paralyzed polio patients. Paul comments that Sister Kenny's techniques were far ahead of customary practices in the United States and that her methods marked an important shift in treatment methods. In 1946, actress Rosalind Russell starred in a movie entitled *Sister Kenny* (available today on VHS).[3]

◆   ◆   ◆

Although I became aware that I could not move my legs, I don't recall any fear of long-term paralysis, or if I even knew what that meant. I do have one distinct memory of a trip to the bathtub. The nurse or assistant placed me in a tub of water, and then left the room. She had forcibly pulled my legs up toward my chin. As I sat in the tub, I was acutely aware that I could not move my legs or save myself if I started to slip into the water. I'm sure that the nurse was gone only a few minutes, or, maybe she was behind me the whole time. But I was alone, or felt alone, and I couldn't move. I can still picture that white porcelain bathtub. I can still recall my fear.

Children were brought to the whirlpool area in groups. We were placed on stretchers, and our bodies were wrapped very tightly in wool blankets. Each of us received a special treat on the way to the therapy area. We were allowed our choice of ginger ale or tomato juice. The nurses gave us different brands each day; we became very proficient at differentiating the distinctive flavor of each brand. Cheryl and Patty Munson, my friends from Moses DeWitt, always chose tomato juice. I always chose ginger ale.

In the whirlpool area, I was placed on a cot, hoisted up, and slowly lowered into a large shallow pool. I was strapped onto the cot so that I would not fall off, but I recall being terrified of drowning. The therapists were very kind as they moved and stretched my legs and arms up and down. Yet, even their kind voices and gestures could not dispel my fear. Frankie and I had learned to swim at a very young age, and by six, I was quite the little fish. Now, unable to move, I felt utterly helpless in the water. I remember a large bank of windows to the right of the whirlpool area. While receiving my water therapy, I often looked out those windows and pretended that I wasn't in the room. My "pretend game" helped to lessen my fear.

To this day, I'm not a gal who wants to spend much time in our bathroom Jacuzzi. As for hot tubs, you'll never find me in one. I've always loved swimming in lakes, but backyard pools are not to my liking. I suppose there's no way to have experienced daily water therapy without developing a few quirks. I also have a "thing" about any encumbrance near or around my feet. I hated those wool blankets that were tightly wrapped around my legs and feet. I couldn't shake them loose because I couldn't move. Over fifty years later, I continue to have a dislike for fabrics that touch me below my ankles. I don't like slacks or long gowns; thank God for cropped pants. If I have my way, I will spend the rest of my days never feeling constrained by any article of clothing.

I've tried to remember whether I was lonely for Frankie while I was in the hospital. My memories of those early days seem limited to my own physical condition. I wonder if I was just too sick to begin the grieving process. Or, perhaps the reality of what Frankie's death truly meant was still too difficult for me to comprehend. Whatever physical and emotional mechanisms might have been at work in those early days, I would not be granted a reprieve from grief for much longer. Within a few months, the sadness would overwhelm me.

◆   ◆   ◆

City Hospital records of the era indicate that the average length of stay for polio patients was just over eleven days. I assume, therefore, that I was discharged from the hospital after about a two-week stay but my parents are no longer here to confirm that, and the hospital records are long gone. While in the hospital, my orthopedic care was provided by Dr. John Kalamarides. He continued to monitor my progress until I departed for college. Upon discharge from the hospital, I was moved to my Grandmother Flood's home for private daily physical therapy.[4]

Some area children, who required additional therapy and surgery, had to be transferred to a nearby rehabilitation facility in Ithaca, New York, called The Reconstruction Home. Many children, who required such extended care in facilities across the country, have haunting memories of long, lonely, painful hospitalizations. I have been shocked and saddened to read of the horrific experiences of some of my peers who were forced to endure the behavior of cruel caretakers. I was so blessed to be able to receive my therapy at home and to have received care from loving, professional healthcare workers.

Until I was able to return to DeWitt after the holidays, I remained at my grandmother's home. My Aunt Rose Geis, who had always lived with my grandparents, helped as well. My grandparent's home accommodated all of my needs on one floor. As my bedroom at home was on the second floor, this temporary arrangement seemed very practical. Moreover, I'm certain that my parents welcomed a little time to mourn for Frankie without fear of upsetting their surviving twin.

I loved seeing my parents each day, yet, I have no memories of being lonely or afraid when they weren't there. I'm sure that Grandma and Rowie (my great aunt's nickname) pampered me twenty-four hours a day. Nor do I have any memories of dwelling on Frankie's death while at my grandmother's home. Did the fact that I was away from our home, a home full of memories of Frankie, play a part in my delayed grief? Or, was my lack of reaction in those early days more a function of my concentration on physical therapy? Before I started writing this book, I had never questioned the fact that my grief work only began with my return to our home in DeWitt—more than two months after Frankie's death.

My grandmother and great-aunt were not young women when I lived with them. They both had to be in their mid-sixties—it must have been physically and emotionally draining for them to have me there. Their hearts were heavy with grief for Frankie and worry for me, but that didn't stop them from taking care of me and offering respite to my parents. Until recently, I never thought about how exhausting it must have been for them. They were two slight little ladies who had buried my grandfather just a year and a half earlier.

◆　　◆　　◆

I can vividly picture my therapy area—the kitchen table—but I have no recollection of how I was transported. Was I carried from the bedroom that I shared with Rowie? Did I have a wheelchair? Each day the therapist came to give me treatment. She pulled my legs and stretched them up and down, up and down. The original therapist was quite stern. She yelled at me as she tried to get me to move my neck to my chest and then toward my knees after she placed me in a sitting position. I was unable to move, which made me cry and made the therapist yell some more. This process was repeated over and over again with each session ending in frustration for both of us. Quite quickly, my parents realized that our personalities did not mix well. I wasn't trying to be stubborn. I just couldn't move, and I surmised that the therapist thought that I was pretending. Looking back, I'm sure that the therapist meant well. She saw me as someone who could get better, and she wanted to guarantee that success, but I was just too young to understand her motivation or to appreciate her need to push me.

Soon, another therapist arrived. Her name was something like Miss "Parasol." Oh, how I wish that I could meet her now, give her a big hug, and thank her! I've tried to track her down through the local physical therapy and visiting nurse associations but there's no one listed by that name—she was probably young and soon took a married name. Although I cannot picture her, I remember her kind, patient approach. The exercises were the same as before, but I looked forward to the therapy sessions with Miss Parasol because I knew she wanted to help me.

Shortly before Christmas, she told me that I could try to walk—was I ever excited. Miss Parasol carried me to the hallway that separated the kitchen from the dining area. She stood me up, let go, and told me to walk. Since I had taken ballet from the time I was three years old and had started tap lessons a few months before we got sick, the thought of walking didn't seem half as exciting to me as being a little ballerina once more. So, instead of trying to take a normal walking step, I stood up on my toes and promptly fell flat on my face. Miss Parasol picked me up and told me to try again. I was angry and started to cry, but I tried again and again until I was able to take that first magnificent step without falling. Ask anyone who has learned to walk again, whether due to illness or injury, and I bet each and every one of them can recall that first successful step. Relearning was not an easy task, but I was too young, stubborn, and innocent to be afraid or discouraged. To this day, I love to conjure up memories of that first wonderful step taken at my grandmother's home.

My family was worried about my reaction to our first Christmas without Frankie. So, Dad asked one of his employees, a very nice man named Hodge, to dress up as Santa Claus. Hodge arrived at my grandmother's and presented me with gifts. I later told my parents that I knew he wasn't the real Santa Claus because I recognized his construction boots. After all, Frankie and I had seen the *real* Santa Claus at the North Pole.

◆   ◆   ◆

In January 1954, I was able to attend school for the morning session. The doctors did not permit me to attend full days until shortly before the school year ended in mid-June. Until the end of that school year, my teacher, Mrs. MacDougall, came to our home each day and tutored me. My walking was not exactly what I would call walking. I moved like a little tin soldier for a long time, but I was moving on my own and that's what mattered. Fortunately, only one child made fun of me, and she was mean to everyone. How lucky I was to be spared the isolation and cruelty that so many polio patients experienced. I recently spoke with one of my childhood friends, Pat LaVoy Harris, about my early ambulation problems. She remarked that she doesn't even remember my wooden gait. I was one lucky kid to be surrounded by so many people who accepted me, stiff walk and all.

My cousin Bonne (you'll meet her a little later) has vivid memories of my family's dining room table being used as my physical therapy center once I returned from my grandmother's home. I think it's odd that I have no memories whatsoever of Miss Parasol's visits at my home, or of my parents continuing the therapy sessions when the therapist was not present. My first memories of home are limited to the emotional trauma I endured as I tried to come to terms with Frankie's death. I also recall looking forward to my teacher's visits.

Upon my return to school, a newspaper photographer came to the school to take several pictures of me with Mrs. MacDougall and my classmates. An article appeared in the *Syracuse Herald Journal* on January 13, 1954. At the time, my Uncles Tom and Bud Coolican worked in the newspaper and radio industries, and I'm sure that they were instrumental in providing the photo op. Mom saved the article, so I examined it while researching for this book. I was immediately struck by my reaction. My eyes went right to my shoes. Oh, how I hated those brown orthopedic shoes with the metal arches. I loved my orthopedic surgeon, Dr. Kalamarides, but I did not like the fact that he made me wear such awful looking shoes. I had always loved pretty dresses that looked good with black or white "Mary Jane's," not ugly, cumbersome, brown shoes that were very heavy on my feet.

As an adult, I'm embarrassed to admit my shoe obsession. I was hung up about brown shoes that afforded me the luxury of walking on my own while many of my peers were forced to walk with braces, transported in wheel chairs, or confined to iron lungs. Many patients recall having to trade shoes with other polio patients because their feet did not develop simultaneously after polio. Shoes can still be obtained through the *National Odd Shoe Exchange* (www. oddshoe.org). Still other patients had to have custom-constructed shoes to accommodate severe leg-length discrepancies. Yet, those awful brown shoes provided motivation. Just as my father's newfound mission in life was to make sure that I would walk, run, and dance again, my newfound mission was to throw away those shoes!

◆　　　◆　　　◆

My parents continued to go out of their way to make all holidays special. They didn't want me to dislike Halloween because it was close to the date of Frankie's death. One year, we even traveled to Rochester to purchase a Martha Washington gown complete with wig. My Nichols family has learned to endure my absolute love of holiday traditions. In my world, there can never be enough Christmas trees or too many children who come to the door on Halloween night.

For many years, once Dr. Kopel and Dr. Kalamarides allowed me to resume dancing lessons, Mom drove me to classes at Coy Dare's Dance Studio in downtown Syracuse. At first, the classes were probably little more than an extension of therapy, but, eventually, my agility returned. I was especially fond of a Can-Can routine performed when I was about nine years old. Oh, how I loved that costume. As I recall, it was a rich butterscotch-yellow fabric with a black underskirt. And as for those kicks, I thought I was on Broadway!

◆　　　◆　　　◆

Note: See the Consulted Works for a list of excellent personal memoirs. For purposes of this book, I have limited my remarks to what I experienced. Because polio survivors have so many unique stories to tell, I urge you to read other books. This is especially important because, in many respects, my physical struggle was far less dramatic than that experienced by other polio patients. The most difficult issues I had to face revolved around Frankie's death.

Surgical and non-surgical intervention, beyond the acute hospital phase, will be discussed in upcoming chapters.

Mrs. Russell (Betty) Wightman—March of Dimes, 1953 Memories

I'm Dodie's sister and Janice's aunt. We were a family of five children: Monne, Bud, Dodie, Tom, and yours truly. Until our parents died, their home was always headquarters and a place where we could all come together to celebrate holidays, Sunday afternoons and evenings, the good times, the sad times. About five years ago, my daughters Chris and Anne began organizing annual reunions for our extended family. We decided that it was important that we all come together at times other than weddings and wakes.

Jan and Dave stopped at my home for lunch when they were on a recent visit back to Syracuse (right after their second trip to City Hospital). I had feared that Jan's return to the hospital would call up too many horrible memories. She wanted to reassure me that she was OK. While enjoying our corned beef sandwiches, my niece noticed three little Rockette figurines that hang off one of my kitchen cabinets. She was instantly smitten with those dancing girls. You see, I've always dreamed that my tap dancing feet would take me to Broadway with or without the dancing feet of my two sisters. During the early days of Jan's rehabilitation, all she could dream about was putting on her pink ballet slippers.

I don't recall any time during my childhood that there was not talk of polio. I think that's why our mother would not allow us to take swimming lessons, since it was commonly believed that you could contract polio from public swimming pools. We were numb when we received the telephone call from Dodie and Frank on that Halloween morning. Polio had hit *our* family.

Growing up, I knew of other families who had been affected by polio. Our friend, Marna Martin, walked with a limp and bore one of polio's cruel side effects—atrophied muscles in one of her legs. I also remember hearing a little about Franklin Delano Roosevelt and his bout with polio. But, even as a teen and young adult, I was never aware of the extent of Roosevelt's disability. Looking back, it might have served polio patients and their families well if we had all been aware of FDR's braces. Roosevelt's public appearances were carefully choreographed to deemphasize the extent of his disability. Roosevelt apparently thought that the country needed to see him erect and resolute. Today, we know that the ability to overcome or go on in spite of illness or injury is testimony to the strength, not weakness, of the human spirit. But, that was a different time.

◆   ◆   ◆

Roosevelt's polio story began in 1921. While vacationing at his family retreat at Campobello Island, the virus struck suddenly and virulently. Determined to walk again, our future president began visiting Warm Springs, Georgia, in the mid-1920s. Since ancient times, people had flocked to the waters of warm springs and mineral spas in a desperate attempt to seek relief from muscle and joint maladies. In April 1926, Roosevelt purchased the Georgia retreat with a $200,000 investment.[1]

Although the resort thrived as a therapeutic retreat, it soon became a financial liability. Roosevelt, in consultation with his law partner Basil O'Connor (who eventually lost a daughter to polio), decided to turn Warm Springs into a nonprofit organization whose sole purpose would be to find a cure for polio and provide aid and comfort to patients and families affected by the disease. On September 23, 1937, FDR announced the creation of the National Foundation for Infantile Paralysis, known today as the March of Dimes. The Foundation was incorporated in January 1938. Dependent upon braces, FDR had found a way to turn his personal tragedy into one of our country's most successful charitable organizations.[2]

A nationwide fundraising campaign was launched in 1934 to provide additional resources for Roosevelt's Warm Spring's facility. To raise money for the cause, public relations genius Carl Byoir opted to capitalize on Roosevelt's birthday. With a $25,000 donation made by powerful business tycoon Henry L. Doherty, the National Committee for Birthday Balls was launched. Birthday Balls became annual events across the country, with the first ball taking place on January 30, 1934. That first year, 4,376 communities joined in 600 separate balls to raise over $1 million for the Warm Springs Foundation. Subsequent balls split the money between Warm Springs and the local communities sponsoring the events. Newspapers and radio stations joined the effort through publicity and advertising campaigns. Over time, Roosevelt and O'Connor determined that a more permanent fundraising venue was required to sustain charitable giving once Roosevelt retired from office (FDR died in 1945 during a fourth unprecedented term). Moreover, Birthday Ball proceeds had started to decline.[3]

Comedian Eddie Cantor was solicited to devise a campaign strategy to fund the 1938 California Birthday Ball. As a play on the popular newsreel, *The March of Times,* Cantor commenced a radio appeal asking everyone in the country to contribute a dime to fight polio. He coined the campaign name The March of Dimes. Hollywood celebrities including Jack Benny, Bing Crosby, Rudy Vallee, Kate Smith, Edgar Bergen and his famous puppet Charlie McCarthy, Judy Garland, and Mickey Rooney all offered their support.[4]

The first March of Dimes radio appeal took place during the week preceding the 1938 Birthday Ball. Citizens were instructed to send their contributions directly to the White House. At first, the flow of contributions was only a trickle. In the two days following Cantor's initial radio broadcast, only $17.50 was received. But, by the end of January, more than 80,000 letters containing contributions had overwhelmed the White House mailroom. With gratitude, President Roosevelt gave a radio address thanking all Americans for the contributions—an astounding $268,000 (or 2,680,000 dimes) had been received. Today, FDR's face appears on all U.S. dimes.[5]

The fact that Hollywood stars, our popular culture heroes, lent support to the polio effort made an enormous impact on the nation. When Howard J. London became the director of the National Foundation's Radio, Television, and Motion Picture Department in the 1940s, he arranged successful tours, radio spots, and benefits by requesting the help of such stars as Jack Benny, Doris Day, and Bob Hope. The department even produced informational films about polio. Two that I can remember were *In Daily Battle* and *Your Fight against Infantile Paralysis.* Some male stars (including that gorgeous Tyrone Power) joined the ranks of mothers in the annual Mothers March. They wore badges professing, "Tonight I Am a Mother."[6]

Baseball greats Ty Cobb, Babe Ruth, and Willie Mays were just a few of the famous athletes that gave their support. The Dodgers baseball team even took part in a number of bowling tournaments. A poster campaign featuring the pictures of children afflicted with the disease also proved immensely popular. Can you imagine refusing to donate when you've just looked at a poster of a beautiful little boy or girl smiling proudly while balancing with the aid of braces and crutches?[7]

In 1954, the year of the Salk vaccine trial in which my niece Janice participated, the National Foundation raised $55 million (plus $20 million during the special summer campaign). Although the Salk vaccine came too late to benefit Frankie and Jan, the 1953 DeWitt polio outbreak would prove one of the last our area would have to endure. With over fifty years of history to reflect upon, I am proud that all Americans banded together to fight a common invisible enemy. The first half of the twentieth century was a period of immense global challenge. World War I, the Great Depression, and World War II had impacted us all. But, we remained a plucky crew. We were an optimistic nation on the brink of many medical and technological advances. I have often wondered if the development of the Salk vaccine in the 1950s and the Sabin vaccine in the early 1960s would have been delayed without the backing of the March of Dimes, our entire citizenry, and the determination of one of polio's most famous victims, our thirty-second president.[8]

◆   ◆   ◆

Memories of that awful 1953 fall are a blur. One day, the twins were happy and healthy six-year-olds; in less than a week, one was dead. Our family had fallen in love with the twins from the time we first peeked at them in the nursery at Syracuse General Hospital. Although they looked like little dolls when they first came home, they were two busy bees in no time. They could be good and angelic one minute and double trouble the next. I can remember Dodie telling me that Jan once asked if she had kept baby books. My sister responded by telling her daughter that when she had a few minutes free from surveillance duty, she just took a much needed nap. Dodie often dressed the twins in matching boy and girl outfits. Frankie could have cared less about his clothes. Jan, on the other hand, loved her pretty dresses and party shoes. I was still single when they were born, so I was a ready-made babysitter. I remember telling one of my dates (my future husband, Russ) that I had to make it an early night—Dodie, Frank, and the twins were visiting and I just wanted to play with the little ones.

At the wake and funeral we tried to comfort Dodie, Frank, and Jan as best we could. Thank heavens so many of the DeWitt neighbors sent food. We were all too numb and heartbroken to do much cooking. We felt so helpless. There was no way to make it better—to make the nightmare go away. Until that time, I had never looked at my parents as getting older. That week they seemed to age overnight. I don't think any of us ever thought that it could get any worse. As you already know, it did.

When Jan announced that she had a severe headache after the funeral and burial, we braced for the worst—could it be happening all over again? My sister Monne made an immediate visit to the Dominican Cloister on Court Street (a local convent that continues to house a group of nuns who practice silence and complete detachment from the secular world) to ask for God's mercy. As a family who had always derived strength from our faith, I gave Dodie a copy of St. Francis deSales' writings. She continued to seek comfort from his words for the rest of her life. Faith, family, and friends were the only things that got us through those dark days. I'm thankful that I can't remember many of the details.

Several months after her hospital discharge, Jan was able to resume her ballet classes. To this day, she speaks fondly of Charleston marathons with her mom and aunts. We're still a family of dancing feet. I'm still waiting to make it on Broadway.

Dave—Surgical Care

Let me introduce myself: I'm Jan's husband. I'm also an orthopedic surgeon. As a kid growing up in the 1950s on Long Island, my memories of polio were pretty standard. I was not permitted to swim in public areas like the nearby Casino Pool. As stoic, silent Scandinavians, my parents never fully explained why they would not allow me to swim in the idyllic Olympic-size concrete salt water pool that drew its water from the nearby inlet to Great South Bay. My pleadings were always denied. Did my parents think that if we didn't talk about polio we could somehow escape its wrath? Fortunately, an epidemic never hit my neighborhood. I didn't know anyone personally affected by polio until I met Jan.

By the time I entered orthopedic residency in the mid-1970s, the incidence of polio infection in this country was negligible. Exciting advancements such as total joint replacement and finger reattachments after traumatic amputation were the hot topics. Thus, the study of surgical and non-surgical intervention for polio patients was limited to historical review in our texts. I was never called upon to perform a surgical procedure on a polio patient. Post-polio syndrome had not yet become a considerable issue, though some patients were beginning to voice complaints to their physicians.

Yet, due to my wife's experience with polio, I often sought out an opportunity to discuss the treatment of polio patients with surgeons whose early careers were filled with the ongoing surgical needs of the virus' numerous young victims. Jan especially enjoyed my discussions when they involved conversations with her own orthopedic surgeon, Dr. John Kalamarides, to whom she will be forever grateful. While I was a resident, Jan was employed by the Syracuse hospital that he was affiliated with, and her rehabilitation counseling caseload often included many of his patients.

Jan was a very lucky girl: gamma globulin injections, intensive physical therapy, and long-term orthopedic follow-up were sufficient. Sadly, for many children, long hospitalizations in rehabilitation facilities and several surgical procedures were the norm. Some patient memoirs accuse surgeons of the polio-era of "operating just to operate" because they didn't know what else to do. I'm certain that the memories of painful surgeries, physical setbacks, and separation from parents and siblings haunt those patients to this day. I'm also certain that having the opportunity to provide long-term follow-up to success stories like Jan's did much for the morale of orthopedic surgeons like Dr. Kal. Physicians of that era spent many a weary evening wondering what patients would next be admitted to infectious-disease facilities.

The early years of Dr. Kalamarides' career, though rewarding, were surely saddened by the realities and heartbreak of polio. As a young surgeon, he dealt with children requiring long rehabilitations. When we spoke physician to physician, he would confide that it was always difficult to accept that a beautiful little girl might always require a brace or that a high school athlete might never play football again. The eradication of polio in this country and the explosion of new procedures and rehabilitation devices literally transformed our shared medical specialty. Dr. Kal's professional career spanned a period from polio epidemics, to wild-virus polio eradication in the United States, to the emergence of a series of symptoms that came to be known as post-polio syndrome.

In our conversations, Dr. Kalamarides explained that several surgical procedures were utilized in an attempt to restore some function to limbs or to correct deformity. Many patients endured multiple surgeries. Unfortunately, procedures often fell short of goals. Moreover, patients frequently became frustrated with temporary post-operative restrictions. I will briefly discuss the most common surgical procedures, which included: *osteotomy, fusion, tendon transfer*, and *epiphyseodesis*. The final procedure, *spinal fusion*, will be explained in a later chapter.

Osteotomy

Paralysis can produce problems in addition to the loss of muscle function. For instance, a child's growing skeleton can be deformed by muscles that continue to function unopposed by muscles that would have moved a bone in the opposite direction. Over time, bone responds to muscle forces by permanently bending. Joints that are not stabilized by normal muscle tone can thus become lax and wobbly as the normal supporting ligaments stretch out. A surgical procedure was sometimes performed to correct deformed bone. This was done by cutting the bone and holding it in position via a metal plate and screws. This procedure was called an *osteotomy.*

Fusion

A flaccid, wobbly joint could be made stable by removing cartilage from the involved joint and allowing the bone to grow across the joint. This procedure was called a *fusion*. The obvious downside to fusion was that while the joint was made stable, it could no longer move in any direction.[3]

Tendon Transfer

A particularly ingenious procedure involved taking a functioning muscle and moving its attachment to a different bone or a different part of the same bone—thus, making up for the lost power of a paralyzed muscle (today, surgeons perform this operation when dealing with traumatic nerve injuries). The procedure was called a *tendon transfer*. Let me give you an example: Normally, the calf muscle is used to pull the foot downward, pointing the toes toward the floor. Polio sometimes left this muscle paralyzed, making it impossible to push off by flexing the foot against the ground. Fortunately, we have several muscles that lift the foot upward off the ground. Muscles from the front of the leg (that normally lift the foot upward) were sometimes surgically redirected to the back of the leg and attached to the heel. Similarly, working muscles from the back of the leg were sometimes transferred to the top of the foot. After a two-month period of casting to protect the new muscle attachment, exercises could begin. Although the new muscle would never be as strong as a normal muscle, any return of movement was better than an entirely flaccid limb.[4]

Epiphyseodesis

Leg-length discrepancies were often addressed by prescribing custom-made built-up shoes. A surgical procedure to diminish or prevent leg-length discrepancy involved the fusion of growth plates in the normal leg. The procedure was called *epiphyseodesis*.[5]

Spinal Fusion

This procedure was performed to deal with curvature of the spine (scoliosis). Because the curvature usually developed soon after the acute disease, the surgery was often performed within a few years of contracting polio. For some patients, the curvature and resulting problems developed more slowly. Therefore, I have decided to elaborate on this condition in a later chapter.

◆   ◆   ◆

Medical records of the era indicate that an orthopedic consult was ordered before polio patients were discharged from acute facilities. The consult was necessary in order to coordinate short and long-term surgical and non-surgical needs. Physical and occupational therapy was prescribed to maximize return of function. As mentioned previously, a shift in therapy treatment methods in the 1940s and 1950s greatly enhanced rehabilitation potential. Rehabilitation devices such as crutches and braces were prescribed to not only allow patients an optimum degree of ambulation but also (in the case of braces) to prevent deformities. Many physicians suggested that patients sleep with a wooden board placed under the bed mattress. My wife can still recall her father lifting her bed mattress and carefully placing a piece of precisely cut plywood between the mattress and box spring. Although I am unaware of the rationale behind the suggestion, it probably made patients more comfortable—it was long before the era of firm, high-tech mattresses. Physicians routinely prescribed orthopedic shoes with metal arch support, which patients like my wife despised. Surgeons followed children and adults with residual problems, as well as patients like Jan, to insure that any potential problems or setbacks could be addressed in a timely fashion. Over the years, for instance, Dr. Kal ordered periodic X-rays of Jan's upper spine. He did this to check for any sign of scoliosis (curvature of the spine). Scoliosis became a problem for many individuals in the aftermath of the acute polio infection.[6]

In a later chapter, "Dave—Medical Care Update," I will discuss several orthopedic conditions associated with polio. In order to highlight present problems and needs, I decided to save this discussion for a later chapter. Although medical and surgical intervention and modern therapy have never been able to prevent all problems related to paralytic polio, lack of proper medical care and therapy can certainly exacerbate problems.

◆   ◆   ◆

The children who suffered alongside my wife had a significant impact on her—that was especially true of the Munson sisters. We have tried to contact Mr. and Mrs. Munson but they have either moved or are no longer living. Cheryl Munson (who succumbed from complications of the disease on April 24, 1960) endured at least one surgical procedure, though Jan was too young to understand the details. My wife can still remember sitting at the breakfast-room table, on the next morning, and reading the obituary account in the *Syracuse Post-Standard*. Cheryl's death was very upsetting to Jan.[7]

Jan cannot remember if Patty, who was in her first grade class, required surgeries. Patty and Cheryl's parents were totally devoted to their care. The girls remained at home with their parents carrying them from room to room. Until Jan was able to drive, her parents drove her to the Munson's home so that the girls could maintain their friendship. Jan always mentioned that Patty and Cheryl had numerous visitors. Patty graduated from high school with the assistance of home tutors; she was pursuing college courses at the time of her death on November 5, 1967. Patty and Cheryl were special young ladies.[8]

Although one can never make sense of heartbreak, tragedy does bond families. The Munsons and Floods were two families hammered by polio. Out of the four Munson and Flood children, only one ultimately survived. In the end, polio had its way. Modern medicine cannot and does not always win.

Brett Sagenkahn and Alan and Gary DeMartino—What Kids Remember

Reflection from Jan

Before I introduce you to these three guys, I would like to provide a little background information. As Frankie already mentioned, our neighborhood was full of children. Although we had many friends, Frankie's closest pals were Brett, Alan, and Gary. As I look back, I wonder how many times the boys were coerced into letting me tag along because I was Frankie's twin? After Frankie died, I continued to play with the boys until they finally kicked me off the neighborhood football squad (I was crushed). We ended up at different high schools—Jamesville DeWitt, Nottingham, and The Convent School—making new friends, falling in and out of love, leaving for college, moving away, and making adult lives.

I don't know about the guys, but I've had great fun finding out about their wives and children, their careers, and their religious and political orientations. I've also had a delightful time reminiscing—of Seder meals and my First Communion (Brett came as my special guest), of overnights at the DeMartino's Oneida Lake cottage (I caught my first and only fish in their boat), of somebody (who was that?) getting stuck in the top of the Sagenkahn's weeping willow tree, of size two brown-suede high heels that Mrs. Sagenkahn let me parade around the house in, of roller skating in the Charlton's driveway, and of Aunt Louise's spaghetti sauce.

Our phone-call reunions have rekindled sad memories as well. Fortunately, for Alan and Gary, their memories are sketchy. They remember Frankie dying, the epidemic in general, the gamma globulin shots, the polio vaccine, and of being sad. The human facility to let go and move on has served them both well. They were blessed that Frankie's death probably didn't seem completely real to them. After all, what does death mean when you're only five and six years old?

For Brett and me, our emotional wounds were deeper and have, therefore, taken longer to heal. I'm thankful that we have rekindled our friendship. One thing that startled me is that none of the guys remember our neighbor Christy's death. Her death made such an impact on me. But, then again, at age four boys don't want to play with girls, unless a twin brother forces the issue.

Today, Brett lives in Florida and North Carolina and continues to indulge in his passion for boats. He's a licensed yacht broker and retired from a career in law enforcement. As a young man, he worked as a respiratory therapist—influenced by Frankie's death. Alan and Gary both inherited their dad's aptitude for electronics (translated into the related fields of avionics, communications, and computers). They've made successful careers combining these talents. Today, Alan lives in the DeWitt-Fayetteville area of metropolitan Syracuse and Gary lives in Florida. As a special treat, Alan recently sent me Aunt Louise's sauce recipe. I've told you about Alan and Gary's memories. Now, I'll let Brett do the talking.

Brett Sagenkahn

I'm one of three children, the middle kid sandwiched between an older and younger sister. Like every little boy, I dreamed of having a brother. I thought of Frankie as my brother or as close to a brother as two non-relatives could be. As I reflect, there are two distinct periods in my life: pre-Frankie's death and post-Frankie's death. My early memories of Frankie, Janice, and all the neighborhood kids are great. When Frankie died things changed for me. You can call me a pessimist or a realist, but either way, my philosophical orientation changed. Why did Frankie have to die? Why did other kids, like Janice, get sick? Why was I spared? I'm a logical guy. None of it made any sense.

My memories of Frankie's death are still vivid. My parents wanted to shield me, to protect me. How can you shield a kid when he just looked out the window and saw a hearse in his best friend's driveway? I was told that Frankie had died from polio. How could he be dead? I was just playing with him a few days ago. What does death mean to a six-year-old? I would soon find out as the days went by and Frankie wasn't around. Janice wasn't home either, because she had been admitted to the hospital on the evening of Frankie's burial. I wouldn't see her for a few more months.

Although my family's memories of that period are hazy at best, one of us may have had the polio virus in our system because my mother said that our house was quarantined for six weeks. I've racked my brain trying to remember if any of us were actually sick at that time. My parents can't remember either. Apparently, someone can have the virus in their system but never come down with the disease. Dr. Turek explained, in an earlier chapter, that people can also have what's called abortive polio (something like the flu). But, during that period, the disease can be passed onto others, and thus the need for quarantine. My best friend was dead, and I was imprisoned in my own home. To a six-year-old kid who just wanted to be outside riding bikes, eating Halloween candy, playing with yo-yos and marbles, and climbing trees with Frankie, things could not have been any bleaker.

When Janice and I spoke on the phone recently, many memories came flooding back. Jan had completely forgotten about our temporary classroom in the basement of Holy Cross Church. God, did I hate that place. It was dark and damp and just plain awful. When Janice and I returned to that classroom in the winter of 1954, the room was more depressing than ever. Frankie was gone, Janice could only attend school a few hours each day, and other classmates were absent. Polio had permanently changed the lives of many people in my little world.

During one of our conversations about that period, Janice mentioned that her parents were determined that she enjoy holidays after Frankie's death—holidays had always been a big deal in the Flood house. We recalled some significant dates: October 30 (the day that Frankie went to the hospital), October 31 (Halloween), and November 4 (the day that Frankie was buried).

All of a sudden it hit me. I have hated Halloween (and early November) for as long as I can remember. Although it has taken over fifty years, I think I'm finally beginning to understand why I just can't stand Halloween. Neither Janice nor I can remember the specifics of our 1953 Trick or Treat planning, but we probably had some great costumes picked out. Knowing that Frankie was in the hospital certainly would have colored my perceptions of Halloween; his death a few days later obviously destroyed the holiday for me—forever.

I mentioned earlier that on the day after Frankie died, I saw a black hearse in the Flood's driveway. Did I understand that Frankie was going to be in the Flood's house for a few more days, dead and in a casket? I knew Frankie was dead. I knew what a hearse was, but I don't think I understood the concept of a wake. In fact, I don't know if I had any concept of customs surrounding death because life had been pretty idyllic up until then.

Without understanding why until now, I may have always hated November 4, because it was the day that that big, ugly, black, hearse had transported my dead friend to his religious service and then on to the cemetery. Did I see that hearse drive away for the last time? I would never see my best friend again. It still makes me sad.

More Thoughts from Jan

Our neighborhood enjoyed many wonderful times after Frankie died, but life had changed for some of us more than others. When Alan and I spoke on the phone one evening not long ago, I reminded him that when we were four years old we decided to marry each other when we became adults. We even chose our home in the Nottingham section. Now, would you believe that Alan had no memory of our promise of marriage? Isn't that just like a guy?

Last night, I e-mailed Brett a photo of our kindergarten class picture (isn't technology wonderful?). Frankie and Brett are sitting next to each other on the far left. Alan is on the right in the front row and I'm in the second row directly behind him. I told Brett that after Frankie's death, my parents explained that I would never be alone, that Frankie would always watch over me from Heaven. That gift of simple faith, reinforced by my parents, has served me well all these years. But, it's not necessarily a concept that most adults (especially guys) find easy to embrace. In my heart, I know that Frankie has always watched over his special Earth pals and will continue to do so. Frankie must be very proud of his friends, Brett, Alan, and Gary!

Frank and Dorothy—Aftermath

Psychologists appreciate that adults and children often grieve in different ways. Adults seem to be stuck in grief, incapable of "coming out the other end" until we have worked through the various stages of grief—shock, denial, anger, bargaining, depression, acceptance. Not everyone makes it through all the stages; it's especially hard for parents who have lost a child.

In those first few months following Frankie's death, we sometimes woke up in the morning, and just for an instant, forgot that Frankie had died. When reality surfaced, we both wanted to crawl back under the covers and never come out. But, out of bed we crawled—especially to continue to care for Janice. All those little things that we wanted to go away, like dirty laundry and a bare refrigerator, forced us to move on. Bills needed to be paid, professional commitments had to be honored, and we needed to attend to Janice's rehabilitation needs. We survived in a place where both of us could coexist *and* in two distinct private hells reserved only for parents who lose a child.

Jan's grief, on the other hand, came and went in waves. One minute she would be so sad, the next minute a friend would ring the doorbell and out she'd go. Yet, all too soon, her little world came crashing down again. Perhaps she was fortunate, in the long run, that she was too young and innocent to know how to stop the grieving that she had to endure. It was such a painful time in her young life. She desperately needed to cling to something of Frankie. She insisted that we paint her bedroom that she had shared with Frankie maroon. Frankie had loved that color; therefore, Jan was going to love that color. Frankie must have seemed closer to her if the color of the room was his favorite. Her bedroom remained maroon until she became a teenager.

Nightmares haunted Janice for the first few months after she returned from the senior Flood's home. We believe that Jan had the dreams until she finally came to terms with the fact that Frankie was dead, that she would never see him again in this world. The dream was always the same:

Janice and Dorothy were wheeling Frankie down the street in the twin baby stroller, but he'd be six-years-old. Half-way down the street, Frankie disappeared.

Further down the street, he reappeared. At the end of the dream, Frankie disappeared for good.

During that brief painful period, Jan was afraid to go to bed at night; she knew that she would have the dream. Night after night, we rushed to her bedroom to console her as best we could, and explain that yes, Frankie was dead, and yes, she didn't want him to be dead. Oh, how her grief broke our hearts. Just as we could not spare Frankie the ravages of polio, we could not spare Janice the ravages of grief.

As time went on, we adopted patterns and traditions to ease our collective grief; some were more positive than others. Apparently, many families attempt to erase the memory of a dead child by removing photos and refusing to speak the child's name. Even if we had been so inclined, Jan would have never tolerated it. She understood that you cannot and should not bury memories of someone you love—memories of her twin were to be cherished. Our daughter insisted that we recall stories of her time with Frankie over and over and over again. As sad as it was for us to relive the six years that we were a young, carefree family of four, Jan was adamant that we never forget Frankie. Is this what that strange twin bond is all about? To forget Frankie would have been akin to cutting out her heart and soul.

We chose to remember Frankie in special ways. Although he could no longer enjoy holidays with us, we always dubbed a special white poinsettia plant, "Frankie's Christmas plant." At Easter time, there was always a special white Easter plant for Frankie. To this day, Jan continues these Christmas and Easter traditions.

Sadly, we developed a pattern that is quite common among families who have lost a child. After Frankie died, we avoided family photos. At a subconscious level, we knew that there was always someone missing. Unfortunately, we didn't recognize that we had developed such a pattern for many years and, then, not until a friend called our attention to the peculiarity. By that point, we had missed many opportunities to capture our family as a whole.

Although two more miscarriages would befall us (one on the day of Jan's eighth birthday party), our daughter Carol was born a few years after Frankie's death. Never was a child more loved and wanted than she was. She was not a replacement for Frankie; she was her own little person, loved for who she was. Jan had prayed hard that her new sibling would be a girl. Looking back, it was better that another child did not enter our lives too soon after Frankie's death. We needed time to heal. We allowed Janice to choose her sister's name.

Thoughts from Jan

As a student of psychology and counseling, I have always viewed my dream as something that forced me to accept reality—a reality that I wanted to resist. My dream seemed to be an expression of the bargaining associated with mourning, that period when we say to God: OK, let me just see him (or her) one more time, when deep inside you know it's impossible. Since Frankie's death, I've experienced the death of many people that I dearly loved, including the death of my parents. But, I have never endured devastation equal to what I felt when Frankie died. I didn't know how to stop the hurt. It just had to run its course.

Yet, the day of my sister's birth was a joyous occasion. I can remember running to my parent's bedroom phone to hear the news. I looked out the window at a beautiful full moon. I know Frankie was smiling from Heaven.

Frankie and Jan at age six months—one of Mom's favorite
photos. Jan likes the photo op. Frankie is not so sure.

What's wrong, Frankie? Can I help?

Here, Frankie. Doesn't this taste good?—*Photo reproduced by David
Nichols with permission from the Syracuse Post Standard. Picture from the
Society Section of the Syracuse Herald American, December 4, 1949.*

Frank and Jan hugging—looks like the birthday party was successful. Frankie broke his arm on this spot at age four.

Frankie, Jan, and Dad at Skaneateles Lake—Jan is practicing her baseball swing to keep up with the guys.

Moses DeWitt Elementary School kindergarten class in 1952—Frankie is in the front row, far left with Brett next to him. Alan is in the front row, second from the right with Jan directly behind him. *The photo is included with permission from Jamesville DeWitt Central School District Superintendent, Dr. Alice Kendrick.*

Frankie and Jan with the *real* Santa Claus at the North Pole,
Adirondack Mountains—voted our best family vacation (1952).

The Floods before polio struck in 1953—a happy family with rambunctious twins.

Frankie gave Jan this ten-dollar bill and two silver dollars a few weeks before he
died—very out of character for the self-appointed "keeper of the money." *This
photo has been sized in accordance with U.S. Secret Service reproduction regulations.*

Frankie was waked at home. This is the Memory Book supplied by Schumacher-Whelan Funeral Home. In spite of the fear of polio, a few hundred friends and family members came to the wake. Jan insisted upon attending the wake, funeral, and burial. This page notes the numerous signatures made by Jan. Frankie and Jan had been practicing what they called "curly writing." To this day, Jan wonders what possessed her to sign her name so many times in the book. Did she want to make sure that Frankie knew she was there, that she loved him and would never abandon him?

Dr. (Jaros) Turek was a pediatric resident at SUNY College of
Medicine at Syracuse. She cared for Frankie and Jan when they were
hospitalized at City Hospital and signed Frankie's death certificate.
She is the medical voice in this book. Jan was reunited with her,
by phone, in March 2006. *Photo supplied by Dr. Turek.*

John J. Kalamarides

Dr. Kalamarides was Jan's orthopedic surgeon; he supervised her
rehabilitation. Jan will always be grateful for the excellent care she
received from Dr. Kalamarides, Dr. Kopel, Dr. Alsever, Dr. (Jaros) Turek,
the staff at City Hospital, and her physical therapists. Dr. Kalamarides
died on January 10, 2007. *Photo supplied by Mr. John Kalamarides.*

Back to school—with those awful brown orthopedic shoes. First grade teacher at
Moses DeWitt Elementary School, Mrs. Jean MacDougall, visited Jan each day
until she was able to return to school for both morning and afternoon sessions. Jan
will never forget Mrs. MacDougall. *The photo was reproduced by David Nichols with
permission from the* Syracuse Post Standard. *The photo appeared on January 13, 1954.*

PART TWO: PROGRESS

Mrs. Betty Anne Read and Mrs. Jeanne LaVoy—Mothers Unite

The concept of a house-to-house solicitation had been successfully tried by several March of Dimes local chapters since the late 1940s, but in 1950, the Maricopa County (Phoenix area) Arizona chapter organized what would become the first of many Mothers Marches. On January 16, 1950, porch lights were lit to signal the event. Mothers from all over the city, armed with Mason jars to hold the donations, rang the doorbells of their neighbors. Within one hour, they had raised just under $45,000 from 42,228 donors. The campaign had been well publicized with the help of local radio, billboard, and newspaper ads, and children came home from school that day with a flyer advertising the event. Trucks with large loudspeakers clamped to their tops canvassed neighborhoods heralding the commencement of the 7:00 PM event. The Mothers March slogan was simple: "Turn on Your Porch Light, Help Fight Polio Tonight."[1]

The National Foundation decided to turn the successful local event into a national campaign. If 2,300 mother volunteers in Phoenix could collect close to $50,000 in one night, what could mothers across the country do? Between 1951 and 1955 the National Foundation raised $250 million, due, in part, to the success of the annual Mothers Marches. From 1951 to 1961, actress Helen Hayes was the National Chairperson. The Foundation desperately needed money if it was to realize its ultimate goal for a cure or a vaccine.[2]

Mrs. Read

As the mother of five children under seven years old, I was more than happy to help Dorothy with the January 1954 Mothers March. The DeWitt polio epidemic had devastated us. Most of our friends knew at least one family in our peaceful, eastern suburb who had been targeted by polio in 1953—they were our children's playmates, our fellow parishioners, our neighbors, our friends. My husband and I had attended Frankie's wake; we sent a funeral arrangement of white and yellow mums. My oldest daughter Carol and Jan have been close friends since childhood. My husband's mother and Frank's parents had been friends as well.[3]

For several months, we had heard that a vaccine was on its way. Money raised by the Mothers March could help pay for some of the vaccine development costs. How could I say no to the local chapter of the National Foundation? So, on a cold snowy evening in January, I donned my navy wool cape and canvassed our street. Everyone was generous. I had officially become a Mothers March "Contact Mother." I believe Dorothy served as a "Section Lieutenant" that year. Like most of the young mothers in our area, I continued as a volunteer for several years.

In 1957, we carried vaccine cards along with our mason jars. We presented a card to each mother. The card explained the importance of the vaccine and served as an easy way to keep track of our family members' inoculation schedules. Every mother appreciated that card; I certainly know that I did (our twins would be born later that year making us a family of nine). Ten thousand mothers in Syracuse and Onondaga County participated in the 1957 Mothers March.[4]

Those Phoenix mothers were really on to something. Soon we (the mothers who marched to fight polio), became the largest group of charitable volunteers that the country had ever seen. That's an amazing accomplishment when you think about it. But, then again, when it comes to protecting children mothers make the best warriors!

Mrs. LaVoy

Like the Reads, our families have known the Floods and Coolicans for many years. Jan has been a close friend of our daughters Pat and Marty since they were little girls and my brother Ray enjoyed tennis matches with Dorothy's brother Bud. Although we were unable to attend Frankie's wake, members of our Altar and Rosary Society sent a beautiful pink aster plant. Both Dorothy and I had been active in the society for a few years.[5]

Our own son, Jim, had contracted polio in 1945 and was hospitalized for about a month. The poor child was in an iron lung for a short time. Fortunately, he recovered completely, but the fear of polio (and what it had done to Jim) was never far from my mind. Our family had been blessed, and I wanted to help in anyway I could. As I recall, my involvement in the Mothers March began in 1954 and continued throughout the 1950s. Many of the mothers who knew the Floods and other DeWitt families affected by the disease volunteered as well. Polio had struck far too close to home.

Although my involvement was limited to the Mothers March, local chapters of the March of Dimes sponsored numerous fundraisers including parades, street theaters, piggy banks, rummage sales, coffee parties, carnivals, you name it. Polio directly or indirectly affected all Americans. Those families who had been spared lived in dread of the yearly polio season. In the winter of 1954, soon after the Mothers March, Lucille Ball, Desi Arnaz, and their children hosted a special TV show to benefit the March of Dimes. The entire country must have watched that program. The polio trials were only a few months away and *I Love Lucy* was everyone's favorite show. First Lady Mamie Eisenhower was named "First Lady of the 1954 Mothers March on Polio." Perhaps at no other point in the peacetime history of our country did our citizens unite in greater numbers to fight a common enemy.

◆   ◆   ◆

Under the direction of Elaine Whitelaw, the Women's Division of the National Foundation sponsored activities throughout the country. Local sewing bees made "polio blankets," and telethons were introduced as a successful fundraising venue. From 1945 to1960, an annual celebrity fashion show was held at the Waldorf-Astoria Hotel in New York. *Life, Look, Ladies Home Journal, Vogue,* and other magazines featured the event each year. The shows were gala affairs with fashions supplied by Christian Dior and other famous designers. Movie stars including Grace Kelly, Marilyn Monroe, and Joan Fontaine modeled the fashions. In 1954, Salvador Dali created a victory statue stage set, symbolizing a hopeful triumph over the disease. Fashion shows took place in many cities throughout the country including Buffalo, Baltimore, Dallas, Chicago, and San Francisco. Even the famed jeweler, Harry Winston, became involved in the crusade. He sponsored an exhibit called "The Court of Jewels." The public was allowed to view the gems in exchange for a small donation to the March of Dimes.[7]

There seemed no end to the creativity exhibited by fundraisers. Beginning in 1939, a "Mile of Dimes" campaign challenged citizens to contribute enough dimes to measure a mile when placed end to end. Probably every child in the country learned that there were 92,160 dimes in a mile. Major corporations and small businesses alike gave of their time and talents to support the cause. In 1953, American Airlines took a small iron lung replica on a ten-thousand-mile tour across the United States to raise money. A "March of Dimes Tobacco Auction" took place in Lexington, Kentucky, in 1954, while a "Sunkist Orange Auction" took place in 1952. The auction was held on the Hudson River's Pier 21 in New York. The oranges had been donated by the Tulane County Fruit Exchange of Porterville, California.[8]

Expenditures during summers of 1949, 1950, and 1954, some of the worst epidemic years, seriously depleted National Foundation funds, so "Emergency March of Dimes" campaigns were held throughout the country. In 1954, Basil O'Connor, President Roosevelt's former law partner turned National Foundation executive and spokesperson, declared the two-week period between August 16 and August 31, an emergency fund-raising period. Although most Americans were happy to participate in the fund drives, some local organizations and individuals complained that the summer drive was interfering with their efforts. One such complaint was lodged by a Syracuse, New York, newspaper reader. [9]

Every kid's favorite TV program, the *Howdy Doody Show,* actively supported the March of Dimes. In 1955, "Doody Dime Day" raised $30,000 for the cause. School campaigns encouraged children to bring their dimes to school. Every older baby boomer probably remembers contributing to the school programs. Even today, those "kids" speak of their contributions submitted on cards shaped like schoolhouses with slots for dimes. [10]

◆   ◆   ◆

How Did the March of Dimes Spend the Millions of Dollars Raised?

The March of Dimes was committed to finding a cure or a vaccine, and it was equally committed to assisting polio patients and their families with the cost of ongoing care.

According to John R. Paul, MD, author of *A History of Poliomyelitis,* one of the most important contributions made by the National Foundation was the establishment of respirator centers to care for patients suffering from the bulbar form of the disease. The Foundation provided special training for physicians, nurses, and technicians and organized mobile teams to be dispatched to areas dealing with large epidemics. During the 1950s, the National Foundation responded to both national and international requests, transporting polio patients as well as lifesaving equipment. [11]

Although many patients were able to be weaned from iron lungs and rocking beds, many patients could not be freed from the equipment. Thus, the National Foundation decided to invest in respiratory technology that would be better suited to home use. One of the machines was a chest respirator that offered a distinct advantage over the perpetual confines of a metal cylinder. In the 1950s, home care was a radical philosophy but one that would prove to not only be cost saving but would eventually become the preferred method of treatment. Studies have consistently shown that disabled patients do far better, both physically and emotionally, if they are allowed to remain at home with their families.[12]

Fundraising figures were staggering but so were the medical expenses that included hospital costs, physician fees, iron lungs, wheelchairs, braces, chest respirators, household help, orthopedic shoes, transportation costs, and attendant care. Even with the assistance of the Foundation, families often incurred enormous expenses making home and auto modifications to accommodate the disabled family member.[13]

In 1954, the National Foundation provided assistance to over seventy thousand people, many of whom had contracted polio in earlier epidemics. For severely involved paralytic or respirator patients, annual expenses often ran between $10,000 and $20,000—an astronomical sum when one considers that the average annual income for men was only $3,200 while the average annual salary for women was little more than $1,000. Some insurance companies offered polio insurance coverage that paid up to $5,000 for care but most people had no health insurance. Even wealthy families found the costs overwhelming. Between 1938 and 1962, 59 percent of National Foundation income was devoted to direct patient care needs and medical expenses.[14]

Alice (Jaros) Turek, MD, MPH—The Salk Vaccine

Within months of the 1953 DeWitt, New York, polio outbreak that struck the Floods and so many other families, the March of Dimes undertook the largest clinical field trial in the history of the United States to test the safety and effectiveness of Dr. Jonas Salk's new polio vaccine. Soon the horror of annual polio epidemics in our country would end.

In order to appreciate the significance of the Salk vaccine, we must first examine the steps (and missteps) that motivated and frustrated the scientific community for several decades. Since 1908, due to the work of Drs. Karl Landsteiner and E. Popper, we had known that poliomyelitis was caused by a virus. Yet, it was nearly fifty years before advances in the field of medicine yielded a way to prevent the spread of the disease.[1]

As is true with most scientific advancements, a number of factors had to come together before success could be declared. This was certainly true of the polio vaccine. It's so easy to forget just how much our world has changed in the last one hundred years. A hundred years ago most Americans still used outhouses and chamber pots. The first horrific polio epidemic that affected a major portion of the United States did not occur until 1916.

Trained in the years immediately following WWII, I was all too aware that medicine was still a very young discipline. An understanding of what medicine terms germ theory (the belief that small organisms, too small to be seen by the naked eye, caused many diseases) had not been validated until the late nineteenth century. It was not until the 1930s that scientists dared try vaccination on human subjects because the process of causing immunity by injecting a subject with viral material was a laborious, trial and error endeavor that first had to be tested on animals. But, in spite of the slow pace of research, progress in related fields was yielding important research tools. For instance, with the 1931 invention of the electron microscope viruses could finally be directly observed rather than inferred.

To facilitate an understanding of the various additional factors that led to the successful production of the first polio vaccine, I'll divide our discussion into a number of categories. Of course, such organization begs the proverbial question: What came first, the chicken or the egg *or* what came first, the money or the scientific knowledge? When it comes to the development of the first polio vaccine, the money and the science came together at around the same time.

Financial Requirements for Vaccine Production

Obviously, an enormous amount of money was needed to fund vaccine research and development. As was described in an earlier chapter, an effective polio vaccine may have been several years or decades longer in the making if it had not been for the motivation of President Franklin Delano Roosevelt. Disabled by the disease in the 1920s, Roosevelt was committed to find a cure or a vaccine for the virus. With the establishment of his National Foundation for Infantile Paralysis in 1938 (known today as the March of Dimes), a unique partnership between the scientific community and the general public was forged.

With the determination of a United States citizenry who had been emboldened and hardened by two world wars and a devastating financial depression, there was hope that sufficient funds and manpower could be raised to yield an effective polio vaccine. It is estimated that by 1954, two-thirds of the population of the United States had donated money to the Foundation. Seven million United States citizens had donated their services. Propelled by the fear of polio epidemics that were getting worse, Americans were as determined as Roosevelt to end polio's reign of terror. While some parents coped with a child (or children) killed or disabled by the virus, other parents lived in fear that their children would not be spared for long.[2]

Once manpower and fundraising issues had been addressed, a number of other issues needed to be settled before a vaccine could be developed. An important breakthrough came during the tenure of Harry Weaver, the Director of Research at the National Foundation from 1946 to 1953. Under Weaver's direction, the system of how large scientific research grants were awarded to universities was revised. Using grant formulas favorable to universities, it had finally become feasible for academic institutions to adequately fund research teams and facilities.[3]

Basic Science Requirements

There were a number of details that scientists call "basic science issues" that had to be verified before vaccine production could commence. Most importantly, it had to be established that the results obtained by earlier researchers (that there were only three Types of polio virus) were correct. This information was necessary in order to develop an effective vaccine, since the serum would have to be capable of producing immune responses to all virus Types. Moreover, a safe and adequate supply of the virus would have to be developed to produce the vaccine and researchers would have to determine which vaccine type (killed-virus or live-virus) would provide the best immune protection, without risk of contracting the disease from the vaccine.

Sadly, early vaccine attempts had not gone well. In 1935, field trials on two different vaccines named for their researchers—Maurice Brodie, William Hallock Park, and John Kolmer—were conducted with unsatisfactory results. In the end, the Kolmer vaccine killed and paralyzed several children. The Brodie-Park vaccine, tested in North Carolina, Virginia, and California, caused the death and paralysis of children as well. Throughout the 1930s and 1940s, several other researchers investigated live-virus vaccine possibilities and scientists continued to debate the pros and cons of both vaccine types. Researchers lined up on both sides of the argument, but because of the problems related to the early vaccine trials it was some time before the medical and scientific community dared to consider another large polio vaccine trial. Yet, in spite of setbacks and fears, the National Foundation was determined to find a vaccine. To that end, the organization's Director of Research, Harry Weaver, canvassed several well-respected polio researchers—among them was a young Dr. Jonas Salk.[4]

Choosing the Vaccine Research Team

In 1948, Jonas Salk was hired by the March of Dimes to confirm the work of previous investigators. From 1949 until 1951, Salk's lab at the University of Pittsburgh tested dozens of polio strains from stool and throat cultures as well as from central nervous tissue obtained from autopsies. The final results of the typing program indicated that of the 196 tested strains, all fell into three distinct Types (I, II and III). Type I accounted for over 80 percent of the strains, with the *Mahoney* strain considered the most virulent Type I strain (this fact would prove significant a little later).[5]

Eventually, Dr. Salk was able to grow the three known Types of poliovirus in his lab. With this knowledge, Salk and his team developed a killed-virus polio vaccine, also known as an inactivated polio vaccine, or IPV vaccine for short. The team subjected the vaccine to pilot trials in the Pittsburgh area between 1952 and 1954. Salk even gave the vaccine to his own children. Many disabled individuals were used as trial subjects. Today's sensitivity to the rights of the disabled would never allow such testing procedures.[6]

Several other researchers were busy during the early 1950s testing alternative vaccines in animal and human subjects. Some, most notably Albert Sabin, remained convinced that a vaccine based on live but weakened or attenuated virus was the only way to establish a lifetime immunity. Sabin also feared that it was difficult to prove that the polio virus had been completely killed using Salk's production process. Sabin argued that although his vaccine contained live polio virus, it was virus material that had been weakened. He felt that Salk's killed-virus was potentially more dangerous than his because if any viral material remained live, it would be injected into patients with full potency.[7]

The National Foundation Announces a Field Trial

Salk's vaccine had the important advantage of being preferred and financially backed by the National Foundation and its most vocal vaccine-crusader, Basil O'Connor. O'Connor's own daughter had contracted polio in the summer of 1950; sadly, she succumbed from the disease in 1961. As was true of many people involved in the polio fight, the war against polio had become all too personal. For instance, Actress Helen Hayes, who chaired the March of Dimes Fashion Show for a number of years, had lost her nineteen-year-old daughter, Mary Elizabeth, to the virus in 1949. Similarly, many of the millions of volunteers who participated in the Foundation's yearly March of Dimes campaign had joined the effort because someone they knew or loved had contracted the disease.[8]

On March 26, 1953, with the backing of the National Foundation, Dr. Salk gave a CBS radio address regarding the status of his research. Soon, Basil O'Connor announced the creation of the "Vaccine Advisory Committee," a group of distinguished scientists who were charged with designing a vaccine trial. As I mentioned earlier in this book, a polio vaccine could come none too soon. But, following established scientific protocol, the vaccine would have to be tested for safety and effectiveness before it could be considered for mass distribution.[9]

Under the direction of Dr. Thomas Francis Jr. of the University of Michigan's School of Public Health, a double-blind study was designed to test the Salk vaccine throughout the country. The term double-blind means that neither the researchers nor the study participants knew who would receive the vaccine. Concerns about Dr. Salk's vaccine and the ethical issues involved in a mass clinical trial produced many detractors and much discussion and revision of methods. Yet, by early 1954, the March of Dimes was on track to commence what was referred to as its "Shot Heard Round the World." The massive field trial was scheduled for spring 1954. Unfortunately, additional problems and setbacks would plague the effort.[10]

Scientific Debate Continues

To say that there was dissent and disagreement among the scientific and medical communities would be an understatement. While ego and political forces were certainly at play, there were several legitimate concerns. There was long-term debate as to which type of vaccine (live or killed virus) would be the safest and most effective. There was debate as to whether a vaccine should be developed at all; some practitioners favored the "passive immunity" attributed to gamma globulin intramuscular injections. It was even suggested that rather than a placebo, another type of vaccine should be given so that all participating children would derive some benefit from the trial. A placebo is an inactive substance used for control purposes in scientific experiments. Some scientists were concerned about Salk's choice of the Type I *Mahoney* strain in the development of his vaccine because of its documented virulence. Development of a trial design caused additional debate with some proponents favoring the methodology chosen by Francis and his team and others favoring a design proposed by Salk and the National Foundation—this conflict (and the resulting compromise) will be covered in more detail in the "Polio Pioneer" chapter of this book.[11]

Vaccine Production Begins, Problems Soon Arise

Since Salk's lab was not equipped to manufacture a sufficient quantity of vaccine for a mass trial, Basil O'Connor approached Parke-Davis in the spring of 1953 to gauge the company's interest in the manufacture of the polio vaccine. There were a number of financial, logistical, and public relations issues that had to be weighed by the company, but the firm was deeply committed to the development of vaccines. Opting to accept the challenge to mass produce the vaccine, Parke-Davis elicited the cooperation of well-respected Connaught Laboratories (in Toronto). Soon, Connaught began providing weekly supplies of live-polio virus to Parke-Davis in Detroit and Eli Lily in Indianapolis. The Canadian laboratory cultivated the live virus in a solution called Medium 199, and was able to provide a sufficient supply of the virus culture for the massive field trial planned by the National Foundation. Ultimately, nearly two million children would participate in the spring 1954 undertaking.[12]

Once vaccine production commenced, it was soon learned that the scientists were having trouble making the vaccine from the instructions provided by Salk. Because Salk continued to modify his production protocol, Parke-Davis and its employees were kept in a constant state of confusion. With pressure to complete vaccine production within a relatively short period of time, errors were made. Salk blamed the errors on the company, while Parke-Davis cited Salk's ever-changing instructions as the reason for production mistakes. Moreover, it had been documented that some lots of the vaccine did not adequately pass tests for safety since some lots contained live virus. This was especially important given that Salk had decided to use the *Mahoney* strain for the Type I element of his trivalent vaccine (a vaccine that provides immunity to all three Types of polio in one dose). As mentioned previously, the *Mahoney* strain had been shown to be the most virulent. By late 1953, due to manufacturing problems, several other pharmaceutical companies, in addition to Parke-Davis, were invited to participate in the production process.[13]

The 1954 Field Trial Is Back on Track

After instituting additional safety and quality control standards and refining vaccine production methods, the National Foundation's polio vaccine field trial was back on track. One day before the planned April 26, 1954, startup date, it was announced that the trial would take place. Production problems, as outlined in the above paragraph, had temporarily placed the commencement of the trial in serious jeopardy. All vaccine used in the field trial was manufactured by Parke-Davis and Eli-Lilly.[14]

◆   ◆   ◆

It can be argued that too much pressure had been exerted to quickly develop a vaccine, but one must also consider the climate under which the National Foundation, polio scientists, medical personnel, drug companies, national and local governments, and the global community were operating. Polio season was fast approaching, and worldwide epidemics were getting worse. The 1952 epidemic, the worst in U.S. history, had demonstrated what had been known since the 1916 epidemic. Polio had the ability to devastate entire families with cunning speed. During the 1940s and early 1950s, there were incidences where as many as three and four children in one family died of bulbar polio. Eleven out of fourteen children in one Iowa family contracted the disease in 1952—no children died but two were paralyzed. Epidemics had clearly demonstrated that a vaccine was desperately needed. Although polio killed far fewer children than many other diseases, the vision of children struggling for breath in iron lungs or struggling to walk via cumbersome, heavy braces and crutches pulled at the heart strings of every parent in the world.[15]

◆   ◆   ◆

<u>Note</u>: For additional information regarding the development of the Salk and Sabin vaccines, the 1955 trial results, and the Cutter situation, you may wish to consult the books written by John Paul, Paul A. Offit, and David Oshinsky (See Consulted Works).

Mrs. Louise DeMartino—"Parental Request to Participate"

There was no community in the country that prayed for an end to polio more than DeWitt, New York. We had relived the horrors of the fall 1953 polio epidemic each and every day for the past several months. As neighbors, we had watched one little boy die while his twin sister battled the emotional aftermath of his death and her own physical rehabilitation. Other children from our suburb continued their battle as well. We had the added burden of trying to explain death to our children.

However, we were encouraged by the news of the day. There was talk of a vaccine trial and an opportunity for our young children to participate. As winter snows gave way to spring thaws, our hearts and minds began to turn to summer and another polio season.

A plan for the field trial clinic at Moses DeWitt took shape. In spite of the risks of an unknown vaccine, the thought of doing nothing to protect our children seemed riskier still. I was astonished to learn from newspaper articles after the trials that a much higher percentage of DeWitt parents gave permission for their children to participate in the study than was true across the country. But, then again, DeWitt parents knew polio's wrath all too well.[1]

In early April, radio and newspaper gossip columnist, Walter Winchell, opened his radio show with his usual salutation. Then, he proceeded to tell us that the National Foundation was planning on vaccinating our children with an unsafe virus that had killed several monkeys. The next week, he added that the Foundation was stockpiling "little white coffins" in which to bury the children who would be killed by the dangerous polio vaccine. Can you imagine the panic that Winchell's radio addresses caused? Pediatricians' office phones must have been ringing off the hooks during that period.[2]

◆   ◆   ◆

On April 25, 1954, (one day before our son Alan was to participate in the trial) word came that the National Foundation's Vaccine Advisory Committee and the Public Health Service had given permission to begin the trial as planned. But, because of the Winchell broadcast, 150,000 children were pulled from the trials by ambivalent parents. When we brought Alan to Moses DeWitt School that morning, LJ and I prayed that we had made the right decision for our little boy. Because our younger son Gary was in kindergarten, he did not participate in the field trial. The trial was limited to first, second, and third graders.

We have never regretted signing the National Foundation's "Parental Request to Participate" form. I now understand that the wording of the permission form was chosen to make parents feel that it was an honor for our children to be part of the 1954 trial. We *were* honored. For the first time in history, parents had been given an opportunity to protect their children from the disease that had taken the life of so many (including my older brother and Frankie) and altered the lives of countless more. The form letter, composed by Mr. Basil O'Connor of the March of Dimes, indicated that participation in the trials was a moral act benefiting not only our own children and their peers but future generations of children as well. Jan views the parents and her fellow "Polio Pioneers" as pretty courageous people. I guess we were. But, you see, no fear could match the fear of continued polio outbreaks.[3]

1,829,916 "Polio Pioneers"—The 1954 Salk Vaccine Trials

On April 26, 1954, 1,829,916 children in grades one, two, and three from 211 counties in forty-four states, as well as children from Canada and Finland, took part in a study designed to prove whether the Salk vaccine was safe and effective. This age group was picked because it was considered the most vulnerable. In 1954, 50 percent of all polio cases occurred in children under ten (75 percent of cases occurred in people under twenty). It would be nearly a year before the University of Michigan's Vaccine Evaluation Center, under the direction of Dr. Thomas Francis, announced the results of the trial. One report indicates that the trial cost $7.5 million (the equivalent of $5 billion today).[1]

The chosen counties in the United States included areas across the country that had experienced especially high incidences of the disease. According to an excellent 1999 retrospective written by Dr. Arnold S. Monto, several other factors were considered when choosing participating areas. For instance, it had been noted that population centers with 50,000 to 200,000 residents had experienced a higher infection rate than had been noted in more populated areas; smaller geographic pockets had even larger incident rates but were deemed less suitable for the study. Designers also felt that it was important that trial sites be held in willing school districts since schools would be used to identify potential participants. Since the polio season had commenced in the southern United States by the time of the trial, children in some states were disqualified from the study because scientists would have been unable to differentiate between children who had developed antibodies as a result of the vaccine versus those who had been exposed naturally to the virus. As mentioned above, Canadian children in forty-eight health districts in three provinces and children in two areas of Finland were included in the study. The trials in Canada and Finland took place in June and July. In Halifax, kindergarten children were included rather than third graders because of their past susceptibility to the virus. In

Finland, children age 5-14 were included. Approximately 60,000 Canadian and Finnish children participated [2]

◆   ◆   ◆

Only after returning their "Request to Participate" forms, were children cleared to participate in the trial. Some children received the Salk vaccine; some were given placebo injections. A third group of children acted as observed, non-injected control subjects. Children had to be divided into these three groups because, based on principles of scientific method (a word used to describe the overall procedures followed in scientific studies), it was the only way that scientists could validate the effectiveness and safety of the vaccine. According to John R. Paul's, *A History of Poliomyelitis,* the field trial (as conceived by Francis and his colleagues) consisted of a double-blind study in which 600,000 to 700,000 first, second, and third grade students randomly received vaccine or placebo control material. Four hundred thousand second-grade students in some locales received the vaccine, while first and third graders in the same areas acted as observed controls. Due to a professional dispute over correct experimental methods, two different designs were simultaneously used in the actual trial. David M. Oshinsky's, *Polio An American Story,* indicates that while some areas followed the Francis model described above, other areas developed a different model preferred by Salk and the National Foundation. In these areas, only second-grade students received the actual vaccine, while first and third graders acted as observed control subjects. County officials in each locale determined which model was to be used. Before the trials began, each participating county hosted a workshop to educate medical and volunteer personnel. [3]

Participating students received a series of three injections, with all shots given by the end of June. Although the necessity for the series of injections complicated field trial administration, final results indicated that, in most communities, adherence was excellent. Apparently, only a small percentage of children received less than the full three shot series; in fact, 95 percent received the full series. A 1954 cartoon, entitled *Rounding Third,* graphically demonstrated the importance of the three shot series. The first two doses were necessary to produce a primary immune reaction, and the third dose "boosted" antibody levels for optimum immunity. [4]

At the close of the study, letters were sent to parents explaining which group their child (or children) had been placed in. Based on the assigned group, parents were told whether an additional series of shots would be required to provide immunity. The children who participated in the trials were designated as "Polio Pioneers." An estimated 20,000 physicians and public health officers, 40,000 nurses, 14,000 school principals, 50,000 teachers, and between 200,000–250,000 volunteers had been involved in the trial.[5]

As would be expected, some administrative problems arose. In one area, several children arrived for their shot without signed consent forms; at another vaccine site, a child received two doses in one injection. In Schenectady, New York, nurses reused syringes, thereby giving vaccine material to some children who had been assigned to receive the placebo, and vice versa. Vaccination records were stolen in one Iowa town. In a North Carolina community, doctors absconded with vaccine supplies, which they promptly used to vaccinate their own children and the children of their friends. Yet, all in all, the study was considered an administrative success.[6]

◆   ◆   ◆

National Trial Summary: 650,000 children received the vaccine, 750,000 received a placebo, and 430,000 children acted as non-vaccinated controls. The National Foundation dubbed a six-year-old boy named Randy Kerr of Fairfax County, Virginia, as "Polio Pioneer #1," although it was impossible to determine which child in America actually received the vaccine first.[7]

◆   ◆   ◆

Newspapers throughout the country ran articles featuring the young "Polio Pioneers." On May 3, 1954, the *Syracuse Herald Journal* printed a story about the DeWitt vaccine trial activities. Onondaga County had been chosen as one of the participating counties, and clinics were set up throughout the area. Although the field trial came too late to prevent the outbreak that struck the DeWitt area in 1953, two survivors of the outbreak were able to participate in the study. According to Moses DeWitt principal, Ted Calver, 307 children took part in the clinics at Moses DeWitt, Lyndon, and Pebble Hill Schools. Eighty-nine percent of eligible children received permission to participate in the trial. Among the participants was Janice (Flood) Nichols, author of this book.[8]

Jan, as a first grader, was one of the children who received the vaccine—indicating that the local officials had chosen the model proposed by Francis and his colleagues. Jan's parents had explained that she needed the vaccine because her polio case had provided immunity to only one Type of polio. It is interesting to note that across the country, only 60 to 70 percent of eligible children received permission from their parents to participate in the 1954 trials (far lower than the DeWitt participation level). The parents of the eastern suburbs of Syracuse were obviously anxious to protect their children. They did not want a repeat of the horror of fall 1953.[9]

The *Syracuse Herald Journal* article included photos of Jan and other "Polio Pioneers" (the Coolican uncles must have organized another photo op). Jan's mother gave her the article a few years before she died. In one of the photos, Jan has just been inoculated by physician-volunteer, Dr. John Holmes. She has a very serious expression on her face. Although she appears slightly anxious in the photo, Jan recalls that her thoughts were of Frankie. Whether newspaper observers were aware of it or not, they were looking at the photo of a very sad little girl who was grieving for her twin. The vaccine had come too late to save his life.[10]

Alice (Jaros) Turek, MD, MPH—Salk Results, the Cutter Situation

The 1954 field trial results were announced on April 12, 1955, (the tenth anniversary of President Franklin Delano Roosevelt's death) by Dave Garroway of NBC's *Today* show. Garroway proclaimed that the Salk vaccine was safe and effective as the American public huddled around televisions, radios, and public address systems to hear the long-awaited results. A May 1954 Gallup poll had shown that more Americans were aware of the Salk vaccine trial than were aware of the complete name of their president, Dwight David Eisenhower.[1]

Results

As the general public celebrated the trial results with family and friends, Dr. Thomas Francis Jr. of the University of Michigan's Vaccine Evaluation Center, was occupied with a technical lecture at his university's Rackham Hall auditorium. Highlighting the results of the trial with slides and charts, the Center's analysis indicated that the vaccine was considered 60 to 80 percent effective against paralytic polio, 60 percent effective against Type I polio, and 70 to 80 percent effective against Types II and III. Striking a cautionary note, Francis acknowledged that while the vaccine was safe, individual lots had varied in quality.[2]

Francis had always been skeptical of the cultural and economic differences that had been inherent in the design study. Consequently, he qualified the remarks he made to his peers. According to David Oshinsky's excellent volume, *Polio,* Francis had conducted his own analysis that had shown that the parents who had given permission for their children to receive an inoculation (whether it resulted in a vaccine or placebo injection) tended to be better educated with higher incomes than the parent group that had refused inoculation. Moreover, the inoculated group's living conditions largely protected them from exposure to the virus, and, therefore, made their immune systems less able to deal with the polio virus once exposed. Thus,

Francis had more confidence in the vaccine and placebo groups where the test populations were so closely matched. He concluded that effectiveness in this "injected population" might be 80 to 90 percent against paralytic polio, 60 to 70 percent effective against Type I virus, and 90 percent or more effective against Types II and III virus, and therefore, different from the result statistics listed in the previous paragraph.[3]

Because of the analyzed differences between the injected and non-injected groups of children, Francis felt that the 1954 trial design had been carried out with unavoidable flaws. To his scientific audience, Francis was free to discuss the difference in the statistical analysis. But, Francis knew that in order to protect the public, he had to rely on the most conservative results on which to base his team's conclusions and recommendations.

Jonas Salk also spoke at the assembly. His remarks indicated that he had made significant improvements over the vaccine used in the 1954 trials. He boasted that his new improved vaccine and inoculation procedures might lead to 100 percent protection from paralysis. Sadly, Salk never thanked the scientists who worked in his University of Pittsburgh lab, and some of his co-workers were deeply hurt by the slight. However, to his credit, Salk never sought a patent on the vaccine.[4]

Some scientists believed that Salk's remarks had undermined the trial's results and that Salk had been unfairly singled out for praise above other critical pioneer researchers. More importantly, many scientists still doubted the safety of the killed-virus Salk vaccine. Yet, later that day, U.S. Secretary of Health, Education, and Welfare Oveta Culp Hobby announced a unanimous recommendation to license the Salk vaccine. The National Foundation had already ordered and paid for nine million doses of the vaccine that were ready for distribution.[5]

1955 Mass Polio Immunization Begins

Throughout the world, governments clamored to purchase American-made vaccine supplies. President Eisenhower signed an executive order requiring that vaccine production protocols be provided to seventy-five nations free of charge. The United Nations announced that it had set up regional centers at Yale and the Hadassah Medical School in Jerusalem. The country and world breathed a collective but short-lived sigh of relief.[6]

With the completion of the 1954 trial results, control and oversight of the vaccine was turned over to the federal government. During the next few weeks, the federal department known as the "Laboratory of Biologics Control" approved vaccine lots made by Cutter Laboratories, Eli Lilly, Parke-Davis, Pitman-Moore, and Wyeth. Between April 12, 1955, and May 7, 1955, children across the country received 4,844,000 million doses of the vaccine.[7]

On April 22, 1955, Dr. Jonas Salk received a special citation presented to him in the White House by President Dwight D. Eisenhower.[8]

Problems

Unfortunately, alarm bells sounded soon after the trial results were announced and mass immunization began. Specific killed-virus lots made by Cutter Laboratories (and to a much lesser extent, Wyeth) contained traces of the live virus. A member of Salk's team, Julius Youngner, had warned Salk of the problems he had observed at Cutter, but there was no proper follow-up. Moreover, it had become well documented that all the vaccine companies had experienced continued problems inactivating the polio virus and that safety tests and quality control mechanisms remained unreliable and inadequate.[9]

A final report indicated that at least 220,000 people had been infected with tainted vaccine from Cutter alone—70,000 of them developed muscle weakness. A total of 204 vaccine-associated cases of "true polio" were identified. Seventy-nine cases were among children who had received the vaccine; 105 cases were among family members of vaccinated children; and twenty cases were the result of community contacts. Three quarters of the cases were paralytic, and eleven people died (one source cites ten deaths). It was a terrible tragedy, with devastating consequences for the affected patients and their families.[10]

The virus found in the intestines and spinal fluids of the victims were all *Mahoney* strain Type I. Children injected with a dose containing some residual live *Mahoney* strain were actually exposed to a more lethal agent than children infected by the natural polio virus. This was true because the natural virus was not necessarily the *Mahoney* strain, the most virulent of strains that had been identified by scientists; moreover, injecting the tainted vaccine had introduced the virus directly into muscles of the arm. More alarming still was the fact that people who came in contact with individuals who had received a shot from one of the lots containing live virus could also contract the disease.[11]

After frantic deliberation, U. S. Surgeon General Leonard Scheele announced a temporary suspension of all polio vaccination programs on May 6, 1955—drug companies held back 3.9 million doses of the vaccine. On May 8, the Surgeon General addressed the nation on television, as he tried to reassure the apprehensive public. This suspension led to similar suspension programs in several countries throughout the world. After reanalyzing vaccine supplies, some countries opted to continue the suspension while others opted to resume planned immunization programs. The Canadian government, after reanalyzing the vaccine supply manufactured by Connaught Laboratories, decided that the vaccine was safe and that its immunization program should proceed as planned; nearly 500,000 Canadians had already received a dose. Like the United States, Canada had suffered devastating polio epidemics in recent years.[12]

Changes, Resumption of 1955 Immunization Programs

Scientific analysis, congressional hearings, and political and scientific fallout continued; careers were destroyed. Significant changes to manufacturing techniques, designed to safeguard the public, were instituted. Thus, on May 14, 1955, the Surgeon General released one million doses of the polio vaccine. However, many scientists and physicians remained skeptical, prompting the American Academy of Pediatrics to recommend that vaccination be suspended for the time being. But, inoculation programs proceeded in many areas, including Syracuse.[13]

The nation and the world faced a difficult decision. Polio season was fast approaching. If children *did not* receive the vaccine, they were susceptible to infection. If children *did* receive the vaccination, they might be vulnerable to vaccine-induced poliomyelitis. By the summer of 1955, polio had once again struck with a vengeance across the United States. Non-vaccinated people were two to five times more likely to contract the disease than those who had been vaccinated. Though there were clearly no guarantees, it had been quickly demonstrated that risks were significantly increased if mass vaccine programs were discontinued. In 1955, there were 28,985 reported polio cases of which 13,850 cases were paralytic. There were 1,043 deaths. Authorities believe that the high incidence of polio cases was probably due to the fact that inoculation programs started late and were not available in all communities because of the Cutter backlash.[14]

Success, Consequences

Between 1955 and 1961, polio incidence in the United States decreased by nearly 90 percent due to inoculation with the Salk vaccine. Four hundred million doses were distributed. Experts who studied the Cutter crisis instituted important changes to safeguard the public, including a surveillance unit at the Communicable Disease Center to monitor outbreaks of polio. Quality control methods were refined and inoculation schedules were modified. The *Mahoney* Type I polio strain was replaced, by some worldwide manufacturers, with a less virulent Type I strain. Lawsuits resulting from the 1955 incident continue to influence vaccine development. Because of liability factors, pharmaceutical companies remain reluctant to engage in vaccine production for any disease.[15]

In part because of what author Paul A. Offit has described as the "Cutter Incident" and in part because of continued disagreement among scientists, health officials began to take a closer look at the live (but weakened or attenuated) virus vaccines developed by Albert Sabin and other researchers—more on that development in a later chapter.

In 1985, President Ronald Reagan proclaimed May 6 as "Dr. Jonas E. Salk Day."[16]

Janice—Soul-Searching

There comes a point when most of us begin to ask the ultimate metaphysical question: Why am I here? Such reflection usually occurs in our late teens and early twenties. But, for me, the introspective journey began as a little girl. I have to say that I was a pretty weird kid. While most of my peers were busy playing with dolls or climbing trees, I was contemplating what Heaven and Earth were all about. My cognitive development appears to have been a peculiar blend of both concrete and abstract thought. Looking back, that particular stage may have made it easier for me to ultimately resolve all of my Heaven questions, including my belief in some kind of connection between this life and the next. As a child, I had the benefit of not having to deal with such issues as logic or scientific validation. I was still young enough that imagination and childlike reasoning were easily intertwined.

In my family's religious tradition, we are told that guardian angels watch over people on Earth. At the ripe old age of six, that was about as sophisticated a theological concept as I could comprehend. Thus, when my parents explained that Frankie would always watch over me, I immediately accepted the idea. I knew that Frankie was dead, but if he was allowed to watch over me he would always be a part of my life—I would not be completely alone. That belief tempered my "grief work" in a very important way. That did not mean that I would escape mourning and all the stages that mourning requires of us.

At first, I was a very sad, lonely, little girl. I wanted Frankie alive. I wanted us both alive. Until he got sick, I had not known one day without Frankie by my side. After he died, I hated the dream I had about Frankie (my parents recalled that dream in an earlier chapter), and I dreaded bedtime because I knew I'd have my nightmare. But, one day the dream stopped. My parents told me that that meant that I had accepted that Frankie was in Heaven and that he would not come back, no matter how much I wished for it.

In those early months following Frankie's death, I remember having many questions. Could Frankie play baseball in Heaven? He had to play baseball; I had put his baseball and bat in the casket. Did Frankie go to school? Were there books in Heaven, or did Frankie just know things without reading about them?

Did Frankie get to see Mittz the First, our grandfather Flood, and Christy? If Frankie didn't know anyone he'd be lonely and afraid. If God calls people to Heaven for a reason, what did He need Frankie to do? Where is Heaven? How did Frankie get to Heaven? If he flew there, did his baseball and bat fly up with him? My questions went on and on.

Although I imagined that you could do many wonderful things in Heaven, I didn't know if it was as much fun as Earth. I wanted Frankie to have fun—that was extremely important to me. Looking back, a major part of my torture in those early days was based in my fear that Frankie might not be happy. I spent time wondering if Heaven was the same for everyone and eventually came to the conclusion that Heaven had to be different for everyone because different things make different people happy. I decided that that meant that Frankie could play baseball. I also decided that Frankie would get to see Christy and our Grandfather Flood and meet lots of new kids. The whole special guardian concept came in handy in another way. Just as I would not be alone if Frankie could watch over me, he'd also get to check on Mom, Dad, Brett, Alan, Gary, and all our friends and relatives whenever he wanted to. If he was able to look down from Heaven and see everyone whenever he wanted to, he wouldn't be so lonely for us.

I tended to think of Frankie's life in Heaven in terms of what I was experiencing here on Earth. I didn't want him to miss anything that I was enjoying. I don't know if I was a more religious child than most little kids or not, but many of my questions and concerns had something to do with the religious traditions and stories that I had been told. I had been fascinated by the story of Fatima. In 1917, Catholics believe that the Blessed Mother appeared to three children over a six month period of time. The site of the apparitions was a rural village in Portugal called Fatima. The children were given three secrets and Mary told them not to divulge the details until she gave them permission. Two of the secrets were made public in the 1940s, but the Pope decided that he would not release the details of the third message. While Frankie was still alive, our nuns and priests told us that, someday, the Pope would release the contents of the last secret. I could hardly wait to hear what that letter said. I probably conjured up quite a few scenarios in my mind; I wish I could remember them now. Following Frankie's death, I was very sad that Frankie would not hear the details of the letter, so I decided that there must be newspapers and radios in Heaven. That way, Frankie could keep abreast of important Earth events, like the Pope's announcement of the details of the third secret. I've always had a vivid imagination—it came in handy in those early years.

I was also troubled that Frankie would not be alive to make his First Communion with me. We had already started talking about that big event before he died. Like every little girl, I was very excited about the beautiful white dress and veil that I would wear. I prayed that God would let Frankie make his First Communion in Heaven.

I can't remember whether Frankie and I had learned about Halley's Comet from our parents or from our first grade teacher, Mrs. MacDougall, but we were certainly looking forward to its visit in 1986. Frankie and I knew that we'd be very old in 1986 but we planned on looking at the comet together. I wondered if you could see Halley's Comet from Heaven. Just to be safe, I asked God if He'd make sure that Frankie was able to see it. Fatima and Halley's Comet had to be the two most exciting things I had ever heard of. I couldn't bear the thought that Frankie would miss either event. I don't know how typical or atypical my concerns were, they were just the concerns that were on my mind—important enough that I can still remember them today.

◆   ◆   ◆

As I worked through the grief process, I took up the serious study of eternity. I used to lie on my back and try to imagine just how long eternity really was. That was a big issue for me, because I had learned from my parents, nuns, and priests that when we die we remain in God's presence for, yes, eternity! I tried to think so hard about what that really meant that I would actually get headaches. Similarly, I was fascinated by what Heaven must look like. I therefore spent hours drawing maps of Heaven. Always an animal lover, I could not imagine Heaven without pets. So, I placed "People Heaven" in the center with a dog and cat area on either side of our human space. I reasoned that although humans love both cats and dogs, the cats and dogs do not usually care for each other. My map thus allowed for equal access to people without causing fights between the four-legged critters. I wasn't sure if dogs and cats could start getting along just because they were in Heaven. I wanted Frankie to be able to see Mittz the First every single day. All in all, I spent a lot of time thinking about things most kids have no need to consider.

For some reason, I also began drawing maps of Pittsburgh, including the area's famous coal mines and steel plants. My mother, in particular, was baffled by the Pittsburgh maps.

"Why, are you drawing maps of Pittsburgh?"

"Because I'm going to go to school in Pittsburgh someday," I replied.

"Why would you want to go to school there? What about schools in New York City or Boston?"

"No, I'm going to go to school in Pittsburgh."

There were many such conversations but they always ended with the same assertion. Why have I always felt such an affinity to western Pennsylvania and the city of Pittsburgh?

◆   ◆   ◆

When I was about eight years old, an older playmate asked me what would have happened if I had contracted polio before Frankie. From the time of Frankie's death, my parents had always told me that there must be a very special reason why God had called Frankie home. I was young enough to accept the explanation at face value, but my friend's question really shook me.

It's overwhelming to contemplate that the circumstances of our birth may have been the very reason why I survived the 1953 polio epidemic. Because of the benefit that I might have received from the multiple gamma globulin injections, one could argue that Frankie's life was taken in order that mine might be spared. Would I have died if I had contracted polio first? Would I have died if I had not had a twin, or other close relative, whose speedy diagnosis afforded me an opportunity to receive multiple gamma globulin shots? My odds would have certainly been much worse—talk about guilt-producing facts!

I just thought of something else: I don't know if my parents ever received gamma globulin injections. I don't ever remember asking them—I was always afraid to ask questions for fear that I would make them sad. Likewise, they never volunteered much information.

Had I ever considered questions about the order that Frankie and I came down with polio before my neighbor asked me directly? I'm not sure, though I do remember asking God soon after Frankie died if I could change places with him. Why would I have asked that question if I had not felt luckier to be alive and on Earth? I seem to have been perfectly willing to do anything that would allow Frankie to come back to Earth. Isn't that an expression of guilt? Or, is it just an expression of the complete love that most twins have for each other? Even though the nuns and priests talked about how great Heaven was, I needed more time to consider the pros and cons of Heaven. Heaven was a hard sell for me when it came to Frankie. I remember talking to God frequently as a little girl.

Whatever those feelings of guilt might or must have been back then, I'm thankful that they do not plague me now. Today, psychologists speak of a term called "survivor's guilt." Such guilt has certainly scarred many lives. I don't think Frankie's death has scarred me as much as it has focused me. Perhaps the innocence and concreteness of early childhood thought patterns shielded me from such adult issues, at least over the long haul. Perhaps my ultimate view of what Heaven was like for Frankie allowed me to move beyond guilt feelings. As a young child, I had eventually conjured up a fantastic image of what Frankie was experiencing. Just think, he could know everything about everything without even having to go to school.

◆   ◆   ◆

The writing of our story has necessitated some pretty serious soul-searching. It just dawned on me that the dynamics of our special Earth relationship did not change after Frankie died. Although I missed him terribly, my early heartache was much more based in worry for *his* well-being (I guess I remained his "little mother" as well as his lonely twin). Life was much easier for me once I made up my mind that Frankie could keep on enjoying all the things that he loved about life on Earth. I couldn't move on until I had reasoned that Frankie was OK. It was the only way that I had to come to terms with the loss of my birth-partner. In my own mind, things had to be right for Frankie. Once I had things all worked out for Frankie, I could begin *my* deeper quest.

What was I here for? My parents told me that we would never understand why Frankie had contracted polio just months before the Salk vaccine or why the vaccine had not been developed earlier. We would never know why I was spared and Frankie wasn't. They explained that focusing on "why" and "what if" would never bring consolation—it would only bring sadness and bitterness. They continually reinforced the idea that God had wanted me to live, for a reason. I don't know whether their support was based on any questions I might have raised, whether they wanted to make sure that I would not be plagued with guilt later in life, whether they were just passing on the religious orientation that had served them well all their lives, or whether their parenting was based on all of these considerations. Regardless of their intentions, I'm thankful for the parenting I received. Their counsel offered a general road map, the rest was up to me.

Although I've never felt compelled to be a famous person, I found direction at a very young age. What a gift that is. Unfortunately, many people stumble through life never knowing what they want to do, or should do. I decided when I was eight-years-old, that I would pursue some aspect of medicine in college and beyond. I knew that I had suffered physical and emotional pain.

Therefore, my life's experiences had to equip me with the ability to provide some measure of care and comfort to others. By high school, I had become a candy-striper at Memorial Hospital and had become a volunteer at the VanDuyn Home, a county facility for the infirmed, and at a nursing home on East Genesee Street.

Did my playmate's question influence my metaphysical quest? Did I begin that quest earlier in life because of her confrontation? I have no idea. If so, I should thank my friend; she was the realistic child in our neighborhood. When I was seven, she told me that there was no Santa Claus or Easter Bunny—I wasn't ready for those revelations either. Or, was the timing of my early quest due exclusively to Frankie's death and my physical recovery?

Our polio experience has colored every day of my life since fall 1953. Today, I don't ask many questions or demand many answers. Maybe I ran out of questions when I was a little girl; God knows I had plenty of them. Maybe I decided that you get far more answers when you're not looking for them.

In preparation for this book, I decided to read narratives of other polio survivors. Many of us have asked such questions as: What would I be like if I had not had polio? Would I be a better person, a nicer person? Or, would I have become self-centered and insensitive to the needs of others? Would I have enjoyed a rebellious stage during my teen years? I certainly had a "free-spirit" aspect to my personality, and I was definitely a product of the tumultuous 1960s. But, I distinctly remember not wanting to hurt my parents. Given Frankie's death, I felt that they had had enough anguish. Frankie's death taught me early on that we have to consider other people's feelings as well as our own. Life was not just about me. I would have preferred learning that important life-lesson another way.

As I pondered these narratives, I found myself asking a question that I had never considered: If polio had escaped the Flood house, would Frankie and I have remained as close as we were as little ones? I believe so, I hope so.

My mother often commented that she and my dad felt that God had shown mercy. They didn't feel that they could have endured Frankie's continual suffering and confinement. From what my parents knew of Frankie's condition, every day that Frankie lingered would have been filled with more agony. His condition could not have stabilized or improved. For my parents, therefore, there were things crueler than his death.

But, what if Frankie had defied all the odds and survived as a severely disabled child and adult? I had dared to ask myself that disturbing question on several occasions over the years. Could our vastly different polio experiences have tempered or even destroyed our special twin bond? What a terrifying thought. Would Frankie have felt resentment and anger every time I ran off to a game or party? Would he have seen me as the lucky twin—the one whose delayed illness was less serious and possibly influenced by massive doses of gamma globulin? What would I have expected of myself? I don't think I could have ever gone away to college or grad school or left home to have my own family if I had known that Frankie was left behind. But, would I have accepted that self-imposed fate with love alone or with some bitterness? I'm certain that I would have been terribly burdened with guilt, the lucky twin who recovered only to watch her birth-partner suffer day in and day out.

Although my sadness, loneliness, and worry took a terrible toll in those first few years after Frankie's death, I can't imagine enduring possible ambivalent feelings toward the twin I loved so much. Frankie died at a point in my life where all I ever felt, and would forever feel, was love for him. For that I am thankful and blessed.

Bonne (Paltz) Hall and Bob Paltz—Vaccination in the Late 1950s

We're brother and sister—Monne, our mother, was the oldest of the five Coolican children. We were the first born offspring of the five siblings, and our family placement provided a unique opportunity to get to know all of our cousins in very special ways.

Frankie knew just how to make us laugh. He would wrinkle up his little nose and talk in that cute stuffed up way of his. Even after the twins had their tonsils and adenoids out, Frankie remained our "Little Snuffles." We were very close to the twins and remain so with Jan. We were the official supervisors at all of their birthday parties. In many ways, we were more like Frankie and Jan's older siblings than first cousins. We have wonderful memories of our childhoods—of Skaneateles Lake, Frank's antique Chrysler with the rumble seat, and Dodie's famous recipe for Spanish rice. But, because we were older, our memories of Frankie's death and Jan's sickness are equally vivid. We learned as adults that we had always been Jan's role models, the big kids she always tried to emulate.

Over fifty years later, we can still remember the horrible phone call our family received on the evening of November 1. Frankie was dead. After much adult discussion on the topic, Mother decided that it was important that we attend the wake, funeral, and burial. As children whose family had been involved in the funeral and hearse business, we had been brought up to accept the fact that death is an inevitable part of the human condition, even when it involved the tragic death of a child we loved. Mother sent a basket of white pompoms and pink roses to the wake just from us.

A second terrifying call came on the evening of Frankie's burial. Jan had been admitted to the hospital. We were so afraid that she'd die too. Because we were with Jan and tried to keep her busy at the family gathering and dinner following the burial, our pediatrician, Dr. Kopel, decided that we should have a gamma globulin shot. No kids like shots, but we were old enough to appreciate the importance of the precaution. We were old enough to understand what polio could do.

Reflection from Jan

During a recent holiday dinner, Bonne mentioned to me that our extended family feared for my life. Although I did not respond at the time, her comment really touched me. I was shocked to observe the degree of sadness and fear still so evident in my cousin's eyes and words. Even today, I am reminded of how much our polio ordeal extracted from our family and friends. My cousin Bob can hardly discuss that period of time with me.

As Jan began compiling information for this book, she asked us to recall our memories of receiving the polio vaccine. She knew that we could provide insight into the experience of older children in the Syracuse area from the mid 1950s to the early 1960s. This information would, in turn, shed light on early vaccination opportunities for older children when the polio vaccination program became a national public health initiative. What we have concluded is based on a combination of our own recollections and Jan's research. We have distinct memories of receiving the Salk vaccine at John T. Roberts School in Syracuse. But, we also have memories of receiving the later oral vaccine at the same school. Could both memories be accurate?

We weren't in the 1954 Salk trials; the trials were limited to grades one through three. According to newspaper accounts, the 1955 Syracuse school vaccine program targeted children in grades one through four who had not participated in the 1954 trials or who had received a placebo. Syracuse was the first city in New York State to begin the May 1955 inoculation program following the temporary suspension of vaccination clinics after the Cutter vaccine problem. Other New York cities began their programs a few days later. Apparently, many health officials and parents had sided in favor of inoculation in spite of the Cutter situation that Dr. Turek discussed in an earlier chapter.[1]

Based on Jan's review of the Cutter incident, it appears that private physicians were able to purchase vaccine supply from pharmaceutical companies in order to inoculate patients, family, and friends with the serum (ignoring age restrictions and guidelines). Jan has not been able to locate figures indicating the percentage of private pediatricians and family physicians throughout the country that had access to the vaccine in 1955. We have no memory of receiving the polio vaccine in our pediatrician's office; moreover, we are certain that Dr. Kopel would have strictly adhered to New York State Medical Society, federal government, and National Foundation guidelines. Thus, on the basis of our ages, local and national newspaper accounts of the period, and histories on polio, we have concluded that we did not receive the vaccine in 1955 but we would have certainly received shots in 1956 and 1957.[2]

Throughout the country, vaccination programs in the latter half of the decade were coordinated to reach a greater segment of the population—from infants and young children to older children and young adults. Here's what Jan's research of the period, gleaned from Syracuse newspaper accounts, concluded about likely nationwide inoculation efforts in 1956 and 1957:

1956:

A February 1956 *Syracuse Post Standard* article indicated that the local campaign focused on the inoculation of children who had not received the full Salk vaccine series in the 1954 trials or in the 1955 mass inoculation clinics. The program included children from age six months to fifteen years (as more vaccine became available, pregnant women were to be added to the group). The article stressed that older children had a very low rate of vaccination. Only 4 percent of children aged ten to fourteen had previously received the vaccine.[3]

A January 27, 1957, *Syracuse Post Standard* article reported findings from the Syracuse Health Department that indicated that only four Syracuse residents contracted the disease in 1956 (another article cited twelve cases). According to health officials, the decrease in reported cases was due to the Salk vaccine. The same article indicated that in Syracuse, 100,000 doses of the Salk vaccine had been administered since its release. Three out of every four Syracuse children had received at least one dose of the vaccine.[4]

1957:

In 1957, Syracuse began an intensive campaign to inoculate the group that had not been allowed to participate in the 1954 trials and the first large-scale, country-wide vaccination programs either because of age or parental objection.

On January 20, 1957, the *Syracuse Herald-Journal* reported on a new polio vaccination campaign in Onondaga County. It appears, from the article, that our county might have been a national trendsetter in initiating a campaign to inoculate all vulnerable age groups. The Onondaga County Medical Society, headed by President Charles A. Gwynn, MD, had been instrumental in convincing public health officials of the necessity and urgency of such an expanded program. The two age groups targeted were junior and senior high school students and young adults age twenty to forty. Although it was known that 75 percent of polio cases occurred in people under twenty, it was also known that the incidence of paralysis and death increased with age and that young adults accounted for the highest number of deaths.[5]

A January 29, 1957, *Syracuse Herald Journal* article discussed the upcoming program that had been coordinated by Syracuse Commissioner of Health, Dr. David E. Bigwood Jr. School medical staffs were to carry out the inoculations with the assistance of volunteers from church groups, PTA organizations, and the local chapter of the March of Dimes. The National Foundation's program was to be coordinated by the local chairperson of the women's activities, Mrs. C. Eugene Farnsworth.[6]

In a February 16, 1957, *Syracuse Herald Journal* article, Drs. William Ayling and Virginia Harris (directors of public and parochial health services) announced that the school-based clinics would begin on February 25. Approximately 28,000 seventh through twelfth-grade students would receive two of the first three shot series at no cost during the mass vaccination campaign. The children were to receive the final shot from their family doctors. Adults would pay a maximum of $3 per inoculation.[7]

The 1957 Onondaga County initiative was financed by a combination of New York State and county funds. To help underwrite the program, the local chapter of the March of Dimes also contributed $15,000. The entire effort was estimated to cost $30,000. Similar initiatives, through local, state, federal, and private sector partnerships, took place throughout the country.[8]

While the 1954 Salk vaccine trials had been underwritten by the National Foundation of Infantile Paralysis, the *Polio Vaccination Assistance Act* of 1955 transferred responsibility to the federal government. This act allowed the federal government to appropriate funds through the Communicable Disease Center to help states and local communities acquire and distribute the vaccine.[9]

As for our memories of receiving the Sabin vaccine, Jan has an interesting thought:

Many of Jan's friends also remember getting the oral vaccine, even though they recall getting the Salk series of shots in the 1954 trials. Some authors have indicated that people were encouraged to get the Sabin vaccine even if they had already received the Salk series. Perhaps we (and many of Jan's friends) received the oral vaccine once it became available in the early 1960s. Jan does not recall whether she received the oral vaccine; her memories are only of the 1954 trials. Our memory of receiving the oral vaccine at Robert's School may stem from a 1961 polio epidemic in central New York. Nearly four-hundred thousand residents received the vaccine in an effort to stop the spread of the disease (a little more on that in a later chapter).[10]

In spite of the fact that our family was acutely aware of the importance of receiving the polio vaccine and continuing with pre-vaccine precautions, we wanted Jan to appreciate that many of our contemporaries enjoyed carefree days in public pools. Jan's research has since indicated that many health officials were alarmed at the cavalier attitude many Americans exhibited in the late 1950s. Polio was no longer front-page news, but polio had not been eradicated. Non-vaccinated individuals were playing with fire.

A 1959 National Foundation report warned that although more affluent children had often contracted the disease in the past, children in poorer urban neighborhoods were now the group most at risk because they had not been vaccinated.[11]

Mrs. Pat (Marshall) Coolican—March of Dimes, Changes

At the time of Frankie's death and Jannie's hospitalization (I've often called my niece "Jannie"), I was dating their uncle Bud. We married in 1954. Although Bud would ultimately own a successful advertising agency with his brother Tom, he worked for *WOLF Radio* (the radio station owned by my parents) at the time of the DeWitt polio epidemic. Both my parents and I attended the wake and funeral. My parents had been friends of the twins' maternal grandparents for many years. While members of the immediate family congregated in the living room, I tried to occupy Jan as best I could. We read together in her upstairs bedroom and colored at the dining room table.

A few years ago, at an annual Coolican reunion at my niece Chris' home, Jan thanked me for taking care of her during Frankie's wake. Months before, Jan had started her polio research although she had yet to decide on the book's format. Her initial research and reflection had brought many buried memories to the surface; fortunately, she remembers many of the ways we all tried to comfort her during those horrible days. When we spoke that afternoon, Jan acknowledged that it was important to her that I know how much she appreciated my show of love and concern. Both good and bad times bond a family.

When Jan asked me to lend my voice to this story, she asked me to recall my memories of polio epidemics and discuss the role *WOLF* played in getting the March of Dimes message out to the public. Since our family didn't move to Syracuse until 1936, my early memories of polio revolve around my childhood home in Mount Vernon, New York. One summer, my parents arranged for us to vacation with another family, in Torrington, Connecticut. Getting me out of the city during polio season was their primary motivation. Reviewing the history of polio epidemics, it appears that families had attempted to escape the virus in similar ways since the 1916 New York City epidemic. Sadly, but ironically, the mother in the other family contracted spinal meningitis. Polio and other contagious diseases knew how to track potential victims no matter how or where they tried to hide.

As a community-focused radio station, *WOLF* ran March of Dimes public service announcements on a daily basis during that frightening time in the mid and late 1950s. Although the Salk vaccine dramatically decreased the incidence of polio, we were all aware of the problems associated with the 1954 vaccine trial and the 1955 vaccine problems. We were terrified of polio, but many people were equally scared of the vaccine. Yet, the 1955 country-wide epidemic had shown that people who had not received the vaccine were the most at risk. And, so, we encouraged the public to heed the March of Dimes' message that stressed the importance of vaccination.

Perhaps because of our family's background in radio and advertising, I closely followed March of Dimes activities. Following the introduction of the Salk vaccine, the March of Dimes organized many volunteer groups to ensure that the vaccine reached all American children and young adults. The Veterans of Foreign Wars (with its Ladies Auxiliary), the U.S. Marine Corps, and Parent Teacher Associations across the country performed services such as transporting iron lungs, raising funds, repairing equipment, and educating the public regarding the disease and its prevention. Teenagers throughout the country joined "Teens against Polio" groups to encourage their peers to be vaccinated. Others organized mobile vaccination clinics.[1]

The National Foundation used every available means to get out its vaccination slogans, *Advertise to Immunize* and *Let's Finish the Job*. Because the business world, like the private sector, was anxious to eradicate polio, companies were eager to lend assistance. Throughout the country, companies sponsored billboards highlighting the fact that polio was still a menace, and that vaccination was imperative. In 1957, the General Outdoor Advertising Company of Chicago paid for a huge billboard that read: "Where Will Polio Strike Next?–Not with You If You Knock Out Polio with All 3 Salk Shots." Another initiative in Salt Lake City featured a street parade with a pony-pulled cart full of children who had been vaccinated. A banner on the side of the wagon proclaimed: "We've Had Our Polio Shots, Have You?" Local television stations covered the event.[2]

◆   ◆   ◆

In the late 1950s, due to the dramatic decrease in polio cases, the March of Dimes opted to expand its mission to include the prevention of birth defects, infant mortality, and arthritis (the arthritis component was eliminated in 1964).

When Jan and I spoke about her current research, I told her that many people were opposed to the change. The March of Dimes had been founded for the sole purpose of eradicating polio. People that I knew who were opposed to the change were not opposed to the new mission, but they felt that the March of Dimes should be disbanded, a victim of its own success, so to speak, and that the expanded focus should be christened with a new name and a new organizational structure. Jan had never read, or heard, about the objection.

Although severely afflicted patients would require lifetime care, much of the public had moved on. For many, polio was a thing of the past. The National Foundation was forced to abandon paying for many services as funds diminished and the organization shifted its efforts to birth defects. In spite of the fact that private health insurance plans would become more prevalent, many did not provide coverage for ongoing care at home. The mid-1960s ushered in Medicare and Medicaid, but individuals continued to fall between the cracks.

Polio patients have been a driving force behind federal and state legislation designed to protect the rights of the disabled. Their voice has stressed the value and importance of independent living, vocational training, and remunerative employment. Their struggle for equal opportunities, access, and federal funding continues into our new century.

◆   ◆   ◆

When Jan had her photo taken for the 1954 Salk vaccine trial newspaper article, she wore a dress that my husband (a bachelor at the time) had brought her from Sarasota, Florida. Bud always enjoyed showering his nieces and nephews with gifts. It was a tailored dress of yellow and gray polished cotton. While researching, Jan took out the old photos that Dodie had always saved. Jan immediately recognized the dress—it had always been one of her favorites.

Note: See Appendix D for additional information on the March of Dimes, including its change of focus in the post-polio-epidemic era and its activities related to polio survivors.

Janice—Progress, Struggles, Reflection

By mid-year of second grade, my parents, doctors, and therapists determined that I no longer required daily therapy. Over the next few years, I continued to make steady physical progress. Although one leg was over a half inch shorter than the other, I practiced thrusting my hip and leg in a manner that hid any limp. Only in recent years has that limp become visible when I'm fatigued. Soon, I was enrolled in multiple dancing, skating, and swimming classes. My dream of discarding the ugly, brown orthopedic shoes was eventually realized. A day was never better than one spent with my baseball bat in one hand and my bow and arrow in the other. I think my father really enjoyed my tomboy stage. Apparently, my mother used to worry that I'd never turn back into a girly girl—my father dreaded the day when I would. Although I have a few other residuals from polio that I'll describe later, I'm convinced that my father's determination and ability to cater to my physical needs made an important difference in my recovery.

In the late 1950s, my parents purchased a copy of Roy Campanella's inspiring story, *It's Good to be Alive*. Campanella suffered paralysis following a near-fatal auto accident. They also bought the play, *Sunrise at Campobello*, the story of Franklin Roosevelt's struggle with polio. Mom and Dad wanted me to identify with those stories. They wanted me to see myself as a fortunate survivor rather than as a victim. Although it has been fifty years since I read those books, I recently purchased a used copy of Roosevelt's story and intend to read it once I'm done with this book.

Today, when I tell people that I had polio and had to learn to walk again, individuals old enough to remember the disease instinctively look at my legs. Many polio patients have one leg that is smaller than the other (atrophy is the proper medical term). I'm very fortunate to have been spared that residual. Some polio survivors walk with a decided limp or walk with a built-up shoe. Though I now wear what I'd refer to as "sensible pumps," my teen, college, and early adulthood years were full of shoes that were far from sensible.

◆   ◆   ◆

Just as my father zeroed in on my need for physical recovery, my mother concentrated on my emotional needs. As well as addressing the concerns I was able to verbalize, she used her own experiences to help me come to terms with my own sadness. She frequently spoke of overcoming her own "demons." Dorothy Coolican Flood was the consummate "window shopper" whose theme song could have easily been the tune, *Downtown*. From the time we were little, Mom had declared Wednesday afternoons as "her time." I'm sure that we enjoyed our babysitters just as much as she enjoyed her weekly escapes. Her favorite pastime was driving downtown, checking out the store windows, and making an occasional purchase; she said it always "cleared her head."

After Frankie died, Mom found it difficult to look at little boys who were his age. Seeing the neighborhood boys didn't bother her but looking at little boys she didn't know broke her heart. She said her downtown sojourns often ended with a flood of tears that seemed to come out of nowhere. Realizing that she could not allow herself to be cut off from young children, she continued her Wednesday trips. She was determined to overcome her reaction and eventually she did. Over time, she learned to accept the realities of her own son's death without transferring her sadness to other innocent, healthy little boys. Until Mom died, she remained a lover of downtown, store windows, and browsing (oh, my, was she the browser!).

There was one little boy in the neighborhood—Ricky Shannon—who brought much joy to my parents. He was younger than we were, and he loved to talk to my father about bulldozers and dump trucks. He'd knock on the front door, walk over to my dad, and sit down next to him to watch a game or whatever else was on TV. Ricky reminded my parents of their own little boy, but in a way that only brought joy and laughter. There was no room for tears when Ricky was around. I've often wondered if that little guy sensed my parents' need to enjoy the sweet, innocent ways of little boys. I thank him for the happiness he brought to our home and for the memories I now recall.

My mother developed a dread of emergency rooms. I'm sure that she worried that any routine trip to an emergency room could have a deadly outcome just as Frankie's sniffles had turned to tragedy in 1953. So, after Frankie died, Dad always took us to the emergency room if we needed stitches, X-rays, or whatever. Most of the time, Mom couldn't even ride in the car with us. A terrible fear tortured my mother when it came to the health of her children—a fear that she just couldn't overcome.

My father, on the other hand, was occasionally known to overreact (to put it mildly) when I became ill. I'll never forget a conversation I had with my parents when I was a student at Seton Hill College. I actually fainted while on the phone, in the middle of one of our weekly Sunday evening chats. My dad flew my mother out on the next plane. He called the Dean of Women, Sister Zoe, at least fifty times until he knew that my mother was by my side in Greensburg, Pennsylvania. Sister Zoe never let me forget that episode.

As a teenager with an adventurous spirit, I occasionally found my father a little too overprotective for my liking. I can recall one situation in particular. One of my Convent School friends had been born in Paris. She was going to spend the summer after our freshman year in France and invited me to come along. As far as I was concerned, this was a chance of a life time. How could my parents say no? My father's decision was swift and cruel. After World War II, he had vowed to never return to France or Germany—too many haunting memories, I guess. He told me that he could not allow me to travel to any place that he could not visit if I needed him. Oh, how I must have carried on! But I promised to never be so cruel to my own children. God was definitely listening: our son Kevin was born with a serious case of wanderlust. I've been eating those words vowed at age fourteen for a long time.

◆   ◆   ◆

This chapter in our family's life would be incomplete if I failed to mention the strength and sensitivity my parents found to reach out to other families in need. A few years after Frankie died, another family in the neighborhood suffered the loss of an infant from crib death. Mom reached out to that grieving mother in a very special way, in a way that only mothers who have suffered such a loss can understand.

My father, being an action kind of guy, reached out in other ways. When my sister Carol was a toddler, he learned of a family that had three children who suffered from cystic fibrosis; the children required frequent checkups in Boston. At the time, my mother's car was a large Oldsmobile station wagon that my dad had retrofitted with a backseat playpen for my sister. He even had the back seat area configured to accommodate a seat belt of sorts for Carol. Upon meeting the family, Dad offered the car for any trips they needed to make to Boston or elsewhere. Whenever the family needed the car, my father would modify Carol's playpen to accommodate the three little children. To this day, I continue to think of that family.

Reflection

As a little girl, I didn't look at my parents as having personalities. They were individually defined, in my mind, by what they did. Dad played games with us and gave us big bear hugs. Mom made wonderful meals and made us wash our hands and say our prayers. Dad made us giggle and taught us how to swim and always smelled of Old Spice. Mom was beautiful, smothered us with kisses, and always smelled of Shalimar or Lily of the Valley perfume. They both took care of us when we were sick, comforted us when we got hurt, made us feel safe.

It has been relatively easy to reconstruct the dialogue in this book as I've simply recalled conversations that I had with my parents over the years. But, as an adult I have come to see my parents through another lens. It has taken this project, perspective that only fifty years of living can bring, to make me fully appreciate just what my parents endured in the early years following Frankie's death—and for the rest of their lives. Yet, in spite of my adult insight, much of their individual stories remained locked inside their hearts. My parents carried on, but there was a part of each of them that died on November 1, 1953. Living is a daily struggle after you lose a child.

The element of guilt, that human emotion that only good people ever seem to suffer from, was alive and well in my mother's mind. Her main source of guilt was the issue of cleanliness. Could she have cleaned the toilets better? Did she insist upon us washing our hands several times a day? Could she have recognized the signs of bulbar polio earlier? Would that have made a difference? Mom was a private woman who learned to cope with Frankie's death by not letting many people get too close. She went on for us, living the maxim, "Let go and let God," though it took her several years to completely let go of her guilt. As a young mother, she had learned, the hard way, that many things are completely out of our control.

My father could talk about funny things that Frankie did, or good times that we shared as a family, but that was it. Talking about November 1953 was as off limits as talking about World War II. I don't ever remember talking to him about Frankie's death until he was in the hospital, dying. Having learned that Frankie died in Daddy's arms provided new insight into my father's refusal to talk or cry. But, my mother's revelation about that came only after Dad had joined Frankie in Heaven. I think there was always a part of my father that was afraid that he'd lose his daughters as well. He had to stay connected: he wrote to me every day through college and grad school and called me every single day until he died. Mom always said that it ripped my father apart to see her cry; he thought that he should be able to cheer her up. Mom needed to cry, something that most men have so much trouble understanding. I don't think my father ever understood that.

When Frankie died and I contracted polio, my parents comforted me when I cried, told me that I could walk again, that I would walk again. In terms of their parenting, nothing had changed: they were taking care of me just like always. But, in their eyes things had changed. Weren't they supposed to keep their kids safe? All parents of deceased children live at least part of their remaining years on Earth in a private hell of self-doubt and fear.

Alice (Jaros) Turek, MD, MPH—The Sabin Vaccine

In an earlier chapter, I mentioned that, although polio plagued the entire globe, incidence in the United States was far greater than in other industrialized nations. When comparing these figures, it should be cautioned that the United States also had a much larger population that the other countries cited. In the late 1960s, the World Health Organization reported the average annual number of cases found in selected countries. From 1951 to 1955, the United States averaged 37,864 cases of polio per year, while the United Kingdom reported an average of 4,381 cases of polio. Denmark reported 1,614 cases. Its neighbor Sweden indicated that there had been an average of 1,526 cases each year. New Zealand, Austria, and Belgium reported an average of 405, 707, and 475 cases respectively.[1]

With the licensing of a live-virus vaccine developed by Dr. Albert Sabin, the World Health Organization report indicated that from 1961 to 1965 the United States had an average of 570 cases per year. Czechoslovakia reported no cases between 1961 and 1965; Denmark reported an average of 77; and the United Kingdom recorded an average of 322 cases during that same time period. In 1963, the United States reported only 396 cases. In 1964, only 121 cases were reported.[2]

◆　　　◆　　　◆

Sabin Gets His Chance

The story of the Sabin polio vaccine is an interesting one that began before the licensing of the Salk vaccine in 1955. You may recall that in my chapter entitled, "The Salk Vaccine," Albert Sabin was a serious researcher who had always voiced opposition to Salk's vaccine. Sabin had long proclaimed that his live-virus polio vaccine, made with weakened or attenuated virus, was superior to Salk's killed-virus vaccine. Other prominent polio researchers held like views. But, until the 1955 Cutter situation (that I discussed in a previous chapter), Salk reigned supreme.

In early 1956, Sabin received a call from the U.S. Public Health Service indicating that a group of Russian scientists were planning a trip to the United States. Although their primary purpose was to study Salk vaccine preparation, the Russians had expressed interest in speaking with other prominent polio researchers, including Sabin. The Russians were alarmed by the recent spread of polio in their country (until 1930 Russia had the lowest incidence of polio in Europe). They had also found the Salk method expensive and difficult to mass produce. Sabin expressed interest in visiting Russia and continuing the scientific dialogue. Salk was not interested in forging a United States-Russian scientific partnership, and his wife opposed the venture—it would require too much time away from his family.[3]

Ultimately, Sabin provided the Russians with serum that they used in 1959 to vaccinate millions of children. Most children received three doses, each dose containing one of the three polio Types I, II, or III. A much smaller group received a trivalent vaccine with all three Types in each dose. The Russian trials did not incorporate the double-blind research design demanded in the 1954 U.S. trials. Soon, the Russians decided to vaccinate their entire population under the age of twenty—77 million children and young adults. For his efforts in helping Russia stamp out the disease, Sabin became an Honorary Member of the Russian Academy of Medical Sciences. An independent study, suggested by Sabin, validated the Russian study.[4]

In 1960, a Russian delegation attended the Second International Conference on Live Poliovirus Vaccines, held in Washington DC. When an American researcher questioned the results of the independent study that had evaluated the Sabin vaccine, the assembled body stood in applause after one of the Russian scientists rebuked the skeptical American.[5]

Live-Virus Polio Vaccine Trials Commence

Sabin and another live-virus advocate, Herald Cox, received permission to conduct trials in the United States in 1960. Sabin taught at the University of Cincinnati and he chose Cincinnati and Hamilton County, Ohio, for his studies. Commencing on April 24, 1960, and continuing for several weeks, nearly two-hundred thousand children received the oral vaccine. The clinics were held on what came to be known as "Sabin Oral Sundays." Cox conducted trials on his trivalent vaccine in Dade County, Florida. More than four-hundred thousand individuals received the Cox vaccine, and six people contracted paralytic polio within seven to fourteen days after swallowing the liquid serum. The Cox vaccine was quickly rejected, fearing a repeat of the 1955 Cutter situation.[6]

During this period, pro and con Salk and Sabin contingents ramped up their rhetoric, a situation made sharper because of sporadic polio outbreaks since the introduction of the Salk vaccine. In 1961, the American Medical Association became embroiled in the controversy. Declaring that its membership was confused, the AMA intended to consult its own "Council on Drugs" for guidance. At its 1961 annual convention, the AMA recommended that the Salk vaccine be replaced with the Sabin vaccine once it could be licensed and marketed. Some accused the AMA of bias.[7]

Like Salk, Sabin never sought a patent on his vaccine. Salk remained convinced that his was the superior vaccine and sought, without success, to slow the development of the live-virus alternative.[8]

◆   ◆   ◆

In 1962, Congress passed the Vaccination Assistance Act which provided $36 million over three years to states to subsidize polio, diphtheria, whooping cough, and tetanus vaccination programs for children with no access to school inoculation programs. President John F. Kennedy signed the act into law.[9]

◆   ◆   ◆

Sabin Vaccine Licensure

In 1961, the HEW licensed Sabin's Type I and II polio vaccines. In 1962, the HEW licensed Sabin's Type III vaccine, and in 1963, the trivalent vaccine was licensed. In contrast to the shot-administered Salk vaccine, the Sabin vaccine had the advantage of being administered orally, at first via serum-saturated sugar cubes and later by drops.[10]

Early vaccine success was soon evident: Central New York experienced thirty-two new cases of polio during the fourth week of August 1961. With the assistance of SUNY Upstate Medical professor Harry Feldman, a sufficient supply of Sabin's new oral agent was secured in an effort to limit the outbreak. Between August 29 and 31, nearly four-hundred thousand doses of the Type I vaccine were given to residents of the tri-county area of Onondaga, Madison, and Oneida counties in emergency clinics set up in public schools. The press, radio, and TV provided excellent publicity. Sadly, a patient diagnosed with bulbar polio died of the disease one day before the clinics commenced, but the new Sabin vaccine proved successful in stopping the spread of the crippler.[11]

A Cautionary Note

Despite the successes, each year the country experienced a small number of new polio cases. Although the live-virus vaccine had provided unprecedented protection from the disease, it had also caused a small incidence of vaccine-induced polio. One of the advantageous by-products of the vaccine was that vaccinated individuals shed live virus in their bodily waste, thereby helping to immunize non-vaccinated individuals through environmental contact with the virus. But, at the same time, the viral shedding had the deleterious effect of occasionally causing the disease in vaccinated individuals or in people who had come in close contact with a vaccinated person.[12]

In 1962, sixty-two cases of polio were reported soon after the victims received the oral vaccine. Although the bulk of the cases would eventually be linked to epidemic conditions, sixteen cases were determined to be vaccine-associated. All of the affected individuals had received the Type III monovalent vaccine between January and September 1962. Risk of contagion seemed to be higher for adults.[13]

As would be expected, scientific debate continued. Some experts believed that since the incidence of polio dropped dramatically for persons over thirty, the live-virus vaccine should be restricted to individuals under age eighteen. Others feared that such restriction could result in the collapse of the polio prevention program. The majority of scientists reasoned that the risk of contracting polio for non-vaccinated individuals was far greater than the extremely small risk of contracting polio from the vaccine.[14]

Between 1980 and 1996, six to eight children in the United States were diagnosed with paralytic polio each year after receiving the live-virus vaccine or coming in contact with someone who had recently received the vaccine. But, the Sabin vaccine remained the only vaccine in use in the United States for the remainder of my medical career (I retired in 1983). In fact, it remained in exclusive use until 1996.[15]

In 1979, the United States was declared free of the wild-type polio virus, but much of the world continued to be plagued by the virus.[16]

◆   ◆   ◆

Congress passed The National Childhood Vaccine Injury Act in 1986, which provided for a no-fault alternative to suing manufacturers. In addition, the CDC and the Drug Enforcement Agency set up a reporting system to track adverse reactions to the vaccine. In October 1988, the National Vaccine Injury Compensation Program was created.[17]

The Salk-Sabin vaccine debate was not over. We'll pick up the latest chapter in the saga a little later.

Janice—Life Direction

Although I had decided to pursue a career in health care as an eight-year-old, I began to seriously weigh specific fields as a teenager. On the one hand, I thought that becoming a physician might be the most rewarding of professions. But, I was concerned about whether I would be able to pursue an active medical career and, at the same time, meet the demands of being a wife and mother. In spite of the fact that many women have been able to juggle the demands, I was not sure that I could. Fearing that I might end up unable to meet the competing challenges, I decided to discuss the matter with my high school biology teacher, Miss Williams. She suggested psychology with a counseling concentration as the balance that I was seeking. That sounded like just the compromise I was looking for.

Since my own recovery had been so complete, my need for ongoing orthopedic care was limited to periodic checkups at Dr. Kalamarides' office. The acute and physical rehabilitation stages of polio were in my past, and post-polio syndrome problems would be a long way off. I continued dancing, swimming, and skating and was quite certain that life could never be more perfect than when, in my junior year, I became a sub for Christian Brother Academy's cheerleading squad. At the time, CBA's enrollment was limited to boys; my school, the Convent School, was all-girl. We referred to CBA as our "brother-school." For a little girl who had walked like a "wooden soldier" in ugly orthopedic shoes, I had come a long way.

◆　　◆　　◆

Yet, as much as my physical recovery had been complete, I could not forget the Flood twins' polio experience or the physical challenges that my friend Patty Munson experienced each day. While my mother continued her involvement with the March of Dimes, I continued to visit Patty. As my teenage world revolved around such events as tomorrow's chemistry test, what boy would ask me to the movies on Friday night, or what I would wear to a weekend party, I marveled at Patty's disposition. Sometimes I wondered if my visits made her sad as she witnessed my complete recovery, but she always welcomed my visits, so I kept visiting. I would have never abandoned her, but I didn't want to force myself on her either. There was something "other-worldly" about Patty. Her face, with sandy blonde hair framing its fragile features, was the picture of serenity. Did she understand, because of her physical needs perhaps, just how precious life and breath truly are?

By the 1960s, polio had been largely reduced to a private matter. Many survivors continued their difficult physical, social, and emotional struggles, but some, like me, were blessed with complete physical recovery. Polio was no longer front page news. In 1963, there were only 396 cases reported in the United States. In 1964, the year before I graduated from high school, the United States reported only 121 cases. I had no idea that many, many people continued to suffer worldwide. My view of polio did not extend beyond what the families of DeWitt, New York, had suffered a decade earlier. Unfortunately, I was not alone in my perceptions. I would not meet another polio survivor until I entered graduate school. And then, not again, until I met the obstetrician who delivered our son.[1]

During high school, I made many new friends, some of whom remain in my life forty years later. As we got to know each other better, sharing the things that only girlfriends can discuss for hours on end, they all became familiar with Frankie and our polio story. Of course my DeWitt friends had known our story for a long time. Even though we all had earth-shattering issues to discuss like the ugly navy orthopedic shoes that we were forced to wear for a few years at The Convent School (would I ever be rid of awful shoes?), my friends always listened. I wanted to keep ... I had to keep ... Frankie's memory alive. I had to remain connected to my twin—it's something that I just can't put into words.

Following Miss William's wise counsel, I entered Seton Hill College in Greensburg, Pennsylvania, in 1965 and declared psychology as my major. I was excited to start college, but it was hard to leave my parents and my kid sister. I was never cut out to be an only child.

In addition to offering an excellent psych curriculum, Seton Hill introduced me to many gals who remain a special part of my life. The chair of the Psychology Department, Sister Maurice, spoke often of a new, innovative health-related counseling program at the University of Pittsburgh. I found myself drawn to that new field.

◆   ◆   ◆

On November 5, 1967, my friend Patty Munson died—the last of the DeWitt children to succumb to the complications of the 1953 polio epidemic in our community. Polio had now claimed the life of both of the Munson children. Patty's death came fourteen years and one day after Frankie was buried and I was admitted to City Hospital. I trust that Frankie and Cheryl were waiting for Patty in Heaven.

◆   ◆   ◆

In 1969, I accepted a graduate fellowship and stipend offer from the University of Pittsburgh (yes, a university located in the city I had drawn maps of since I was a little girl). My program in rehabilitation counseling allowed me to choose an internship and field placements in my declared area of specialization. As you have probably guessed, I chose to work with physically disabled patients. My practical experiences took place at the Veteran's Administration Hospital located in Oakland and Shady Side's Home for Crippled Children. Without a car, I was fortunate to obtain placements in the university area close to my courses and apartment.

Although I was trained in nondirective counseling techniques, my program stressed practical intervention as well. The "rehab philosophy," incorporated into my courses, fit perfectly with my worldview. I knew all too well that illness or injury affects an individual (and his or her family) in a variety of ways. There are spiritual, physical, social, emotional, financial, and vocational needs that must be addressed.

Rehabilitation counseling was a young, exciting field at the time I entered grad school. No longer were individuals with special needs described as "handicapped," a word that implied a deficiency. The new word was "disabled," a word that implied ability with a need for special accommodations. Finally, emphasis was being placed upon eliminating the physical barriers that had, in the past, made it more difficult for the disabled, like many of my fellow polio survivors, to gain equal access to higher education, employment, or entertainment venues. As a large interest group that came of age in the 1960s and 1970s, baby-boom polio survivors have made their concerns known and sought solutions. But, their fight continues. Post-polio syndrome is demanding that many old adaptations be readdressed.

My college friend and grad school roommate Michele (Moore) Ridge, the gal who sent me the copy of the *Rotarian* a few years ago, and I shared an apartment in Oakland. I found it exciting that I was walking some of the same streets and hospital corridors that Dr. Jonas Salk walked as he and his team developed the polio vaccine. I was proud to be in his city and thankful that both the Salk and Sabin vaccines had proved successful. I had no idea that Dr. Turek, the physician who cared for both Frankie and me at City Hospital in 1953, had also walked those same streets and hallways. I wouldn't learn that for over thirty years.

◆   ◆   ◆

Reflection on being a twin

I've often wondered why it has always been so important to me to continue to acknowledge Frankie's life, his death, and the fact that we are—not were—twins. For me, being a twin is totally tied up with who I have always been and always will be. I am what you would call a "natural-born sharer." I have often joked that it's easy for me to share with others because I even had to share the womb. I don't know what words fit best—mystical connection, spiritual connection? I don't know. Maybe there aren't words. But, I've never met a twin who didn't feel "it"—whatever "it" is.

Why do I mention my twin relationship and my belief in a connection in a book about polio? The answer is simple. I have lived my life not only as a woman who polio has taken much from but also as a woman who has gained sensitivity because of her experience. Polio, the disease, has always been a powerful, brutal force in nature. But, in some inexplicable way, the nature of twinship has been an equally powerful force in my life's physical, theological, and philosophical journey.

Twins have always intrigued researchers and the public at large, although the bulk of scientific studies have involved identical twins. Excellent twin research is conducted at California State University under the direction of Dr. Nancy Segal (a fraternal twin). Dr. Segal has written extensively on various aspects of twinship, including grief reactions among surviving twins. The Minnesota Center for Twin and Adoption Research is also involved in the study of twin-loss issues.

Many twin studies have concentrated on the old nature versus nurture debate. Technology now exists that enables viewers to observe the activities of multiples in the womb—bonding, touching, caressing, playing, and sparring. Is it any wonder that twins are different? We have literally "known" something of the other from a profound, miraculous, cellular beginning.

Of late, I've taken a good look at our family photos, many of them displayed on the Nichols' family wall. Until now, I had never paid attention to how often Frankie and I are touching each other. Although we do not usually have our arms around each other, we are touching somewhere. I still "feel" Frankie's touch even though I know that he is not physically by my side.

Some studies have examined the lives of twins who have lost their birth-partners. As could be expected, my parents became intrigued and puzzled by my "sixth sense"—evident from the time of Frankie's death. When I was a teenager, a relative suggested that my parents enroll me in a study involving twin psychic phenomena, but I had no interest in being studied. I was perfectly comfortable with my heightened sensitivity; I still am. Besides, as a teenager, I had much more important things on my mind. I had moved on from being the weird little kid who needed to know exactly what Heaven was like to the typical teenage girl caught up with friends, clothes, and boyfriends.

There are now international support groups to help twins who have lost their birth-partner through death, unavoidable separation, or alienation. The support group, Twinless Twins, has provided invaluable support and information to its members (see the Consulted Works for contact information).

Many twinless twins (as they sometimes call themselves) endure an unbearable sense of loss, a loss often described as similar to that experienced when someone loses a child or a spouse, but a loss that sometimes remains unresolved. They describe themselves as being disconnected. Some studies indicate that the surviving twin is left with a drive to "succeed for two," while others go through life with little direction. Research indicates that reaction to the loss of a twin tends to be especially profound and enduring when the loss occurs suddenly and at a young age.[2]

Fortunately, in my heart, I remain connected to my twin. My strong religious background provided an opportunity to embrace the concept of an afterlife. As a little girl, my parents told me that Frankie would always watch over me. I decided to hold onto that belief, and it's made all the difference. I do not feel alone. Some may call my belief foolish, childlike, a convenient defense mechanism, even disturbed. My life's experiences tell me otherwise.

As an adult, I've wondered if my parents truly believed in a guardian concept or whether they just searched their minds and hearts until they came upon something that they thought I could hold onto. If they were skeptics, they certainly succeeded in convincing me. Even as a child, I often suggested that my mom "talk" to Frankie. In my mind, my twin needed to be connected to us just as much as I needed to remain connected to him. But, Mom would always respond, "Oh, I can't talk to him. He's just a little boy. I don't want to bother him." That confused me. Frankie was a part of our family, a part of me.

Would I believe so strongly in a connection between this life and the next, if I had not lost my twin? I'm not sure about that. But, I can't seem to think as a "non-twin." As I've said before, there's just something different about twins. You'll never convince me that something very profound doesn't go on between Heaven and Earth dwellers, especially between separated twins. There are some things stronger than the polio virus.

Mary Jane (Reid) Maidment—Anniversaries

Jan and I met when we were eighteen, just days after arriving at Seton Hill College (a few years ago Seton Hill achieved university status). Within weeks, we were fast friends, and for the next three years we were roommates. In spite of never living in the same city after college, our friendship has endured, thrived, and deepened. Several years ago, I suggested a weekly morning coffee klatch via phone. We both cherish our weekly chats that used to be on Tuesday mornings but have recently moved to Wednesday late afternoons (how dare our jobs try to interfere with our friendship time). We'll always find a way.

We've shared so much together—falling in and out of love, our weddings, the neurotic fears that accompany motherhood, the death of our parents, the dreams and aspirations of our children, college tuition payments, how young age sixty is beginning to sound, Jan's obsession with anti-wrinkle creams, you name it. But, today, I just want to talk about Jan and Frankie.

As you have already learned, Frankie died on All Saints' Day. In our religious tradition, it is a Holy Day of Obligation, which means that we are required to attend Mass. Before Jan left Syracuse to attend college, her family always observed the anniversary of Frankie's death by attending Mass together. It was a day of sadness and remembrance for the Floods, a day that brought forth old memories that remained dormant throughout most of the year. But, it was also a day of special bonding for the Floods, a day that their Church held sacred by honoring all Heaven-dwellers. Jan's parents believed that the fact that Frankie had died on All Saints' Day was a special sign from God—Frankie had truly been reunited with his heavenly Father. Jan embraces the same belief.

Just a few months after entering college, my friend boarded a plane bound for Syracuse to observe the anniversary of Frankie's death. Each year thereafter, Jan's parents mailed a plane ticket so that the family could all be together on the anniversary. My roommate always told me that she hated the early fall days leading up to the anniversary date. There was something about the chilly days, the fall foliage, the smell of the earth, the fading sunlight that could make her feel melancholy. It was a time when she would recall not only the special times she shared with Frankie but also the tragic events of his hospitalization and death. Within a few days after her annual trip, I noticed lightness in Jan's step—another anniversary had passed. To this day, members of Jan's family and friends make certain that she is never alone on the first of November. We're sharing in a tradition that Jan's parents began more than fifty years ago.

Reflection from Jan

Every woman should have a Mary Jane in her life. Since we graduated from college at age twenty-one, Mary Jane has never forgotten to make a November 1 phone call to her old college roommate. Thank you, my dear friend.

MJ's older brother, Charles, contracted non-paralytic polio as a teen. Fortunately, he made a complete recovery. It's hard to find anyone in my age group who has not had some connection with polio.

Janice—Polio's Surprise, Wednesday's Child

Upon completing graduate school, I returned to Syracuse and accepted a position at Community-General Hospital. It was good to be home. Working in an acute care facility was the perfect mix for my personality—the pace was fast, the caseload was varied, and we could often see the fruits of our work. I was also afforded an opportunity to teach. The graduate students in Syracuse University's School of Social Work certainly kept me on my toes. In addition, our hospital department supervised many graduate students who desired hospital field placements. I had finally realized the goal that I had set for myself when I was eight years old.

A hospital is such a unique environment—it's the only place in the world where someone may be dying in one room while just down the hall a baby may be making his or her first triumphant screech. I think that's what I loved most about my hospital work. The rhythm of an acute care facility pulses with the reality that everything truly does have a season: life, death, rebirth. I always told my grad students that a quick trip to the nursery viewing area could bring joy to the hardest of days. I still believe that.

As my husband mentioned in an earlier chapter, Dr. Kalamarides (the orthopedic surgeon who cared for me when I was a polio patient) was on staff at my hospital. The little girl he had helped to rehabilitate was now a member of his health care team.

◆　　　◆　　　◆

Within a few years of my hiring, the orthopedic wing at Community-General played an even more important role in my life. One autumn morning, after visiting one of my orthopedic patients, I stopped in the floor's "chart room." I had to make a note in my patient's chart to allow her attending physician to be updated regarding her post-hospital plans. I immediately noticed a nurse who was openly flirting with a young, cute guy dressed in surgical scrubs. I finished my chart note and promptly left the room. I shook my head as I left the room, mildly disgusted with the nurse's obvious attempt to "snag a doctor."

I made a quick stop at another floor and headed for the hospital cafeteria. A few minutes after I sat down at a table, I heard the hospital operator page me over the central intercom system. When I picked up my page, it was the voice of a guy who introduced himself as Dr. Nichols. He said that he had seen me in the 4W chart room. When I left the area, he had approached my patient and asked what my name was. He asked if he could meet me in the cafeteria. Since the cafeteria seemed like a perfectly safe place, I agreed to meet him. Five minutes later, I was paged to report to the emergency room; he was paged to return to the orthopedic wing. Before exiting the cafeteria, he asked if he could make me dinner the next evening. Now, that offer intrigued me—a guy making *me* dinner. That chance meeting in the chart room changed my life. We were married in the spring of his intern year. I remained an employee in the Social Service Department until Dave finished his residency. And yes, we're still enjoying that "happily ever after" stuff.

◆   ◆   ◆

Soon after marrying, we began planning for a family even though Dave had several more years of training. But, getting (and staying) pregnant, became a daunting task. Following fertility testing, my physicians informed me that my odds of getting pregnant were about 15 percent—certainly not great odds. Therefore, we attempted to add our names to an adoption agency list, but we were refused. It took so many years to match a couple with a baby that the adoption agency limited its list to couples who would definitely remain in the area—we couldn't promise that we would stay in Syracuse. We decided that when it finally came time to choose a place to practice, we would make every attempt to move to a city where adoption might be possible.

A few years into Dave's residency, I finally became pregnant—with twins no less. I believed that our family had been granted a second chance to delight in the special world of twins. When I miscarried, Dave and I were both devastated. Because of the pregnancy prognosis that I had been given, I was afraid that I might never conceive again.

I've had many years to reflect upon that time in my life. It's best that things did not work out. I may have sought to live vicariously through the twins, a situation that would have been unfair and destructive to the children. Most importantly, I can't imagine life without the little guy that you'll meet in a few pages.

◆   ◆   ◆

After experiencing a fertility problem and the traumatic miscarriage of twins, I was elated to learn that I would soon become a mother. As my husband began making our post-residency transition to the world of private practice, I reveled in my pregnancy. But, all too soon, polio would invade my life once again.

I had an uneventful second pregnancy, experiencing all the regular stuff—morning sickness, the thrill of that first little 'kick," and a sonogram to rule out the possibility of another multiple birth. I had no idea how fearful Dave was of becoming the father of twins. My husband's face lit up with relief when he saw only one baby on the sonogram. Our son's first photo op remains enshrined in a frame on our family room wall.

Dave and I enjoyed preparing the nursery. We chose Kevin and Erin as our favorite names. My obstetrician monitored me closely, and we made preparations for an end of November delivery. Although I reminded Dave that babies don't necessarily adhere to due dates, he was certain that the baby would arrive just on schedule. He closed his office in anticipation of the blessed event and arranged to have my mother present for the delivery as well. As you may have guessed by now, our baby had no intention of being born just to accommodate us. So, the end of November came and went, and there was no baby. The first and second weeks of December came and went, and, still, there was no baby. By that point I was so uncomfortable that I could hardly move. I had endured terrible pain at the base of my spine for about a month. As I walked, I often felt as if my body was going to break in two. I think I dismissed my complaints as typical of those voiced by most women in the last month of pregnancy. We would soon learn that there was more to it than that.

On December 15, my doctor decided that it was time to induce labor, but opted for an X-ray before injecting me. Even though Dr. Kalamarides had ordered numerous X-rays of my upper back to check for signs of scoliosis when I was a teenager, there had never been a need for pelvic X-rays. The child he had watched grow up had never complained of any lower back pain or any problem with physical activity; on the contrary, I was one very agile girl. Similarly, neither my husband nor my obstetrician, Stuart Caplin, (a polio survivor himself), had ever worried about any internal problems that had not surfaced earlier. Dr. Caplin had just been concerned that my pelvic structure might be too narrow to accommodate normal delivery. I will be forever grateful to my obstetrician for insisting upon that simple X-ray.

When I looked at that X-ray film, I saw a darling little baby. I was sure that I was going to have a boy that looked just like his father. Everything was fine until I looked at my husband—all the color had drained from his face. I asked him what was wrong and he indicated that he had never seen a lower spinal structure that looked like mine. Apparently, that area of my anatomy (the five sacral vertebrae) had not grown since I was six. Moreover, my sacrum (the bone located at the base of the spine, also known as the tailbone) was deformed in such a way as to prevent a normal delivery—my sacrum makes a right angle rather than a gentle curve. As my husband discussed in an earlier chapter of this book, bone can become deformed from the aftermath of polio weakened or paralyzed muscles. If I had gone into labor, our baby's little skull would have been crushed as he traversed the birth canal, and my odds of surviving the ordeal would not have been much better. I asked Dave if my condition had a medical name, but he just shook his head. He had never seen such a deformity described in the medical literature—no wonder I felt that my body was about to break in two. A C-section was scheduled for the next day. As I said in the opening chapter, polio has always had plenty of tricks (and surprises) up its sleeve.

Our baby was to be born on a Wednesday. If you recall the baby rhyme, "Monday's child, Tuesday's child, Wednesday's child is full of woe..." I promptly informed Dave that I could not possibly have our baby on a Wednesday. He looked at me, puzzled, and simply asked why I felt that way. When I recited the rhyme, he calmly responded, "Then change the rhyme." Undaunted, I did just that:

In my version, Wednesday's child has a magic glow!

Now, I think I'm a pretty lucky gal. My life was not only spared at age six but my life, and the life of our son, were spared disastrous consequences because for some unexplained reason, I had not gone into labor in spite of Kevin's gestational age. Our son, Kevin, was born on December 16, 1981.

Fearing that another pregnancy could result in tragedy, Dave and I opted to have only one child. We spoke at length about the decision as Dave knew how important motherhood was to me. I had always dreamed of being the mother of a large brood. Dave honestly felt that he could not go through another pregnancy. Given my bizarre bone structure, any pregnancy would have gambled with the life of the child, not just my own life. I didn't think that I had the right to place a baby in such peril or jeopardize the well-being of my husband and son. In my heart, I feel that we made the only decision we could.

Kevin has been a joy in our lives. We gave Kevin two middle names. Since Frankie could not continue my father's blood line, we opted to add my maiden name to Kevin's. I was thrilled that Dave was enthusiastic about the idea. The same priest that married us also baptized Kevin. I'm a woman who has been blessed with "nine lives." I think I have a few of the nine left.

P.S. For all mothers who have babies born on a Wednesday, remember my version of the rhyme.

◆   ◆   ◆

<u>Post-polio update</u>: The late effects of post-polio syndrome eventually forced Dr. Stu Caplin to retire several years ago. Never defeated, he became the president of his area's post-polio sports group and currently serves on the organization's advisory council. When ambulation became progressively more difficult, necessitating his use of a scooter, this special guy decided to take up table tennis. He won the U.S. Table Tennis Title in both 2005 and 2006. He recently retired as the president of the Medical Society of Clay County, Florida. Hats off to Stuart Caplin—he is a credit to his profession and offers inspiration to the millions of polio survivors living with post-polio syndrome.

Janice—Choices, New Adventures

Although my chosen profession often left me feeling pretty burned out (and our department secretary exasperated with my aversion to record keeping), I did not contemplate temporary or permanent retirement until I became a mother. A product of my era, I was taught that work outside the home was required for fulfillment. My life's direction had been determined at age eight. But, when I held our son in my arms, all thoughts of work outside the home evaporated. I have never regretted my choice.

In addition to experiencing the joys and frustrations of everything from the terrible twos to a full blown case of the empty nest syndrome, my at-home status provided me with an opportunity to care for our aging parents and engage in numerous charitable activities. I think I've made a pretty good medical wife, as I've never been jealous of my husband's profession. I've been on the other side. Medicine is a most demanding mistress.

◆　　　◆　　　◆

Over the years, as Mom and I both learned to speak of Frankie without crying, our conversations became more frequent. As a child and teenager, I had been terrified to ask if Frankie had suffered. I just couldn't bear to learn that he had been in pain. But, when I held our own son in my arms, I suddenly viewed Frankie as if he could have been my own child. And, so, I mustered the courage to ask Mom the one question I had always feared. You can imagine how relieved I was when Mom reassured me that Frankie was so sick that she was certain that he had never known what hit him. I had not been ready to hear the truth, whatever that might have turned out to be, until I became a mother.

It was then that Mom also divulged that Frankie had died with my father's arms cradling him. I had been told as a child that Frankie had died before an operation to help him breath could be performed. I also knew that my dad had accompanied the medical staff to the operating room area,

160

but I did not know the specific details of my father's involvement. What a terrible burden my mother and father had carried. I wanted to hug my dad but it was too late for hugs—he had died nine months before our son Kevin was born.

I'm so thankful that Frankie was not alone. I can't begin to imagine what it must have been like for my father as he watched, helpless to save his namesake. I hope that the mother-to-mother talk that Mom and I shared that day lessened her burden. She probably knew that someday I would need to ask the one question that I had always avoided—the question that signaled to her that I was finally ready to learn the details of Frankie's final moments.

Mom was never ready to offer any other details; I'm not sure if she even knew anything else. As for me, I had had the most important question answered. I'm not sure if I'd want to know anymore, even twenty-five years later.

◆   ◆   ◆

My mother moved to be near us in 1984. She maintained her own home and independence until she developed medical problems in 1992. She lived in our home after that initial illness. Although she had had the joy of watching her two daughters grow to adulthood, she had never had the experience of watching a little boy grow past age six. I was so thankful that Mom had the pleasure of seeing Kevin on a near daily basis until she died.

The years from 1988 to her death were especially poignant for both Mom and me as we watched our little boy grow beyond the milestones we had experienced with Frankie. I can also remember being apprehensive when Kevin reached age 6, and I breathed a sigh of relief when we began to plan Kevin's next birthday party. As I watched Kevin as a fun loving little guy, I couldn't help but recall the wonderful memories I had of Frankie leading up to the fall of 1953.

While I delighted in the joys of motherhood, polio continued on its rampage. In December 1988, as Dave, Mom, and I made plans for Kevin's birthday party, 350,000 people in 125 countries continued to be infected with the polio virus. Yet, I remained under the false impression that polio was a thing of the past. After all, the United States had been declared polio-free in 1979. Thankfully, Rotary International, WHO, CDC, UNICEF, and numerous private, public, and governmental agencies were not only aware of polio's continued rate of infection but, more importantly, were determined to end the suffering. Kevin just turned twenty-five. Sadly, the eradication struggle continues.

In June 1994, Mom suffered a severe stroke. After a short hospitalization, she returned to our home, where she remained until she joined Frankie and Dad. Within a few hours of being stricken by the massive cerebral hemorrhage, my mother was unable to speak. The last words she ever uttered in the hospital were to Kevin as she looked at him and mumbled, "Love." Death finally reunited her with her other little boy in August 1994. What a reunion that must have been.

◆   ◆   ◆

As a woman who is finding new adventures in this empty nest phase of my life, it's finally a "right time" for me to get back to my original life path. First Stop: Writing this book.

Frankie and Jan with cousins Bonne (Paltz) Hall and Bob Paltz—the happy foursome are sitting at the breakfast nook at Nona and Bompa Coolican's home (1952).

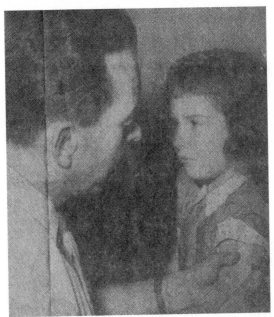

Jan and other students in grades one to three at Moses DeWitt Elementary School participated in the 1954 Salk vaccine trials. Dr. John Holmes participated as one of the physician-volunteers. Jan can recall her sadness on that day. The vaccine had come too late to save Frankie. *The photo was reproduced by David Nichols with permission from the Syracuse Post Standard. The photo appeared on May 3, 1954*

PART THREE: LOOKING BACK, LOOKING FORWARD

Dave—Medical Care Update

Fortunately, Jan has never needed surgical intervention for polio complications, but she wanted me to explain a surgical procedure for scoliosis that some of her contemporaries have required. I will also mention non-surgical treatments for scoliosis and other conditions, and conclude this chapter with a discussion of the plight of many present-day polio patients in Third World countries.

Surgical Intervention

Today, surgical intervention is sometimes required to address lingering foot, toe, knee, and hip problems. Yet, the most common reason for surgery is due to progressive curvature of the spine (scoliosis). Unfortunately, every time a patient requires surgery, rehabilitation must begin again, and this can be very discouraging.[1]

Spinal curvature in post-polio patients results from weak muscles on one side of the spine. Approximately one-third of all polio patients develop scoliosis. The condition usually occurs early in the disease process. Over time, this muscle imbalance can cause the spine to bend either to the right or left, depending upon which side of the body the weak muscles are found. Surgeons can correct the curve by "jacking up" the concave side of the curved spine with a metal rod and fusing the spine in that position by removing the cartilage from the spinal joints and allowing the bone to grow across the joints in a permanently corrected position. According to Dr. Irwin M. Siegel of Rush Presbyterian/St. Luke's Medical Center in Chicago, paralyzed polio patients benefit more from surgery than any other scoliosis group.[2]

Surgical intervention is suggested for patients who are experiencing pain or breathing problems as a result of the spinal curve. In addition, successful surgery helps patients maintain an upright posture and diminish trunk fatigue that they may have experienced because of the curvature. It is important that the anesthesiologist be made aware of the polio history as polio patients tend to be more sensitive to anesthesia. Post-polio patients sometimes suffer from heightened postoperative pain as well as increased blood loss during surgery. Post-surgical prognosis tends to be more variable in adult post-polio scoliosis patients because older patients have stiffer spines than children do, making it more difficult to correct the curve. The procedure used to correct curvature is called *spinal fusion*. Many polio survivors require this intervention early on, while others face a need for surgery only after several years of progressive curvature.[3]

Non-Surgical Intervention

Bracing rather than surgical intervention may be indicated for patients who experience mechanical back pain, for some scoliosis patients not considered good surgical candidates, and for polio patients not anxious to undergo surgery. Bracing is accomplished by means of a plastic "jacket" that surrounds the entire torso. When an adult patient is braced, the brace may be required for life because the curve will continue to progress.

Patients who have used limb braces since contracting polio now enjoy the benefit of technological advances. Modern devices incorporate lightweight designs with energy saving innovations. Wheelchair and respiratory-aid designs have also benefited from improved technology.

Unfortunately, for some successfully rehabilitated patients, post-polio syndrome problems have necessitated a return to braces, canes, or wheelchairs long ago abandoned.

Current Realities in Endemic and Epidemic Areas

Polio patients in Third World countries often have little or no access to modern surgery, therapy, and appliances. When surgical care is available, the same procedures as discussed in my earlier chapter are utilized, including *osteotomy, fusion, tendon transfer, epiphyseodesis,* and *spinal fusion.*

Clinics in developing countries vary in terms of financial backing and the size and scope of adjacent workshops. Sadly, many individuals are forced to make do with crutches made from wooden sticks, physical support limited to that which relatives can provide, or makeshift trolleys that serve in place of modern wheelchairs. But, at the same time, a number of creative individuals have devised simple innovations that can be made in low budget workshops. Current professional literature also stresses that technicians must remain sensitive to the geographical and cultural realities of each community. This is especially true when dealing with patients who suffer from leg-length discrepancies. Thus, clogs may be viewed as more acceptable than boots—especially in a community where villagers walk barefoot. Boots may also be seen as impractical in areas where wet, muddy conditions rapidly deteriorate leather. Many patients, with one leg shorter than the other, will refuse to wear a boot on one foot and not the other but will accept a clog.[4]

As I mentioned in a previous chapter, physical therapy, surgical intervention and non-surgical techniques cannot prevent all deformities and complications related to polio. But, lack of proper medical care and therapy can certainly exacerbate conditions. Orthopedic conditions associated with polio include:[5]

- foot equinus deformity—the foot is stuck in position with the toes pointed down
- valgus deformity—the foot is twisted outward
- varus deformity—the foot is twisted inward
- clawing of toes—toes are curved upward
- cavus deformity—excessively curved arch
- bunion—curved big toe
- genu recurvatum—forward curve of the knee
- flail knee—unstable knee in all directions
- femoral torsion of hip—a twisting deformity of the hip; the leg turns inward or outward
- flexion contracture of hip—hip is bent forward and can't be straightened
- deformities and atrophy (muscle shrinkage) of the upper limbs; atrophy also occurs in the lower extremities

To gain a better appreciation for the degree of disability that many polio patients in developing nations endure, you may wish to view online photos provided by the CDC Immunization Program, "Stop Transmission of Polio (STOP) Teams," and the Global Polio Eradication Initiative:
http://www.cdc.gov/nip/global/stopteam/team-pix.htm
http://www.polioeradication.org

It is a tragic reality that many current polio patients are denied access to rehabilitation services that patients in western countries have long taken for granted. Dedicated relief organizations cannot deliver care without adequate financial backing. Hopefully, renewed attention to the plight of survivors will increase private donations and program funding. Distance from medical facilities and lack of sufficient personnel trained to deal with post-polio conditions also complicate rehab efforts. Although vaccination is the ultimate solution, we must address the needs of patients already afflicted. After-care will be required for several decades to come—even if eradication is realized ...

Likewise, residents must be made aware that vaccination cannot correct deformity once the virus has attacked. I have actually heard of incidences, reported by vaccination program volunteers, in which it is not uncommon to see polio patients crawling to inoculation sites under the false impression that a dose of the polio vaccine can reverse their disabilities. Without proper education and rehabilitation, needless suffering will continue.

Esther and Chet
Sagenkahn—Let Me Thank You

Reflection

These pages have covered over fifty years of my life, and I have introduced you to many people who played a role in our polio story. I'd like to introduce you to the last of the story's voices—our neighbors Esther and Chet Sagenkahn. You've already met their son, Brett. I had not spoken with the Sagenkahns since I was a teenager. For many years they have resided in Florida though they still own Sagenkahn Interiors in Fayetteville, New York, and continue to engage in many philanthropic endeavors.

I have chosen to depart from the first person accounts expressed by the other voices in this book and tell the Sagenkahns' story in my own words. Like members of our extended family and the DeMartinos, the Sagenkahns were an integral part of our acute polio story.

It was wonderful to reconnect with Mr. and Mrs. Sagenkahn, two parents who meant so much to me growing up. We reminisced about the 1950s—when neighbors didn't lock their doors, fast-food chains didn't exist, suburban moms stayed home, black-and-white televisions were high tech, and neighborhood kids were treated to Mrs. Sagenkahn's fudge cake (I could go for some right now). Mrs. Sagenkahn was a very pretty woman (I'm sure she still is). She had beautiful clothes and a sense of style that I could appreciate even as a little girl. When I was about four, she gave me a tiny, sample-size pair of brown-suede heels. Boy, did I think I was something else. (Frankie mentioned those shoes when discussing our tonsillectomies.)

Mr. Sagenkahn told me how reserved my parents became after Frankie's death, something I was oblivious to as a little girl. Children are unaware of the social interactions their parents have with other adults. Our neighbors readily identified with the Floods' overwhelming grief, the way that their grief was bound to change them. It must have been very difficult for our family and friends to watch.

Both Mr. and Mrs. Sagenkahn spoke of the fear that polio would continue to strike neighborhood children, including their own. The helplessness that parents felt in the pre-polio vaccine era is something that I have discussed with many of my friends. As children born soon after World War II, we can all remember that our parents would not allow us to go to public pools or be in large crowds during the warm months. But, we were far too young to understand just how terrified our parents were—how terrified we would have been if our own children had been subjected to polio epidemics and how terrified many parents remain in areas where the polio virus has not been eradicated. In the fall of 1953, many young DeWitt, New York, parents came face to face with the fact that their lives could change in an instant. Certainly the Floods had had their world turned upside down in less than a week. Our suburb had lost some of its innocence. Its young parents had learned that nice homes and excellent schools could not protect their children from many things, including polio.

Mrs. Sagenkahn said that their family was in mourning for months. Although much of their life is now far from Syracuse, the Sagenkahns said that they still speak of that sad time, even to their new friends. When I spoke with Brett, he also commented that he often thinks and speaks of Frankie and the polio epidemic that changed so many lives, including his own. Likewise, Aunt Louise DeMartino has never failed to mention how much she and Uncle Larry loved my parents.

Although I will always cherish our recent phone chats, the voice of Mr. and Mrs. Sagenkahn is included for another reason, as well, for it demonstrates the power of kind, thoughtful gestures. After all these years, it's time that I thank the Sagenkahns for remembering Frankie's death with the annual arrival of a beautiful floral bouquet. Until my mother's death, she often spoke of the flowers that were delivered on November 1 each year. I don't think the Sagenkahns had any idea that a simple gift could mean so much. In their minds, as they mentioned on the phone, they just wanted to let our family know that they cared. It was a way of expressing friendship and solidarity without invading our privacy on each anniversary.

As neighbors and friends, most of us partake in wake and funeral rituals, make a few meals for the grieving family, send flowers or a donation to a charity chosen by the family, and then move on. A month or so after a death, most of us would be hard-pressed to recall a date of death, yet alone remember that day year after year.

Anniversaries of deaths, especially the first few, are difficult days at best. We have a tendency to recall the events surrounding the sickness or injury in a way that is pushed "out of mind" for most of the year. The Sagenkahns' sincere expression of friendship was testimony to the fact that since we would never be free to forget, they would not forget either. Thank you, Mr. and Mrs. Sagenkahn.

Dave—Post-Polio Syndrome

It is estimated that one million polio survivors live in the United States and that nearly half of those are living with the effects of permanent paralysis. Worldwide, ten to twenty million people live with the aftereffects of the polio virus. During the past twenty plus years, physicians and their patients have learned that polio can rear its ugly head decades after the initial infection, as a condition called post-polio syndrome. Moreover, recent evidence seems to indicate that individuals who were never diagnosed with polio may have actually contracted the disease. These patients may also be experiencing symptoms that are consistent with post-polio syndrome complaints. Jan will discuss her own experiences in the next chapter but, once again, she asked me to provide an overview.[1]

Post-polio syndrome is reported to affect somewhere between 25 and 60 percent of all polio survivors, though physical limitations vary. Post-Polio Health International lists figures that between a hundred twenty thousand and a hundred eighty thousand survivors may be developing the syndrome. It is important to note that it is generally accepted that post-polio syndrome is *not* a recurrence of the virus.[2]

◆　　◆　　◆

Cause

Although its cause is not fully understood, most practitioners believe that the syndrome occurs as the result of degenerating nerve cells. As explained earlier via the voice of Dr. Turek, the initial polio infection attacks nerve cells called motor neurons. Since the virus kills or damages nerve cells, the remaining cells must sprout additional fibers in order to compensate for the cells that have been lost. Researchers theorize that, over time, the neurons become overtaxed—thus leading to the deterioration and eventual death of the neuron itself. Even though everyone experiences a loss of neurons as part of the aging process, polio survivors begin their post-polio life with a neural deficit.[3]

Some scientists believe that the initial polio infection causes an immune reaction in which the body's immune system begins to attack normal cells as if they were foreign bodies, but this theory has not been accepted by the majority of researchers. Another controversial theory, refuted by most scientists, is that the polio virus remains dormant in the body only to be released several years later.[4]

A Swedish institute is studying the effect of administering intravenous doses of immunoglobulins to post-polio sufferers. Since a specific inflammatory agent has been found in the cerebrospinal fluid of polio survivors, it is thought that symptoms may be caused by inflammation. Still other scientists postulate that post-polio symptoms are simply the result of overuse of undamaged muscles.[5]

The October 12, 2006, issue of the *Journal of the American Medical Association* included an excellent article by Mike Mitka entitled, "Aging Brings New Challenges for Polio Survivors."The article reviewed current post-polio research and current theories regarding the causative agents involved in post-polio syndrome. A recent study conducted by Rochester, Minnesota's Mayo Clinic found that most polio survivors do not experience physical decline as a result of post-polio syndrome and that decline in function mirrors age-related changes. These findings may certainly be questioned by many polio survivors currently experiencing the late effects of polio and by practitioners involved in the direct care of post-polio patients. The results of the Mayo study also stand in contrast to results obtained in many earlier investigations. Lauro S. Halstead, a polio survivor and director of the National Rehabilitation Hospital in Washington DC, postulates that the Mayo Clinic's results could be due to the fact that patients involved in the study may have been initially infected by the polio virus Type usually associated with a milder form of the disease. Medical debate will continue for the foreseeable future. It is important that polio survivors continue to educate their personal physicians regarding their post-polio problems *and* that they continue to demand additional clinical investigation.[6]

Signs and Symptoms

Primary signs and symptoms of post-polio syndrome include:[7]

- new muscle weakness in affected limbs or in limbs not previously affected
- general fatigue and exhaustion following minimal physical activity
- difficulty breathing (including sleep apnea), sleeping, or swallowing
- muscle and joint pain
- decreased cold tolerance

Although symptoms are most prevalent in initially affected muscles, many patients complain of weakness and pain in limbs that had not been previously paralyzed. These symptoms are not due to a spread of the syndrome. Most experts believe that the muscle areas newly marked by pain, weakness, or fatigue were initially affected by the virus but went undetected by both the patient and his or her health care providers.[8]

Unfortunately, those most at risk for the syndrome are individuals whose initial cases were the most serious and whose recoveries were the greatest. It appears that this may be due to the fact that the recovery process placed greater stress on surviving motor neurons. Moreover, the strength of surviving muscles may have been overestimated following initial rehabilitation efforts.[9]

Age of onset is also a risk factor in that the incidence of post-polio syndrome increases if the person acquired polio as an adult or adolescent rather than as a young child. Survivors who engage in rigorous physical activity to the point of experiencing fatigue or exhaustion may also be more susceptible to the syndrome. Progressive post-polio muscular atrophy may be especially prevalent in individuals who have engaged in high-intensity use of muscles over the years.[10]

Diagnosis

A diagnosis of post-polio syndrome is made by examining three factors: previous diagnosis of polio, a long asymptomatic period, and a gradual onset of symptoms. Although an asymptomatic period of between thirty to forty years usually occurs before the onset of post-polio complaints, there are incidences of symptoms occurring as early as eight to ten years after onset of the acute infection or as long as seventy plus years after contracting polio. Many post-polio patients indicate that they noticed symptoms over time and thus find it difficult to precisely recall when a particular symptom was first noticed.[11]

Physicians may recommend a series of tests including a nerve conduction study (EMG) and imaging tests such as an MRI or CAT scan. Since a diagnosis is made by process of elimination (to make sure that the symptoms are not the result of other diseases), a thorough examination and yearly follow-up by an informed physician (often a physiatrist, pulmonary specialist, orthopedist, or neurologist) is recommended.[12]

Treatment

Because post-polio complaints are so varied, there is no specific treatment fitted to all patients. Treatment goals for all post-polio patients are simple: retain maximal independence while decreasing discomfort or pain. Suggested treatments include: energy conservation, physical therapy, occupational therapy, sleep apnea treatment, speech therapy, medications, and the use of respiratory aids as needed. Non-steroidal anti-inflammatory drugs may sometimes ease pain, and some of these drugs are currently being examined to see if they can provide relief. While most physicians and therapists believe that exercise to maintain fitness (such as swimming, water aerobics, or walking at a leisurely pace) is important, it is equally important to avoid the overtaxing of muscles. Post-Polio Health International (PHI) recommends that patients suffering from fatigue take frequent, short rest periods. Management of psychological stress caused by the onset and progression of symptoms is also important.[13]

Post-Polio Syndrome: A Guide for Polio Survivors and Their Families by Julie K. Silver provides excellent medical and practical information—my wife has found it to be an invaluable resource. A second edition of *Managing Post-Polio: A Guide to Living and Aging Well,* has recently been published. Dr. Lauro Halstead serves as the book's editor in association with the National Rehabilitation Hospital in Washington DC. Although I have not had an opportunity to read this book, or the earlier edition, it is surely an important volume for anyone living with the late effects of polio.

In general, it is recommended that activities should be avoided that cause fatigue within a short period of time, but the role of exercise remains a controversial medical issue. As a physician who has never experienced polio but whose spouse has, I try to remember that a polio survivor experiencing post-polio syndrome symptoms is probably the best judge of his or her own body, its strengths and limitations.[14]

It is equally important that friends and family members remain sensitive to the limitations required to maintain optimal functioning over the long haul. Post-polio syndrome is a difficult emotional issue for people who struggled to rehabilitate many years ago. No one wants to remain independent and ambulatory more than someone who fought to walk again or breathe without mechanical assistance. Likewise, it can be difficult for family members to accept that their loved one may no longer be able to maintain the degree of physical activity that was once taken for granted.

When one considers the current polio outbreaks in several Third World countries, it is important to stress, once again, that intervention must go beyond inoculation. Most likely, present patients will experience post-polio syndrome symptoms some ten to forty years from now. Moreover, patients in developing nations who contracted polio years ago may already be experiencing symptoms.

◆   ◆   ◆

Post-Polio Health International (PHI) and its affiliated International Ventilator Users Network (IVUN) are invaluable sources of information for polio survivors, home ventilator users, and health care professionals. Both PHI and IVUN utilize education, research, advocacy, and networking to assist their clients. PHI and IVUN publish excellent newsletters that provide a wonderful mix of educational material and human-interest stories. In addition, PHI provides an annual directory that lists post-polio clinics, health professionals, and support groups, by state and country.

Polio Survivors and Associates (PSA), founded by a Rotarian and polio survivor, is another organization dedicated to the dissemination of information to polio survivors throughout the world.

In 1987, the Social Security Administration acknowledged the late effects of polio and issued criteria for its evaluation (listing number D1245080.010E.3). In 2003, the Social Security Administration updated its evaluation criteria for post-polio syndrome (listing number D124580.010 Evaluation of Postpolio sequelae).[15]

Note: Please consult Appendices B, C, and D for additional information on the activities of Post-Polio Health International, Rotary's PolioPlus program, and the March of Dimes.

Janice—Polio, Part II

For many years, the physical aftermath of polio had virtually no effect on my life. Then, along came the realization that polio had left its calling card back in the 1950s—a deformed sacral area that made it impossible to accomplish a normal delivery. Although Dave and I were faced with a difficult decision regarding parenthood, I moved on with my life quite easily. Perhaps it would have been harder for me to accept if I had not had a difficult time getting, and staying, pregnant. But, when Kevin entered our lives, I was far too happy and far too tired to feel anything other than joy. I had been blessed.

The first sign of post-polio problems (other than the one discovered at delivery time and my limp that became more noticeable when I'm tired) surfaced in the early 1990s. As I mentioned in an earlier chapter, I enrolled in several dancing and ice skating classes as soon as my physical condition could tolerate each new activity. Peggy Fleming had nothing to worry about, but I could hold my own on the ice at Jamieson's private rink on Syracuse's Erie Boulevard East. In addition to being great fun, the skating routines were excellent for building ankle and leg strength.

As a teenager, college coed, and young adult I had no problem balancing on everything from spiked heels to crazy platform shoes. Therefore, I was certainly amazed when, as a forty-something, I started having problems following long walks. I would notice that my ankles would literally start caving inward so that the insides of my feet were bent precariously close to the ground. Now, even on the best of days, my right ankle is slightly turned inward. Very recently, I've noticed that my left ankle bends inward as well.

There are some definite benefits to living with an orthopedic surgeon. Dave immediately begins rehab any time I experience a serious cave-in. He wraps both of my ankles with ace bandages and then makes me practice walking with my feet and ankles bent outward. I have to work very hard to accomplish ambulation, but within a few days my ankle muscles are, once again, in fine working order. Today, I travel with a few ace bandages in my carry-on luggage just in case. I've also developed a way of exercising my ankle muscles whenever and wherever I'm sitting or standing. I just push my ankles outward, inward, outward—over and over again. Most recently, I have rediscovered Dr. Scholl's exercise sandals. Because you have to work at walking in them, I trust that they will benefit my weakened ankles.

The most frightening experience I've had occurred a few years ago. Dave and I had taken a relatively long bike ride together along the Erie Canal bike trail. When we returned to the start of the trail, I hopped off my bike, only to be stopped dead in my tracks. I was literally unable to move my legs, though I felt no fatigue. I was terrified—in a nanosecond, I reverted to that six-year-old little girl who could not move her legs. I just stood there. Fortunately, after a few minutes my legs started moving again. But, I was not able to walk normally for an hour or so. Since that day, I have refused to ride my bike. Perhaps I'm being stubborn or foolish, but I don't want to experience that terror ever again. I worked far too hard to walk again to risk my independence over a bike ride—walking suits me fine.

There are only a few other things that I've noticed. The first happens each morning when I try to walk downstairs to make coffee and commence my early morning cleaning routine. I can't make my legs move in unison. Instead of proceeding down the stairs like an adult (right leg, left leg, right leg), I go down the stairs like a little kid (right leg, pull the left leg down to meet the right, right leg again, pull the left leg down to meet the right and so on). It's almost as if my brain and legs aren't in the same body. But, within fifteen minutes or so, I can run up and down the stairs any way I choose.

Now, my other symptoms are stranger still. Sometimes, my hands just won't work properly. I'll try to tap on my laptop or write a note, but my hands just don't seem to know how to hold a pen, write, or maneuver around a keyboard with any degree of dexterity. Though I can't say many good things about my penmanship on a good day, my writing becomes completely illegible when my hands are being stubborn. Often, my hands and arms ache all over even though I'm not arthritic. It's a dull, diffuse pain that is only partially alleviated by aspirin. I find it especially helpful to take an aspirin before going to bed. Could my muscles be telling me to lay off the laptop for a few days?

I've found that stretching out my hands and fingers as well as kneading some silly putty helps immensely. Pens with larger circumferences also help compensate for my lack of dexterity (like a little kid who uses thick crayons when learning to color). I don't remember my physical therapist concentrating on my upper extremities when I was a child. Although I'm certain that I lost some muscle strength in my arms and hands, the first priority was to get my leg and neck muscles moving again. Very recently, I've noticed the same dull diffuse pain in my legs and feet but only in the evening when my muscles are fatigued; by morning, all the pain is gone.

For the past month or so, my right hand has given me additional troubles. When I first wake up, I am unable to move my hand at all. I begin my day by forcibly bending and stretching my hand in different directions. For some insidious reason, post-polio syndrome sometimes enjoys attacking areas not previously affected by the virus or perhaps, more accurately, not diagnosed at the time of the acute polio infection. Hand strengthening exercises are becoming an ever more important part of my daily routine.

As of this writing, my post-polio problems are little more than annoyances; I am not incapacitated. Looking forward to the next few decades of my life, my goal is quite simple: just keep walking under my own steam. During a recent family vacation, I found myself taking note of numerous women (in my age group) who were confined to wheelchairs. I couldn't help but wonder if their confinement was due to the late effects of polio. I must admit that I experienced some degree of fear and apprehension. Could that be me some-day? How would my family react? How would I react to life in a wheelchair? I certainly hope that neither my family nor I ever have to face such issues, but I cannot change my polio history. For anyone who has never experienced an inability to walk, it may be difficult to comprehend what it's like. But, for a polio survivor who has learned to walk again, walking is *never* again taken for granted. I give thanks for all that I am able to do today. I derive comfort from not being able to predict my ambulatory future.

Similarly, I am thankful that to date, my hand problems have not prevented me from participating in any aspects of what therapists refer to as "activities of daily living." I find myself relying more frequently on kitchen aids (or my husband) to open jars. I have adjusted to a light-weight vacuum cleaner and carry fewer items at a time up and down the stairs. Although it's difficult for me to hold even small objects like a coffee cup when I first wake up, within less than fifteen minutes or so my hand strength improves. I am learning to rely on my left hand and my upper arm strength in both limbs. I remain joined at the hip to my laptop, eternally grateful that I am less dependent upon legal pads and ball point pens these days. I will make additional adaptations as needed—I hope without too much complaint.

Both in the acute and chronic phases of polio, I've been more fortunate than many long term polio survivors, and each day I remind myself of that fact. Polio continues to extract much from my peers who suffer the progressive effects of post-polio syndrome. I pray that in the near future, medicine will find cures for polio's latest cruel tricks.

In the end, we are members of a club that totals in the millions. We have made it this far and will continue to adapt. At the same time, history has shown that polio survivors have never been afraid to challenge the status quo. I am confident that we will continue to fight for our peers and for the millions of polio survivors who have yet to experience the late-term effects of the virus. Future practitioners and researchers may yet unravel polio's remaining mysteries.

Alice (Jaros) Turek, MD, MPH—Changes, Eradication Update

As mentioned earlier, a very small number of polio cases related to the live-virus Sabin vaccine were reported each year between 1980 and 1996. In an attempt to eliminate this transmission, a mixed vaccination regime was instituted in the United States in 1996. Children received two doses of the Salk vaccine at age two and four months of age, followed by two doses of the Sabin vaccine at twelve to eighteen months and four to six years of age. When polio cases persisted under this modified protocol, the United States opted to abandon the live-virus vaccine.[1]

The World Health Organization and the Advisory Committee for Polio-myelitis Eradication (ACPE) have both recommended that polio-free countries transition to the killed-virus vaccine. Once the spread of the wild-type polio virus is stopped, the final obstacle to worldwide polio eradication is vaccine-derived polio. Eradication issues and recommendations are discussed, in greater detail, in the first chapter of this book.[2]

◆   ◆   ◆

The last recorded case of vaccine-associated polio in the U.S. took place in 1999, soon before we transitioned back to the killed-virus vaccine. In spite of the fact that our country and 29 other countries have returned to the killed-virus polio vaccine, unvaccinated individuals remain vulnerable if they come in contact with a person from another country who has recently received the live-virus vaccine. Four non-vaccinated children contracted polio in Minnesota in 2005; fortunately, none of the children suffered paralysis. From 2000-2005, there were approximately sixty circulating vaccine-derived cases of polio reported in the island of Hispaniola (Haiti and the Dominican Republic), Indonesia, the Philippines, Madagascar, and China. Vaccine-derived cases have also been isolated in Nigeria, Niger, Myanmar, and Cambodia. It should be remembered that from 1997 to 2007, over 10 billion doses of OPV were administered worldwide with less than 200 vaccine-derived cases of polio. During that same period, there were 31,100 cases of wild poliovirus among non-vaccinated individuals, thus affirming the overwhelming success of prevention through vaccination. Circulating vaccine-derived cases occur in areas with very low vaccination rates. See www. polioeradication.org for continually updated information on all eradication issues.[3]

In February 2006, the CDC reported its first *imported* vaccine-associated case of paralytic polio in a twenty-two-year-old unvaccinated woman who had traveled in Central and South America in 2005. Because of the serious implications of this importation case, a great deal of scientific debate took place before authorities were ready to confirm the young woman's illness as paralytic polio. The final diagnosis was made on the basis of examination of stool specimens, clinical evidence, and the absence of other agents known to produce similar symptoms. As reported by the Immunization Action Coalition, the case highlights the small risk that unvaccinated people face when traveling to countries where the oral polio vaccine is still in use. Risk is obviously greater in areas where polio cases persist.[4]

What is the Status of Polio Vaccination in the United States?

Since 2000, children in the United States have, once again, been immunized with a killed-virus polio vaccine that is administered by shot. It is estimated that the United States spends $350 million each year to inoculate children against polio. In the United States, eligible children are able to receive childhood vaccinations free of charge through a private physician network, administered at a national level by the CDC. The agency contracts with drug manufacturing companies to purchase vaccines at discounted prices. Free vaccine clinics are also provided in many states.

Information regarding eligibility for the "Vaccines for Children Program" (VFC) is currently available at: http://www.cdc.gov/nip/vfc/about.htm.[5]

All states and the District of Columbia require that children receive certain vaccinations (usually diphtheria, tetanus, whooping cough, measles, mumps, rubella, and polio) before entering school or daycare programs, unless documented medical conditions render vaccination inadvisable. However, children may be exempted from the vaccine regulations on the basis of religious grounds in forty-eight states. In recent years, vaccination waivers or exemptions have also been granted in several states for grounds other than religious convictions. As of March 2006, nineteen states allowed personal belief waivers for philosophical, religious, or other unspecified non-medical reasons. It should be noted that each state develops its own waiver criteria. According to 2004 CDC data, 95.5 percent of children in the United States are immunized against polio by the time they enter school. Unfortunately, recent data also indicates that in some cities immunization levels have fallen below optimal community (herd) immunity levels. A trend against vaccination in a state, city, or neighborhood creates clusters where infectious agents can more easily be introduced. Public health officials are alarmed by the growing number of states granting philosophical waivers.[6]

Current CDC data indicates that there are no known serious side effects to IPV vaccines although a serious reaction, such as a severe allergic reaction, can occur with any medication. The CDC concludes that the risk of serious side effects from the polio vaccine is extremely small. According to the CDC, the IPV vaccine available in the United States provides protective immunity to all three Types of polio virus in 90 percent of recipients after two doses of the vaccine. Ninety-nine percent of recipients have protective antibody immunity after three doses. IPV vaccine available in the United States since 1987 is as effective as OPV for preventing polio.[7]

According to the CDC, routine polio vaccination is not recommended for persons eighteen and over living in the United States, unless they are at increased risk for exposure, such as travel to polio-endemic or epidemic areas. Vaccination should be avoided by some children and adults because of certain medical conditions and known allergies to vaccine components.[8]

Current Polio Vaccinations Available in the United States

In 2002, a five-component (pentavalent) combination vaccine became available in the United States. Licensed under the name, Pediarix, the vaccine provides protection from five childhood diseases in one shot: inactivated polio, hepatitis B, diphtheria, tetanus, and acellular pertussis (whooping cough). Pediarix is usually administered at two months, four months, and six months of age and is manufactured by GlaxoSmithKline[9]

The other IPV currently in use in the United States is IPOL. This trivalent vaccine, licensed in 1990, offers protection from the three virus Types of polio. It is manufactured by Sanofi Pasteur and is usually administered at two months, four months, fifteen months, and between four and six years of age. A modified schedule is recommended for unvaccinated children age four to eighteen years of age. When Pediarix is administered, the U.S. vaccine schedule indicates that a fourth dose of IPV should be given between ages 4-6. Sometimes, Pediarix and IPOL are referred to as eIPV vaccines rather than IPV vaccines because of their enhanced potency.[10]

A September 2005 press release from Sanofi Pasteur reported that the company had received permission from the FDA to file a licensing application for its combination vaccine, Pentacel. It is the first DTaP-based (diphtheria, tetanus and acellular pertussis) combination vaccine that includes both polio and Hib vaccine components (Haemophilus influenzae type b). The vaccine is currently licensed in several countries outside the United States.[11]

Sanofi Pasteur has been involved in polio eradication efforts for the past fifty years. In addition to IPOL, the company also markets a monovalent agent MOPV1. In 2001 the Chairman and CEO of Sanofi Pasteur, Jean-Jacques Bertrand, was awarded the Sabin Institute's Humanitarian Award. The Sabin Institute, with national headquarters located in Washington DC, was founded in 1993 (the year of Albert Sabin's death) as a public nonprofit organization dedicated to the development, delivery, and dissemination of effective vaccines throughout the world.[12]

Recommendations

Public health officials caution that a decision to refuse vaccination is not a passive decision. It is, more accurately, an active decision to allow yourself and your family to remain susceptible to a deadly disease. Unvaccinated individuals are at increased risk of acquiring polio. Moreover, individuals who are not vaccinated are putting *other* unvaccinated children at risk who may be too young to have completed the vaccination schedule or who may not be able to be vaccinated because of medical conditions.

It is important that parents address any vaccine concerns or questions to their medical providers, including issues related to the safety of the polio vaccine, medical contraindications, modified inoculation schedules, allergies to vaccine components, and special travel issues. Moreover, before any vaccination is given, parents must apprise the physician if their child is experiencing a fever or any type of illness; this information is needed because the situation may warrant a delay in the vaccination schedule. Some mild conditions do not necessitate delay.

In addition to consulting with their private physicians and Web sites provided by the CDC and the American Academy of Pediatrics, parents may find the following online source both useful and informative: http://www.vaccinecheck. com/vacinfo_2.jsp?vac=2.

Travelers to polio endemic countries or areas where polio outbreaks continue to occur should consult their medical providers. Vaccination requirements and recommendations for international travelers are provided in CDC publication,

"Health Information for International Travel, 2005–2006" (and future updates). See: http://www.cdc.gov/travel/diseases/polio.htm.

Individuals living in other countries must adhere to travel requirements and recommendations stipulated by their country of residence and country of visitation. The Advisory Committee for Polio Eradication recommends that WHO travel requirements be updated. Contrary to popular belief, not all countries mandate routine immunization against childhood diseases.

◆   ◆   ◆

As we contemplate the total eradication of polio within the near future, it is imperative that vaccinations not be stopped while one case of polio remains in the world. Several years ago, a European country stopped mandatory polio vaccination because the country had been polio-free for well over a decade. The vaccination program was reinstituted after a small epidemic was traced to an individual from another country. An outbreak also occurred in the Netherlands in the 1990s in an area where a religious sect does not adhere to vaccine recommendations. It is likewise important to take note of two recent developments reported by www.polioeradication.org: In summer 2007, an Australian student visited his home in Pakistan. Upon returning to Australia, he was diagnosed with paralytic polio. Pakistan is one of the countries where polio has never been eradicated; Australia had not experienced a case of polio in over twenty years. In fall 2007, poliovirus was found in part of the sewer system in Geneva, Switzerland. The virus was genetically traced to ongoing transmission in the country of Chad. Although Switzerland enjoys an excellent vaccination rate, this event demonstrates the importance of continued vaccination. Because polio has not been eradicated worldwide, public health officials warn that polio is a disease that could be "just a plane trip away."

If we reach the end point, we need to evaluate how long the world should be considered polio-free before halting vaccinations. Some health officials and scientists have suggested that vaccination could stop after three years of a polio-free globe. Cost analyses have been calculated to show the cost benefits if and when eradication can take place. The World Health Organization currently estimates that polio eradication would provide an annual savings of $1.5 billion. Yearly financial tolls for every additional year we remain plagued by the disease have also been calculated. Some scientists remain more cautious, questioning whether we can ever stop vaccination or if the disease can ever be completely eradicated.[13]

For many years, critics of the polio vaccine have pointed to sensational articles in magazines and newspapers that only serve to confuse the public and misrepresent the status of present research and vaccine safety. Thus, I'd like to conclude my remarks with an explanation of current screening safeguards and research findings involving the controversies. I'm also anxious to tell you about a very exciting potential use for a genetically-engineered polio virus:

Ever since the development of the Salk and Sabin vaccines, there have been questions as to whether the vaccine contained strains of the dangerous simian viruses (monkey viruses) during the early years of production, 1954–1963. In 1963, the federal government began screening for simian viruses to prevent dangerous problems.

Since the 1990s, there have been occasional reports linking the polio vaccines to AIDS and various cancers. The latest research indicates no correlation between the oral polio vaccine developed by Hilary Koprowski (given to nearly a million people during his Belgian Congo trials in the late 1950s) and AIDS. Similarly, the National Institutes of Health and the National Cancer Institute point to several studies, conducted throughout the world that show no correlation between human cancers and exposure to a particular simian virus. Continued research is underway to definitively address concerns. [14]

Duke University reported the results of a clinical trial crossing a genetically-engineered polio virus with the common cold virus in 2001. The initial trial, with monkey subjects, was conducted to determine if the combination could cure a lethal form of brain cancer. Results from the trial indicated that the combination was very effective in killing malignant cells without damaging normal cells. Who could have ever predicted that the vicious virus that killed or maimed so many in the past would ever be considered as a potential healer? We'll have to wait and see. Scientific research is a long, painstaking process. [15]

◆   ◆   ◆

In addition to eliminating one source of human suffering, a polio-free world would allow resources to be shifted to diseases and conditions that continue to plague mankind like AIDS, cancer, spinal cord injuries, and Alzheimer's.

Dave—Are There Connections?

I decided to tell this story not only because it's a sweet tale but because I've come to accept that when it comes to things between Jan and Frankie, there are things that happen that just can't be explained. As Jan's father mentioned earlier in this book, Jan has known and sensed things ever since Frankie died. Long ago, Frank decided to accept his children's unique bond, evident since their birth.

When my wife received a copy of *The Rotarian* a few years back and announced that she needed to write a book about polio, I decided to go along for the ride. In truth, I had wanted her to write about polio for some time though I had not anticipated quite so many fifteen-hour days, months, or years of researching and writing. Jan believes that Frankie has guided her along her life's journey and that writing this book is just one more stop along the way.

Perhaps because of whom I am married to, I have come to draw comfort from the possibility that there may be a strange, wonderful connection between Earth dwellers and Heaven dwellers. We humans can certainly use all the help we can get. I'm thankful that my wife looks upon the special connection she seems to have with her twin as a gift from God, a silver lining in an otherwise tragic story. If Heaven resembles Jan's childhood concept at all, I pray that Frankie's hope for a polio-free world will soon be realized. Who could wish for an end to polio more than twins, long ago separated because of the vicious polio virus?

I'm an intractable science type. I've been trained to not believe anything without validation, to be skeptical of everything. For years, I struggled with what my wife always described as "her gift." I learned about Frankie, and her bout with polio, on our first date. Jan spoke freely about that period of her life, but she didn't get into any "twilight zone" kind of stuff for some time. I'm certain she wanted to make sure that I had dubbed her solidly sane before telling me any of her stories. As time went on, Jan began to tell me more about her feelings and dreams, her premonitions of imminent death for people who, to the rest of the world, seemed healthy. I listened intently but ever the skeptic, I just couldn't buy Jan's explanations, her insights, or her predictions. I really didn't know what to make of that aspect of my wife's personality.

But, over the years, I've come to accept that there may well be some connection that Jan and Frankie enjoy. I can't believe I'm saying this. So, when Jan had a dream about her father's death at the precise time he died (according to the death certificate), I began to question my own skepticism. When Jan dreamt that her mother would die on an August 3, and then she did, I began to shake my head.

Many of our friends and family certainly believe Jan has some kind of sensitivity or, in her words, some kind of "gift." Many years ago, Jan's father related an incident that occurred while Jan was in college. Now, if you had known Frank, you would have understood that he had absolutely no tolerance for such things as the paranormal. But, he recognized that there was something about Jan that even he could not explain or ignore. Though Frank wrote melodious prose, his speech was often peppered with a few expletives that his son Frankie was known to use as well. One night, Frank recalled a story that took place when Jan was in college. She had called home to ask if her cousin Russ was OK. Startled, Dodie told Jan that Russ had been in a very serious car accident the night before but that he would be OK. Frank's comment to me was succinct: "Now, God___, how in the ____ did she know that?"

Jan believes that this "gift" of hers comes from a bond that she retains with Frankie. I guess sooner or later, I had to accept that my wife was a little different. Let me tell you a story that had my head spinning for some time. Is it coincidence? Or, is there really a connection that defies logic, science, everything except faith?

Back in the 1990s, we were in the process of selling our home. For many reasons, it just wasn't selling. Now, my Irish gal was getting discouraged, even depressed—something very unusual for her. She had loved our home and had wanted just the right family to buy it, a family who would find happiness, fun, and peace within its walls. Dodie, my mother-in-law, had died in the home, making it even more important for the "right family" to be found. We had also built a fantastic clubhouse in the backyard, complete with a deck, slide, sandbox, and rear ramp to accommodate our Golden Retriever, Bailey, and Dodie. My wife was adamant that the new family should enjoy that clubhouse as much as we did. Each Christmas, we decorated it as a gingerbread house complete with four foot-high candy canes, wooden lollipops and gum drops, holiday lights, even a life-size blonde gingerbread boy.

Jan had planted a statue of St. Joseph in the front yard, hearing that the statue would help find the perfect new family. She had placed a special angel (she's always had a thing about angels) in a kitchen cabinet and hid a lucky penny for the new family to discover—but, no luck. So, one day, Jan decided to have a "little talk" with Frankie. Now, don't get me wrong. Jan isn't delusional or psychotic, but she does silently talk things over with Frankie. Apparently, many people have such conversations with deceased loved ones or with God. I just didn't happen to know anyone so inclined until I met Jan. She asked Frankie to help her find the perfect family.

Well, as you can probably guess by now, strange things began to happen. That very afternoon, a friend called expressing interest in buying our home. She had always liked our country-style Tudor but, more importantly, she had always been struck by its peaceful nature. Jan was delighted. Like her own family, this family had lost a child—an adopted special little girl who had died in a tragic house fire. Although the home's asking price was higher than the family could spend, a deal was soon struck. Jan had convinced me that we just had to accept this offer. Frankie had found the right family, for sure! Within days, a contract had been signed contingent upon the family selling their house. Life was good in the Nichols' household.

Like all good stories, there were more twists and turns to come. Five days later, our realtor called and said that another family had made an offer, but not a contingency offer. Jan did not want to accept the offer; the realtor warned that if we did not accept it, we might sit on the house for some time. True to her reliance on her feelings, Jan decided to have another chat with Frankie; she wondered if she was confused about the right family. Had she misunderstood the sign? Was the second family the right family?

Here is where the story gets weirder still. Within minutes, the door bell rang. The UPS truck had left a package on the porch. Jan opened the box to discover that a gal whom she had met on a recent trip to Pittsburgh (yes, Pittsburgh again) had sent her a little gift, a funny ceramic angel with crossed eyes, a near absent mouth, and shoelace-less sneakers on the wrong feet. Jan decided to "speak" to Frankie once again. Was this ceramic figure the sign that she had been right all along, that the first family was indeed the right choice? You see, Annie, the first family's child who had died in a fire, had facial features similar to the ceramic angel. More striking, was the fact that Annie had always worn her sneakers on opposite feet and (as you have probably guessed) she had always removed the shoelaces. It's not that Annie didn't like shoelaces. She just preferred playing with them; keeping them stuck in shoes was no fun at all. There were even significant dates that seemed to point to signs from beyond. Annie had come to live with her new family on an August 25. The ceramic Annie angel had arrived on the porch several years later on, yes, you guessed it—another August 25.

Jan was convinced that Frankie had indeed been sending her signs all along. The deal with the first family was finalized following the sale of their home. Two other offers, both for considerably more money, were presented by the realtor, but we declined their bids. Because we did not accept the higher offers you can conclude one of two things. Either we have absolutely no business sense, or we are a couple who has come to appreciate the unexplainable.

As far as we know, that family still finds peace in that old place of ours. Jan is also certain that Frankie and little Annie keep tabs on it. What have Frankie and Jan done to that intractable science-type guy?

Janice—Back to City Hospital

The First Trip

As I began organizing this chapter in my mind, I decided to canvass the many family photos that my parents had saved. I needed a little inspiration. I've always found one picture particularly poignant. It's a small photo (maybe two by three inches) of Frankie and me in our living room, feet away from where Frankie's casket would be placed a month or so later. We're kneeling in front of the sofa, our hands folded in prayer. On the back of the photo is an imprint of my mother's lips, made by her cherry-red lipstick. When I found the photo several years ago, I placed it in a plastic bag to preserve the "kiss." It made me recall a daily ritual that my mother repeated until she died. On my father's dresser, there was always a beautiful baby picture of my sister Carol. Opposite that photo, was a picture of Frankie and me when we were about six months old. Each morning and evening, I would watch my mother kiss Carol first, then Frankie, then me (and repeat that triple kiss one more time). That beautiful maternal ritual spoke volumes then, as it does now, as I approach the end of our family's polio story.

Soon after commencing my research for this book, I came to the conclusion that I had to visit the hospital where Frankie and I were patients. Known then as City Hospital or Dr. A.C. Silverman Public Health Hospital, it is known today as the College of Health Professions (part of the SUNY Upstate Medical University system). I had always had memories of the hospital, but now it was time to validate or correct those memories if at all possible. So, on July 22, 2006, my husband, Dave, Dr. Eric Luft, his wife, Diane, and I entered the halls that I had not seen since 1953.

Although the building has been completely renovated, my memories seem to have been accurate. We think we found the ground floor whirlpool therapy room with its bank of windows, the front lawn where my parents and our family dog stood as I looked down from my patient window, the door through which the nurse wheeled me to my parents' car after receiving the multiple gamma globulin shots, and the elevator and hallways. We haven't been able to track down original blueprints for the facility.

As we entered, I wondered how I would react to the building that held so many of my memories. What would it smell like? Would the hospital scent trigger additional memories? But, it has been many years since the hospital served patients: there was no antiseptic, hospital smell.

Would I be sad or frightened, like a grieving sister or a scared young patient? I surprised myself; I remained composed. Although Frankie had died in the building, I didn't identify him with the hospital that day. My memories of Frankie are very much tied to the places that we shared together, and I never picture Frankie alone. On that day, this building only had memories for me and I recovered, in part, because of the care I received under its roof. I felt more like a detective than a patient or sister. I was on a mission to check out long-held memories.

In my mind's eye, I've always been the little girl looking outside the window at my parents and Mittz the Second below, or the child looking out the windows to try to forget that she was in the whirlpool tank, or the sister being wheeled to the car after receiving gamma globulin shots. This day, I was a woman looking at that little girl in the window, on the stretcher, in the wheel chair. I was no longer looking out. I was looking in, one step removed. I have done my fighting and my grieving long and hard. Going back to the hospital was in a sense completing a circle of memories, questions and, finally, answers. It was a trip that I would have never made if it had not been for this book.

Late that afternoon, we drove to the cemetery; my wise husband had suggested that we make that stop. Although my father had insisted upon Memorial Day and Labor Day trips to St. Agnes Cemetery, I have learned to live happily without that tradition. But, on that July day, it seemed like an appropriate trip to make. There's something about looking at headstones, I guess.

I think Mom and Dad would be happy with this book project of mine. I sense that Frankie has been guiding me toward this endeavor for some time. When I was a little girl, I needed to have answers to my Heaven questions. It was the only way that I could make it all right for Frankie and, tolerable, for me. As an adult, I don't need such questions answered. I can easily accept those unknowns that can haunt us all. But, I still believe that there is a place called Heaven, that we are reunited with our loved ones in the after-life, that Heaven-dwellers do watch over us, and that we each have a purpose that transcends the material world.

Because of the kindness and assistance of College of Health Professions staff members Annette Sharkey and Bob Fluck and Eric Luft, Curator of the Health Sciences Library, I learned that the building continues to house an old iron lung. According to Dr. Turek, the hospital had two iron lungs. Mrs. Sharkey believes that the facility's current iron lung was once housed in another building. Perhaps the iron lung was taken to another building to assist polio patients requiring hospital services in the age before modern ventilators. But, since all communicable disease cases were cared for at City Hospital, there's a good chance that this iron lung was one of the two originally used during the polio epidemics and, therefore, the machine that tried its best to save my twin's life.

With this knowledge, I realized that I had to see that iron lung, or more accurately, my husband realized that I had to see that iron lung. At first, I balked at the idea. I didn't want to see the machine whose design always frightened me—the machine that couldn't make Frankie better. But Dave kept nudging me. So, I agreed to go back, but I told him I was not going to write about the second trip to City Hospital. I had made up my mind—end of discussion. This trip was just too personal. Dave sensed more than I that this reunion was something I had to write about.

The Second Trip to City Hospital

On Tuesday, August 8, 2006, my husband and I met Dr. Eric Luft, Annette Sharkey, Bob Fluck, and Deborah Rexine in the lobby of City Hospital. After taking a short tour and reviewing architect's drawings of the hospital just prior to the renovation, we descended to the ground floor. I had reluctantly agreed to "meet" the machine that may have housed Frankie's body because I knew, in my heart, that my husband was right. I had to complete my own journey if I ever expected to convince others of the importance of polio eradication. More importantly, I had come to realize that since my parents spoke so little of Frankie's final hours and their final moments with him, the closest I would ever come to getting into their heads and hearts was to meet the metal-caregiver that tried so desperately to keep their son, my twin, alive.

Throughout this book, I've kept Frankie a six-year-old little boy. In my parents' minds, Frankie always stayed a young child. But, I found that as I aged, my perceptions of Frankie changed. I could picture him as a six-year-old, but I could also picture him as a teenager and young adult (was he ever handsome). It just dawned on me that I've never pictured him as a middle-aged man. But, then again, I still have to remind myself that I'm not twenty-one anymore.

Until I reached adulthood, I saw Frankie's death only through my "twin eyes." Oh, I could try to imagine what it was like for my parents. But, my ability to empathize went only so far. I was not then an adult, a wife, or a parent. Parenthood changed my perceptions. My "mother eyes" saw Frankie as my small, desperately ill little boy who could not get better. Growing up, I had mourned the loss of my twin. As a mother, I had come to see that for Frankie only death could release him from pain and suffering. It was not a matter of loss for me. It was a matter of freedom for Frankie.

As I contemplated the hospital visit in my mind, I gave myself a little pep talk. I had no idea how I would react. When we arrived on the ground floor, the seven-foot yellow iron lung was waiting for us in the middle of the hallway. In 1990, a few undergraduates in the College of Health Professions had refurbished the machine as part of an independent study project. Although some parts were not available, the students restored it to the point where the mechanism could be demonstrated.

Upon coming face to face with the iron lung, I felt a mix of sadness, terrible sadness, and a surprising appreciation for a machine that I had always despised. If parents could see this tired machine that lost as many or more battles with nature than it won, they would immediately give permission for their children to receive the polio vaccine.

I wanted to touch it, ever so gently, almost like it was a human. By today's high-tech standards, the iron lung is quite rudimentary, but its design allowed caregivers the ability to meet patient needs. We examined the interior, the exterior "portholes" through which medical staff provided physical care, the "collar," which separated the patient's head and neck from the cylinder, the mirror used so that patients could see what was going on, and the instruction manual.

Bob fired up the machine. Although it had not been restored to full strength, we were able to hear the familiar sounds associated with iron lungs. The manual featured a diagram that illustrated attachments for intravenous feeding and air pressure adjustments. The iron lung could be tilted to help patients clear secretions. An intermittent aspirator attachment could also be used to help keep airways clear. Through the side "portholes" nurses were able to turn and position patients to prevent bedsores and care for bodily needs as well as provide hot-pack therapy and passive exercise to limbs that may or may not have been paralyzed by the virus.

Dave was intrigued by an alarm bell on the top of the machine. We quickly realized that the bell was used to alert the staff in the event of a power failure or a loss of adequate pressure in the cylinder. Bob showed us what the manual described as a "hand operation handle." It was heavy and cumbersome. How could anyone possibly crank that lever, over and over and over again, until power was restored? Those caregivers worked harder to save the lives of many polio patients than I had ever imagined.

While Dave, Eric, Annette, and Bob were occupied with the mechanics of the iron lung and Deborah was busy snapping photos, I found myself picturing Frankie in the iron lung and my parents standing by his side. Being in that room was the closest I had ever come to feeling my parents' helplessness. My heart ached for my parents, and for Frankie. The fact that Frankie required a *tracheostomy* meant that he was literally drowning in his own secretions.

I am thankful that Frankie remained unresponsive throughout his sixty-one hour ordeal, and that my parents never had to see terror in his eyes. Losing him in the end was torture enough. I don't know if I could have ever faced that iron lung if I had not received my mother's assurance about Frankie's last hours. My heart aches for all the patients and families who live without such comfort.

No matter how hard that iron lung worked, the status of medicine in the fifties was unprepared to adequately deal with Frankie's complications. Medicine is not always up to the task of dealing with polio's power today. Coming face to face with that life-saving machine made me see how totally impotent it or any device was against a virus that had morphed into such an efficient killer in my twin's vulnerable body. Like my parents, I have long been thankful that God took Frankie quickly. Thank you, Frankie, for the time I had with you. I love you.

◆　　　◆　　　◆

Reflection

After this second trip, Dave and I stopped at my Aunt Betty Wightman's home for lunch. I wanted to connect with a member of the "Coolican Clan." My aunt had expressed concern about my trips back to City Hospital. She was afraid that this second visit might dredge up too many painful memories. I wanted her to know that I was OK and that this "reunion" was something that I had to do. In some ways, I think my aunt still sees me as that vulnerable child who lost her twin and fought to walk again. Fortunately, that child has grown up and moved on, a more resilient character than she might otherwise be. I am touched by the special relationship that I share with my relatives.

Although my visit was made as part of research for this book, I gained a better understanding of the concept called empathy, of my parents' sorrow and emptiness. Just as my trips back to City Hospital have brought a heightened sense of closure, so has my relationship with Dr. Alice (Jaros) Turek, the medical voice in this book. She is a lovely woman who still speaks with compassion and sadness of the era of polio epidemics. I find it comforting to know that in Frankie's final moments, he was attended by such a loving physician. I am grateful that she played a part in the acute phase of my recovery. I pray that my rehabilitation brings comfort to Dr.

Turek and that she can reflect upon those sleepless nights at City Hospital that were filled with worry and fatigue and conclude that her sacrifices were well worth it. There are many little children from the 1950s who can thank her.

◆   ◆   ◆

Late that evening, I took out my laptop and started writing. Dave just smiled that knowing smile of his. I wish that polio had never invaded our home, that Frankie had never died, that I had not contracted the disease, that post-polio syndrome had passed me by. But, as I've said before, I can't change history. The best I can do is direct my energies, memories, and insights. All I ask from you is that you take this story as yet one more reason to eradicate polio, as a reason to join the fight.

Frankie—Heaven Update

I can't believe how long I've been in Heaven. Has it really been fifty-three Earth years? We don't think about things in terms of Earth-time here. I bet that fact will put Jan's mind at ease. The idea of eternity has always given her a headache. I still greet children who have died from polio, but I'm not nearly as busy as I used to be. There haven't been any kids from Syracuse in a very long time.

When Daddy died, President Roosevelt and I were waiting for him. We told him that his job in Heaven would be to meet parents and reunite them with their children who had died years before from polio. You can imagine how happy that made Daddy. He had been so sad after I died. When Mommy came to Heaven, she was allowed to greet parents with Daddy. I think it's great that God knows just how to pick the right job for each of us. My parents still love to hug and kiss me. I guess I'll always be their little boy. As for Jan, I know she's not nearly ready to join us up here. So, I'm happy to just keep tabs on her.

In 1993, Dr. Sabin came to Heaven. Then, two years later, Dr. Salk arrived. They both work as special guardians to all the medical teams and volunteers who are giving the vaccine to children in some very poor countries. One of the grown-ups told me that they didn't like each other on Earth, but they work as a great team now. No one fights or is jealous in Heaven, and everyone shares. Dr. Sabin and Dr. Salk hope that someday, no one will get polio. I hope that too. Not too long ago, Jan's orthopedic surgeon, Dr. Kalamarides, came to Heaven. God put him on a special team that watches over all the doctors and nurses that have to operate on children still being paralyzed by polio.

I've just been called to the Greeting Area. When I first came to Heaven, the Syracuse girl taught me how to tell when someone is crossing over, but it's a secret. Did you know that some of the children in Heaven get to decorate the Entrance Gate for holidays? The decorations need to be changed all the time because Heaven-dwellers come from so many countries. They have lots of different customs and religions. Right now, the children are planting beautiful yellow flowers. The flowers remind me of the kind that I used to pick for Mommy when I was still on Earth. They always made the grass look extra pretty in the springtime.

The boy I'm going to greet is named Kato. His name means "second-born twin." His family lives in a small village in northern Nigeria. The medical workers hadn't been allowed to visit his area to give children the oral polio vaccine for some time. One of my friends told me that the clinics are open again, but it was too late for Kato's village. Many children and adults have gotten sick this year. Kato hasn't been able to move his legs for a few months. About a week ago, he got a high fever.

Kato's body just couldn't fight the fever anymore—but, his spirit doesn't want to come through the tunnel. Kato's mommy and daddy are kneeling around his bed; his sister is holding his hand and begging him to stay with her. It's my job to help Kato cross over. He doesn't want to leave his twin, Adebanke. He's afraid that she'll get sick, and he won't be there to help her. Even though he was born second, he's always been braver and stronger (just like me).

You know, sometimes I still wish I'd been able to go through the tunnel on my way to Heaven. Maybe God knew that it would make me sick to my stomach, just like that big boat and all the waves on Lake Champlain made me sick on one of my last family vacations on Earth.

I'm going to tell Kato how sad I was when I had to leave my twin sister, Jan. I'll also let him know that God always lets us watch over our families on Earth. Kato's sister's name, Adebanke, is Nigerian for "God is taking care of her." Adebanke will be sad for a long time, just like Jan was. I'll remind Kato of the meaning of his twin sister's name. I think that will help put his mind at ease. After as many greetings as I've done, you get to know what is best to say, and do. I'll put my hand out to him and give him a good tug. I don't know if boys in Nigeria play much baseball. I always keep a spare ball and bat near the Gate. Kids always feel better when they see some toys and bikes around. If Kato doesn't know how to play baseball, that's one thing that I can teach him right away. Somebody told me that Nigerian boys like soccer even better than baseball. I could use some help with my soccer kick. Soccer wasn't a big sport in the United States when I was a little boy. When I died, Jan put a baseball and bat in my casket. I bet Adebanke will bury Kato's body with a soccer ball. Twin sisters love to take care of their brothers.

I think God decided to have me die on All Saints' Day because He knew that it would help my family. They always told Jan that it was a special sign that I was in Heaven.

President Roosevelt says that someday, there will be no more polio.

Postscript

Although a day has never gone by that I have not thought of my twin, recalling early childhood memories for this book has offered me an opportunity to rediscover the little things that were so uniquely Frankie. I have, once again, become the sister who calls out to the grown-ups (readers of this book), "See, honey. See, honey."

Many friends have commented that they are surprised that I have so many memories of Frankie, since they have few early memories of their own brothers and sisters. But, they still had their siblings. There would be new things to share. The fact that Frankie died, thereby leaving no hope for future times together, must have heightened my desire and need to hold on to whatever I could. The fact that my parents always indulged my need to recall stories has, in a very real sense, made the format of this book possible.

There have been times, these last few years, when recollections have brought tears to my eyes, and there have been many more times when my recollections have brought laughter and joy to my heart. My mind's eye can still picture Frankie teasing and terrifying me with one of his jars full of buzzing bees. I can still hear Frankie using one of my father's favorite expressions, a phrase that guaranteed trouble for both my father and twin.

I could never have enough memories. Of late, I've wondered: What was Frankie's favorite flavor of ice cream? Did he take peanut butter and jelly sandwiches to school like I did? I can't remember what his "snuffles" sounded like. What about his laugh, and his cry? I want to see Frankie hold his breath and turn blue. I know that Frankie loved baseball, but I don't remember what position he played. Was he a southpaw like some of our relatives? When Frankie and I are reunited in Heaven some day, I'll have many questions for the twin I've missed for so long. What a party that will be.

I was a serious little kid, spending much time thinking about what Heaven was like for Frankie and equal time contemplating what this life on Earth was all about for me, for all of us. In the end, we all need to make such a philosophical quest if we choose to live life with meaning beyond ourselves. The DeWitt 1953 polio epidemic simply started me down that road a little early.

As outgoing as I am, I am a private, solitary soul in many ways—to some a contradiction, perhaps. It has been much harder to put my sad memories to pen than I had ever imagined. Up until a few years ago, I was more than content to keep my life's journey private, reserved only for those who knew me personally.

Although parenthood has allowed me to see my own parents from a different vantage point, there is so much that I never asked, more still of what they never divulged. I'll never know what was deep inside my parents' souls. The best I can do is draw upon what they said and didn't say, did and couldn't do. Early on in this story, Frankie spoke of my parents' willingness to tell and retell episodes of our short life together so that I would always have wonderful memories to hold onto. My memories are priceless, although I'm quite certain that the retelling of stories was often at my parents' expense. What did it do to them to call up memories, over and over again, of vacations, backyard escapades, and devilish capers? I am thankful that Mom and Dad have been reunited with Frankie. Their sadness is finally over. I am a daughter saddened and angered that so many parents continue to suffer the unimaginable grief of losing a child to the polio virus.

I have spoken of coming to see Frankie as my own child as well as my twin, a change that evolved over many years and life experiences. My heart aches for the little girl who placed a baseball and bat in her twin's casket, though I know that I long ago moved on. There are many children throughout the world who continue to place similar articles of love in their siblings' caskets. Children are more than capable of mourning long and hard. I am a mother saddened and angered that so many children continue to suffer the physical and emotional consequences of polio's wrath—some as polio survivors, some forced to cope with the "grief work" that comes with losing someone they loved, while still others succumb to the power of the vicious virus.

As the twin who believes that her brother was a most perfect specimen, I hope that my words offer a touching glimpse into the life of a real little boy who had so much trouble pronouncing the letter "R," loved to catch bees in a jar, and delighted in baseball games and climbing the Sagenkahn's side yard tree with his pals Brett, Alan, Gary, and Jan.

I pray that our story, and the medical information provided, emboldens you. Through charitable giving, education, political will, advocacy, vaccination, and career and volunteer activities, I'm certain that we can put an end to polio's reign of terror once and for all.

It's up to you. It's up to me.

Frankie and Jan's fifth birthday party—Frankie is on the far right with Jan to the left. Brett and Alan are near the porch with Gary nearby. Note the "party supervisors," Bonne and Bob.

This photo was taken a few months before polio hit the Flood's home. The outfits were purchased for Frankie and Jan's sixth birthday party—their last birthday together.

Frankie and Jan saying their prayers a few months before polio hit.
Frankie's casket was placed in this room during the wake.

Mom's kiss made in her cherry-red lipstick on the back
of the photo of Frankie and Jan praying.

City Hospital (now Silverman Hall) photo taken in 2006—Jan believes
that her hospital room was on the third floor, far right. She recalls
having her hospital bed pushed to the window so that she could see her
parents and dog, Mittz the Second, standing on the lawn below.

City Hospital (now Silverman Hall) photo taken in 2006—Based on Jan's memory of looking out a bank of windows while receiving whirlpool therapy, she believes that the therapy area was in the bottom floor as shown from this angle.

The Onondaga County Health Department requested that all clothing and toys belonging to Frankie and Jan be burned a few days after Frankie died. These sterling baby juice cups are two of the items that the Floods were able to save. Today, the cups are in safekeeping in an oak cabinet in the Nichols' dining room. The cabinet once belonged to family friend, Marna Martin. Marna contracted polio in the 1920s.

Dr. Alice (Jaros) Turek in February 2007—Dave and Jan flew to Florida to meet Dr. Turek. After fifty plus years, Jan was able to thank the physician who cared for the Flood twins with skill, love, and compassion. Jan cherishes her special relationship with Dr. Turek and is thankful that this retired pediatrician and public health official has lent her voice and support to this book.

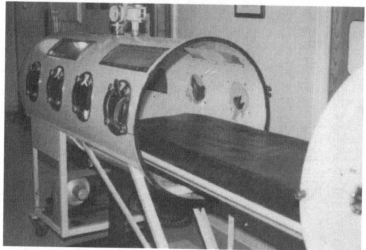

Frankie may have received care in this iron lung. City Hospital utilized two iron lungs for the acute care of polio patients. Permission to include photo received from Hugh Bonner, Dean of the College of Health Professions at SUNY, Upstate Medical University. Photographer: Deborah Rexine.

Appendix

Appendix A
Polio History Timeline and Unsung Heroes [1,2]

Although Drs. Jonas Salk and Albert Sabin are the names that have become synonymous with the polio vaccine, there are many lesser known, yet equally important, men and women who provided invaluable research. Some of these unsung heroes include: Members of the Salk lab (Julius Younger, Byron Bennett, Elsie Ward, Francis Yurochko, Percival Bazeley, James Lewis and those in the group whose names I haven't uncovered), Thomas Francis (and members of his team including Donald Byrne), John Enders, David Bodian, Howard Howe, Thomas Weller, Fred Robbins, Dorothy Horstmann, Hilary Koprowski, Herald Cox, Simon Flexner, Isabel Morgan, Peter Olitsky, John Paul and James Trask. Earlier researchers include: Maurice Brodie, William Hallock Park, Thomas Rivers, John Kolmer, David Kramer, Lloyd Aycock, Joseph Stokes Jr., and William Hammon.

1789–British physician Michael Underwood describes "a debility of the lower extremities"

1840–German physician, Jacob von Heine, publishes a paper describing what would later become known as polio

1841–First U.S. recorded epidemic in Louisiana

1893–Polio outbreak in Boston

1894–The first major polio epidemic hits the U.S. in Vermont. A young physician, Charles Caverly, documents the cases: 50 people are paralyzed, 18 died; 84 cases were in children under six (with boys stricken more often than girls)

1908–Dr. Karl Landsteiner and E. Popper discover that polio is caused by a virus

1909–Simon Flexner, of the Rockefeller Institute, confirms Landsteiner's discovery

1910–Polio outbreak in Mason City, IA

1912–Polio outbreak in Buffalo, NY and Batavia, NY

1916–The first major epidemic documented in the U.S. with 27,363 cases and 7,179 deaths

1915–1950–An estimated 368,000 polio cases reported in the U.S.

1921–Franklin Delano Roosevelt contracts polio

1927–Roosevelt forms the Warm Springs Foundation in Georgia to treat polio patients

1928–The iron lung is developed by Philip Drinker; manufacture ceased in 1970

1934–The first Birthday Ball is held on FDR's birthday to raise money for the Warm Springs Foundation

1935–Drs. Brodie, Park, and Kolmer conduct field trials on their polio vaccines; several children died or were paralyzed from the vaccines. Researchers were reluctant to test other vaccines for some time

1937–Roosevelt announces the formation of the National Foundation for Infantile Paralysis, known today as the March of Dimes

1938–The Foundation is incorporated; awards its first research grants to Yale University, Michigan and Johns Hopkins. Yale and Michigan are to concentrate on the epidemiology of polio while Johns Hopkins will concentrate on polio's pathology

1942–The Sister Kenney Institute opens in Minneapolis

1942–Virus Research Center established at Johns Hopkins with National Foundation funds

1945–1949–Large polio epidemics (20,000 per year average) occur each year in U.S.

1948–Dr. Jonas Salk of the University of Pittsburgh receives a grant from the National Foundation to confirm polio virus strains; studies had started earlier in the decade

1951–1954–160,333 new polio cases reported in the U.S.

1952–The U.S. experiences its worst polio epidemic with 57,879 cases (21,269 paralytic cases and 3,145 deaths)

1954–Salk develops a killed-virus polio vaccine (tested '52-54).

1954–April 26, 1954–the Salk vaccine trials begin

1954–John Enders, Thomas Weller, and Fredrick Robbins receive the Nobel Prize for developing a tissue culture method for growing polio virus

1955–Dr. Thomas Francis, of the University of Michigan Vaccine Evaluation Center, announces that the Salk vaccine is safe and effective

1955–1957–Incidence of polio in the U.S. drops 85–90 percent

1959–Albert Sabin's oral vaccine given to millions in Russia

1960–March of Dimes establishes The Salk Institute for Biological Studies

1961–1963–Albert Sabin's oral polio vaccine licensed in the U.S.

1963–Congress establishes the Immunization Grant Program; U.S. cases fall to 396

1979–U.S. declared polio-free from wild-virus polio; a 1979 outbreak occurs in unvaccinated members of Amish communities in Iowa, Missouri, Pennsylvania, and Wisconsin

1979–Rotary begins its first inoculation program in the Philippines

1981–*Time Magazine* reports that many polio survivors are experiencing late-effects of polio

1984–A conference at Warm Springs Institute for Rehabilitation sponsors a discussion of the growing concerns about post-polio syndrome

1985–Rotary establishes its PolioPlus program; on January 1, 1986, Rotary participates in the Rose Parade with a theme float

1988–Global Polio Eradication Initiative launched: partners include WHO, Rotary, CDC, and UNICEF

1994–Americas certified polio free

2000–U.S. returns to the killed-polio virus vaccine

2000–Western Pacific Region certified polio free

2000–March of Dimes and Post-Polio Health International host an international symposium

2002–European Region certified polio free; Pediarix (IPV) vaccine available in U.S.

2005–Aggressive Global Eradication Initiative in the Horn of Africa— Bill & Melinda Gates Foundation instrumental

2005–Four cases of vaccine-acquired polio reported in Minnesota

2005–50th Anniversary of the Salk vaccine

2005–2006–Smithsonian Museum of Natural History sponsors a new exhibit: "*Whatever Happened to Polio?*"

2008–Latest WHO target date for worldwide polio eradication

Appendix B

Post-Polio Health International, including International Ventilator Users Network

In 1985, the International Polio Network (IPN) was formed to provide information and support to polio survivors. As part of its mission, the group began publishing *Polio Network News* as well as its *Post-Polio Directory*. In 1987, the International Ventilator Users Network (IVUN) was formed, and the following year Joan L. Headley was named Executive Director of IPN. Since 2003, the organization has been known as Post-Polio Heath International, with its affiliated International Ventilator Users Network. [1]

The history of PHI can be directly traced to the work of Gini Laurie. In 1958, she began printing a newsletter, *Toomeyville Jr. Gazette,* for the Toomey Pavilion, a center for polio respiratory patients in Cleveland, Ohio. Four of Gini Laurie's siblings contracted polio in 1912. Two sisters died, one sister was minimally disabled, and an older brother was severely disabled. He died sixteen years later. Laurie understood that most disabled individuals are better served if they can be maintained in their homes rather than in institutions. This remarkable woman and her husband spent the rest of their lives championing the cause for disabled patients through education, networking, and advocacy.[2]

In 1979, Laurie published a letter from a polio survivor that discussed what would come to be known as post-polio syndrome. Three years later, she coordinated a conference entitled "Whatever Happened to the Polio Patient?" Although both her organization and her publications have gone through many name changes, the mission has always remained the same. In 1984, Judith Raymond was hired as the first executive director of Gazette International Networking Institute (GINI). The group published the *Handbook on the Late Effects of Poliomyelitis for Physicians and Survivors,* edited by Gini Laurie, Frederick M. Maynard, D. Armin Fischer, and Judith Raymond.[3]

In 1985, IPN was formed, and in 1989, Gini Laurie died. In 1990, the "Americans with Disabilities Act" was passed. It took effect on July 26, 1992. Ms. Laurie had spent a lifetime fighting for such legislation.[4]

Since the 1980s, the group has continued to coordinate international conferences on issues related to post-polio and ventilator user needs. In 1999, an updated edition of the 1984 *Handbook* was published. In 2005, PHI loaned archival information to the Smithsonian for *Whatever Happened to Polio Exhibit.* PHI recently received a health promotion grant from the Christopher Reeves Foundation. The organization continues to be an advocate for government funding for home care needs. This effort is essential in light of ongoing budget proposals.[5]

Volumes of *Post-Polio Health* from 1996 to 2006 can be purchased individually for $1.00 per issue or $35 for the complete set. Topics include: Aging with Polio, Assistive Technology, Breathing/Swallowing, Clinics/Physicians, Education/Training, Eradication, Exercise/Activity, History, Management/Coping, Management/Treatment, Medication, Nutrition, Pathology/Cause, Polio and Other Illnesses, Relationships, Research, Social Security, Support Groups, Surgery, Travel, and Vaccines.

Joan Headley, the Executive Director of PHI, is a polio survivor who has devoted much of her adult life to improving the lives of other survivors. I asked her to describe the work of PHI in her own words:

PHI's roots can be traced to mimeographed publications written for the past and current residents of the Toomey Pavilion, a respiratory center in Cleveland, Ohio, established to rehabilitate the most significantly affected polio people—those who used breathing equipment, such as iron lungs, rocking beds and chest cuirasses ... Today, PHI continues to fulfill its mission of providing education, advocacy, networking, and supporting research. To the surprise of many, the estimated one million polio survivors in the United States are in need of information and support as they face the consequences of having had polio—new weakness, extreme fatigue, and pain. Research shows that not all survivors are having significant medical problems, but all are aging with a disability, one of the first major disability groups to do so. They are learning as they go and they are teaching others. PHI's goal is to serve its core until they no longer need support and to transfer its wealth of knowledge to younger polio survivors around the globe.

Anyone interested in learning more about *PHI* may contact the organization through the Web site: www.post-polio.org.

Appendix C
Rotary International PolioPlus

Recently, Rotarian Dudley Ericson from Jamestown, New York, mailed me an excellent book on the history of Rotary's involvement entitled *Conquering Polio—A Brief History of PolioPlus, Rotary's Role in a Global Program to Eradicate the World's Greatest Crippling Disease* by Herbert A. Pigman. It is a fine tribute to Rotary's commitment.[1]

Rotary's polio eradication involvement, under its Health, Hunger and Humanity (3-H) Program, began with a 1979 commitment to purchase and help deliver oral polio vaccine to six million children in the Philippines. During the next five years, Rotary operated similar campaigns in other countries. In 1985, Rotary joined Dr. Albert Sabin to develop a global eradication strategy to immunize the hundred million children born each year in developing countries. At the fortieth anniversary of the United Nations, Rotary announced its initial financial commitment of $120 million to fund its PolioPlus Program. By establishing partnerships with health agencies and national health ministries,

Rotary began its global campaign to raise money for vaccine purchase. Rotarians were recruited to aid in the inoculation efforts.[2]

Rotary International chose the name PolioPlus for the project because the name illustrated the organization's two-fold goal of eradicating polio and increasing immunization against other childhood diseases. In 1986, Rotary publicly announced its initiative with a float in the annual New Year's Day Rose Parade prior to the Rose Bowl. The float featured an abandoned wheelchair, a banner heralding the year "2005" (Rotary's target date for global eradication), and a "Stop Polio" symbol (a red circle with a white diagonal slash across the word *polio*). The theme of the float was "Turning Tears to Laughter."

In 1988, the Global Polio Eradication Initiative was launched in Geneva. The successes and challenges of the Initiative are outlined in the first chapter of this book (Janice—A Twin on a Mission). In 1995, Rotary initiated a task force to advocate for financial support and political commitment from donor governments. In 2000, Rotary, in conjunction with the United Nations, spearheaded a private sector financial appeal.[3]

In an effort to continue eradication efforts, Rotarians have developed a variety of creative and informative fundraisers. An example of one such effort was conceived by the Chittenango, New York Rotary Chapter (District 7150). With the cooperation of SUNY Upstate Medical University, the group, under the direction of club member, Carol Anthony, transported an old iron lung (seven feet long and weighing 500 pounds) via trailer to fundraising venues throughout the area. On April 12, 2003, the *Syracuse Post Standard* ran an article and photo showing the iron lung being wheeled from City Hospital to the awaiting trailer. The iron lung is the same machine that is now housed in the basement of the hospital and, therefore, may very well be the same machine that tried its best to save my twin's life. It is believed to be the last of its kind in the central New York area.[4]

Appendix D
March of Dimes
(see text for earlier history related to polio)

Conceived to rid the world of polio, the National Foundation of Infantile Paralysis, known today as the March of Dimes, has spent the last sixty-eight years attempting to alleviate human suffering.

In 1960, the March of Dimes provided the seed money for the creation of the Salk Institute for Biological Studies. Ground was broken in 1962, and the first lab opened the following year. Salk was wooed to locate the Institute in San Diego, California, by polio survivor and San Diego Mayor Charles Dail. Today, the Salk's major research areas include the study of genetics, molecular biology, neurosciences, and plant biology. The Institute has trained more than 2,000 scientists. According to the March of Dimes, the Salk receives $1 million from its research budget each year. An additional $2,117,563 has been awarded to Salk during the past ten years for specific research projects.[1]

In 1958, as the incidence of polio declined, the March of Dimes decided to shift its mission to the prevention of birth defects, though it has never forgotten its commitment to iron lung and ventilator patients and to those who suffer from post-polio syndrome. In 2000, the organization partnered with the Roosevelt Warm Springs Rehabilitation Institute and Post-Polio Health International to offer an international symposium on post-polio syndrome. The March of Dimes was the presenting sponsor of the Smithsonian's National Museum of American History Exhibit, *Whatever Happened to Polio?*[2]

Since the late 1950s, the March of Dimes has undertaken several successful campaigns including: PKU screening, birth defect prevention and treatment, expansion of childhood vaccines, fetal alcohol syndrome education and prevention, establishment of neonatal intensive care units, expansion of birth defect and developmental disability newborn screening, and the prevention and treatment of premature births.[3]

Over the years, the March of Dimes has partnered with hospitals and other service organizations to ease the burden of parents and children. One such group is "Thread of Life," a national sewing group whose members fashion clothes and blankets for sick, stillborn, and premature babies. A July 12, 2006, *Syracuse Post Standard* article highlighted the work of two women, Sandy Meltzer and Peggy Goodell, in the DeWitt, New York, chapter—just one more example of DeWitt residents showing compassion to others.[4]

We are often led to a life direction because of adversity. President Franklin Delano Roosevelt's commitment to the plight of polio patients is a shining example of such determination and dedication. Over the years, I've met many men and women who have turned their personal tragedies into positive endeavors. This is certainly true of Christine Scott, Associate Director of Program Services for New York State Chapter of the March of Dimes. Following the tragic death of her stillborn son, Jacob Wesley Scott, Christine redirected her academic pursuits and career goals to join the March of Dimes. Just as there were no fiercer warriors than mothers who walked door-to-door to raise money for polio in the 1950s, Christine now offers a voice of compassion and understanding that only a parent who has lost a child can possibly provide. I have asked her to lend her voice to this section:

> In 2003, the March of Dimes started their multi-year, multi-million dollar campaign to fight premature birth. Premature birth is the leading cause of newborn death. The alarming increase in premature birth over the past decade has prompted the March of Dimes to launch this campaign to raise public awareness of premature birth and, ultimately, to find ways to reduce the occurrence of premature births. Today, in the U.S., one in eight babies are born prematurely … If I can make a difference in the life of one baby each day, then I know I am where I am meant to be. Our efforts provide hope to more than 500,000 babies born prematurely each year.

Appendix E
University of Pittsburgh Fiftieth Anniversary Celebration[1]

During April 2005, the University of Pittsburgh, under the direction of Chancellor Mark A. Nordenberg, commemorated the fiftieth anniversary of the Salk vaccine with a three-day celebration honoring scientists who participated in the development of the vaccine and individuals who were personally touched by the virus' wrath. The university sponsored an academic symposium focused on the history of past, present, and future vaccine development. An historic marker was dedicated, citing Salk Hall as the epicenter of the fight against polio. *Defeat of an Enemy*, printed in celebration of the anniversary, provides an excellent overview of the university's role in the fight.

Appendix F
Killed-Virus Vaccine[1]

As of October 2006, WHO reported that the following countries have returned to the use of the killed-virus polio vaccine (IPV). Information was supplied by Sona Bari of the World Health Organization: Andorra, Australia, Austria, Belgium, Canada, Denmark, Finland, France, Germany, Greenland, Guam, Hungary, Iceland, Ireland, Israel, Italy, Luxembourg, Malta, Mariana Islands,

Monaco, Netherlands, New Zealand, Norway, Republic of Korea, San Marina, Spain, Sweden, Switzerland, United Kingdom, and the United States.

Appendix G
UNICEF[1]

The United Nations Children's Emergency Fund, known as UNICEF, was established by the United Nations General Assembly in December 1946. Initially, it was involved in aiding the plight of children affected by the devastation of World War II. Today, the organization has expanded its focus to include several specific issues including: child survival and development, basic education and gender equality, child protection from violence, exploitation and abuse, immunization, HIV/AIDS and children's rights. Originally known as the United Nations International Children's Emergency Fund, its name was shortened to the United Nations Children's Fund in 1953. Its headquarters are in New York City, but UNICEF staff members are stationed in over 150 countries and territories. UNICEF's Supply Division (whose role in polio eradication efforts was discussed in an early chapter of this book) is located in Copenhagen. UNICEF is a voluntarily funded agency that receives its funding from governments (accounting for two-thirds of the agency's resources), private groups, and millions of private individuals.

Appendix H
Smithsonian Exhibit—*Whatever Happened to Polio?*[1]

During 2005 and 2006, the Smithsonian National Museum of American History sponsored *Whatever Happened to Polio?* an exhibit coinciding with the fiftieth anniversary of the Salk vaccine. The exhibit opened on April 12, 2005—fifty years to the day after it was announced to the world that the Salk vaccine was safe and effective against the polio virus. On this day in 2005, bells tolled fifty times atop the Institution's oldest building to mark the opening of the exhibit. The March of Dimes was the presenting sponsor with additional funds provided by Rotary International and the Salk Institute for Biological Sciences; PHI supplied archival information for the exhibit. The interactive exhibit allowed visitors to view everything from an iron lung to leg braces used by President Franklin Delano Roosevelt. There was even a piece of cake from one of the Birthday Ball fundraisers. Polio survivors were offered an opportunity to submit their experiences in writing while the general public was able to trace the history of poliomyelitis from the era of yearly epidemics to the era of near global eradication. You may wish to consult *Images of America: March of Dimes* by David W. Rose for an excellent pictorial overview of the subject.

Appendix I
Advisory Committee for Polio Eradication Recommendations[1]

(Taken from an October 2006 Global Polio Eradication Initiative update)

To Stop Transmission in Endemic Areas:

1. Supplementary rounds of immunization should be conducted seven to eight times per year.
2. The Head of State in each endemic area should be briefed on a regular basis.
3. Endemic countries should establish realistic target and planning frameworks.

To Limit International Spread:

1. Supplementary immunization activities should continue in areas that have experienced polio importations.
2. Supplementary immunizations should be conducted in geographic areas bordering endemic areas.
3. The WHO publication *International Travel and Health* should be updated and recommend that all travelers, going to and from polio-infected areas, should be fully immunized in accordance with national policy.
4. A Standing Recommendation regarding the polio immunization of travelers from polio-infected areas should be established under the *International Health Regulations 2005*.

Appendix J
Contact Information for WHO, Rotary, CDC, UNICEF[1]

<u>WHO</u>
> Sona Bari
> WHO Geneva—+41 79 475 5511
> baris@who.int
> Oliver Rosenbauer
> WHO Geneva—+41 22 791 3832
> rosenbauero@who.int

<u>Rotary International</u>
> Vivian Fiore
> Rotary International/Chicago—+1 847 866 323
> vivian.fiore@rotary.org

<u>CDC</u>
> Steve Stewart
> CDC/Atlanta—+1 404 639 8327
> znc4@cdc.gov

<u>UNICEF</u>
> Jessica Malter
> UNICEF/New York—+1 212 326 7412
> jmalter@unicef.org

Appendix K
Received and Confirmed Donor Contributions to Polio Eradication Efforts, 1988–2008[1]

<u>Greater than $500 million</u>
> Public Sector—USA
> Private Sector—Rotary International

<u>$250–500 million</u>
> Public Sector—Japan, United Kingdom

<u>$100–249 million</u>
> Public Sector—European Commission, Canada, Netherlands
> Development Banks—World Bank

$50–99 million
> Public Sector—Germany
> Private Sector—Bill & Melinda Gates Foundation

$25–49 million
> Public Sector—Denmark, France, Norway, Sweden, UNICEF Regular Resources, WHO Regular Budget
> Private Sector—United Nations Foundation

$5–24 million
> Public Sector—Australia, Belgium, Italy, Ireland, Luxembourg, Russian Federation Development Banks—Inter-American Development Bank
> Private Sector—Aventis Pasteur, IFPMA, UNICEF National Committees

$1–4 million
> Public Sector—Malaysia, New Zealand, Spain, Switzerland, United Arab Emirates Development Banks—International Federation of Red Cross and Red Crescent Societies
> Private Sector—Advantage Trust (HK), DeBeers, Pew Charitable Trust, Wyeth

Appendix L
Tribute to Survivors

What determines who we become? It is a common belief that, at least in part, adversity shapes our personalities. Numerous studies have documented that the typical polio survivor develops an A type personality—a spirit driven to hard work, mastery, success. There's something about having to learn to walk again, to accept the assistance of a respiratory aid, to come to terms with post-polio syndrome, to deal with the death of family members and friends that does much to build an inner core of strength and determination. This may be especially true for polio survivors who suffered isolation and discrimination. So, I thought that you might be interested in knowing a *few* of the survivors who have helped to make this world a better place, a brighter place.

Tenley Albright—physician and Olympic gold medal figure skater
Alan Alda–actor, writer, director
Lionel Barrymore—actor
Charles E. Bennett—U.S. Congressman, Florida
Jean Chretien—former Prime Minister of Canada

Arthur C. Clarke—author
Francis Ford Coppola—director
Claudius—Emperor of Rome (lived 10 B.C. to 54 A.D.)
Bill Cullen—game show host
Walter "Buddy" Davis—Broad Jump Olympic Champion
William Orville Douglas—Associate Justice, U.S. Supreme Court
John East—U.S. Senator
Ray Ewry—Track and Field Olympic Champion
Mia Farrow—actress
William Alexander Gadsby—1970 NHL, Hall of Fame
John Hager—Lt. Governor, Virginia
Ida Lupino—actress, screenwriter
Shelley Mann—Olympic Gold Medal Swimmer
Frank Mars—founder M&M Mars Chocolate Company
Paul Martin—former Prime Minister of Canada
Joni Mitchell—singer
Jack Nicklaus—golfer
J. Robert Oppenheimer—physicist
Itzhak Perlman—internationally acclaimed violinist
Franklin Delano Roosevelt—U.S. President
Sir Walter Scott—historical fiction writer
Siptah—ancient Egyptian Pharaoh
Dinah Shore—singer
Lord Snowden—former husband of UK Princess Margaret
Donald Sutherland—actor
Paul Winchell—ventriloquist
Neil Young—rock singer

To the world's polio survivors—Hats off to all of us!

This partial list has been taken from Jann Hartman's "Famous Polio People" Web page. See Notes and Consulted Works for citation and Web page addresses requested by Ms. Hartman.[1]

Appendix M
CDC (Centers for Disease Control)

The CDC is the "behind the scenes warrior" of the Global Polio Eradication Initiative, deploying epidemiologists and public health experts to WHO and

UNICEF. In addition, the Atlanta based agency provides funding for polio vaccine and utilizes its laboratory capabilities to assist in pinpointing not only outbreak strain information but also precise geographical outbreak data that is used to target immunization efforts. The CDC will remain a critical component of GPEI, offering its assistance around the globe.

Appendix N
Vaccine Information

Although it is imperative that vaccine issues be discussed with medical providers, the following resources may help individuals sort out scientific information from misinformation and provide a basis for discussions with health care professionals. Many of these sources have been mentioned in the body of this text.

Books:

Myers, Martin G. and Diego Pineda. *Do Vaccines Cause That?!* Galveston, Texas: Immunizations for Public Health, 2008.

Offit, Paul. *Vaccines What You Should Know, 3rd Ed.* Hoboken, NJ: John Wiley & Sons, Inc. 2003.

Online Sources:

1. www.vaccine.chop.edu – The Vaccine Education Center at the Children's Hospital of Philadelphia. The vaccine education department provides excellent, comprehensive online information.
2. www.ecbt.org – Every Child by Two
3. www.vaccine.org – Allied Vaccine Group
4. www.aap.org – The American Academy of Pediatrics
5. www.childrensvaccine.org – The Children's Vaccine Program at PATH
5. www.immunize.org – Immunization Action Coalition
6. www.pkids.org – Parents of Children with Infectious Diseases
7. www.immunizationinfo.org - National Network for Immunization Information
8. www.i4ph.org – Immunizations for Public Health
9. www.whattoexpect.org – A pamphlet, entitled "What to Expect Guide to Immunizations," is available for free pdf download.

It should be noted that since the initial printing of this book, one more state has added a vaccination philosophical waiver; other states are considering similar waivers.

Please Note: The FDA has approved KINRIX, a combination vaccine made by GlaxoSmithKline offering protection against diphtheria, tetanus, pertussis, and polio. The government has also approved, Pentacel, Sanofi Pasteur's combination vaccine against diphtheria, tetanus, pertussis, polio, and haemophilus influenzae type b.

Appendix O
Eradication Update: 2008

Today, children from endemic and importation countries, where sanitation is poor or non-existent, are especially vulnerable. It has also been noted that non-vaccinated young adults in developing countries where polio transmission continues, are emerging as a new vulnerable group.

Since the initial printing of this book eradication efforts continue in earnest, though the goal of global eradication in 2008 will not be reached. Fortunately, Margaret Chan, Director-General of WHO, Dr. Robert Scott of the Rotary Foundation, and Dr. Julie Gerberding of the CDC remain determined that polio can—and must—be eradicated. The following information has been taken from weekly updates found at www.polioeradication.org (the Web page for the Global Polio Eradication Initiative). Highlights include:

- In 2007, the final global polio case count was 1315, down from 2006 levels.
- A 1/15/2008 GPEI update indicates that the current funding gap includes $175 million through 2008, $350 million for 2009, and $490 million for 2010-2012.
- In order to meet the critical funding gap, the Bill and Melinda Gates Foundation provided an immediate infusion of $100 million in fall 2007. Rotary International has pledged to provide an additional $100 million over the next three years, seeking contributions from both Rotarians and non-Rotarians. As of this update, Rotary has contributed over $700 million to polio eradication. To encourage donations from non-Rotarians, a new Web site has been created: http://www.rotary.org/en/

ServiceAndFellowship/Polio/Pages/040708_announcement_
Newpoliosite.aspx

- As of June 17, 2008, there have been 599 polio cases reported this year with 560 cases among endemic countries and 39 cases in non-endemic countries. Countries that have experienced cases in 2008 include: India, Pakistan, Afghanistan, Angola, Nigeria, Ethiopia, Benin, Chad, Niger, CAR, DRC, Sudan, and Nepal. Both Myanmar and Somalia experienced cases in 2007, but remain polio-free in 2008 as of this update.
- An outbreak of Type 1 polio in northern Nigeria has caused spread to Benin and Niger. Fear of further importation is high, with officials desperately working to prevent the devastating spread that occurred between 2003 – 2006 because of the eleven month Nigerian boycott.
- India is hopeful that they can stop the spread of Type 1 by the end of 2008, with plans to concentrate on Type 3 in 2009.
- Although Type 1 transmission reached its lowest level in 2007, GPEI sees the interruption of Type 1 transmission as its overriding strategic priority in 2008.
- *Whatever Happened to Polio*, the exhibit that had been at the Smithsonian, is now on display at the Roosevelt Warm Springs Institute for Rehabilitation in Georgia, USA. The transfer of the exhibit was made possible through the ongoing work of Rotary. From April 23-25, 2009, PHI will present its tenth international conference, "Living with Polio in the 21st Century." The conference will be hosted by the Roosevelt Warm Springs Institute for Rehabilitation.
- The Harvard School of Public Health reported that between 1955–2005, 1.1 million cases of polio and over 160,000 deaths were prevented by the polio vaccine. During that period, the government spent $35 billion in vaccine costs, but saved $180 billion in treatment costs.
  Please see: www.hsph.harvard.edu/review/spring07/spr07polio.html

About the Author

Janice Flood Nichols is a survivor of a polio outbreak that struck DeWitt, New York (an eastern suburb of Syracuse), in late 1953. Eight of the twenty-four children in her first grade class were diagnosed with the disease. Her twin brother, Frankie, died after a sixty-one hour hospitalization. Two of her childhood friends succumbed as well. In April 1954, she was one of nearly two million children who participated in the National Foundation of Infantile Paralysis' Salk vaccine trial. Influenced by her physical struggle and recovery and her childhood challenge to come to terms with the loss of her twin, she received a bachelor's degree in psychology from Seton Hill and a master's degree in rehabilitation counseling from the University of Pittsburgh. Her professional career included positions at Community General Hospital and Syracuse University's School of Social Work, before leaving the Syracuse area in 1981. For the past twenty-five years, she has devoted her energies to her family, engaging in numerous charitable activities and volunteer positions. Her writing endeavors span a broad range of topics, including medical social work, history, medical care, twin loss, and polio. Her articles have appeared in a variety of newspapers and magazines. She is the author of a practical guide for medical social workers and a local history text. With her son Kevin grown, she has found the freedom to return to her original life-calling. She intends to use her personal story of loss, religious faith, and recovery to support the effort to eradicate polio. First stop: Writing this book. As she likes to put it, she's a woman on a mission! She resides with her husband, Dave, in western New York.

Notes

(Note: Web site citation access dates are listed in the Consulted Works section)

Foreword by Alice (Jaros) Turek

1. Global Polio Eradication Initiative, "Wild Poliovirus Weekly Update, March 7, 2007," http://www.polioeradication.org/casecount.asp; International PolioPlus Committee, "Statements on Current Facts and Figures Relative to Polio Eradication and the Role of Rotary International in the Global Effort," March 2006, www.rotary.org (pdf file); Herbert A. Pigman, *Conquering Polio* (Evanston, IL: Rotary International, 2005), 8.

2. John F. Modulin, "Poliovirus," in *Principles and Practice of Infectious Diseases*, 6th ed., ed. George L. Mandell, John E. Bennett, and Raphael Dolin (Philadelphia: Elsevier Churchill Livingstone, 2005), 2141–2148.

Janice—A Twin on a Mission

1. March of Dimes, "50th Anniversary Backgrounder, Polio Epidemic Statistics, Salk Polio Vaccine, From Polio to Prematurity, the March of Dimes Today," received from Christine Scott.

2. Pigman, *Conquering Polio*, v-vi; March of Dimes, "Polio Vaccine Timeline and Milestones," received from Christine Scott; International PolioPlus Committee, "Statements,"July 2006.

3. Pigman, *Conquering Polio*, 10; International PolioPlus Committee, "Statements," July 2006; March of Dimes,"Polio Vaccine Timeline and Milestones."

4. Pigman, *Conquering Polio*, 10–11.

5. UNICEF, Supply Division Annual Report 2004, "Supplies for UNICEF Priorities,"6, www.unicef.org (pdf file).

6. International PolioPlus Committee, "Statements," July 6.

7. Ibid.

8. Global Polio Eradication Initiative, "Wild Poliovirus Weekly Update," World Health Organization, Media Centre, "Poliomyelitis," "http:// www.who.int/mediacentre/factsheets/fs114/en/index.html; Global Polio Eradication Initiative, "Monthly Situation Reports," January 2006, http://www,polioeradication.org/content/general/current monthly si; Global Eradication Initiative, "Wild Poliovirus Weekly Update, March 7, 2007," http://polioeradication.org/casecount.asp.

9. Global Polio Eradication Initiative, "Monthly Situation Reports," December 2005, File://C:/Documents%20and%Settings/Dave/ Local%20Settings/; World Health Organization Media Centre, Revised September 2006, "Poliomyelitis;" World Health Organization, Media Centre, Joint News Release WHO/Rotary International/CDC/ UNICEF, "New emergency immunization plan launched to protect horn of Africa, as polio is confirmed in Somalia, 13 September 2005," http://who.int/mediacentre/newsreleases/2005.pr42/en/

10. Global Polio Eradication Initiative, "Monovalent oral polio vaccine fact sheet," www.polioeradication.org (pdf file).

11. Ibid.; World Health Organization, Media Centre, "Gates Foundation funds new polio vaccine to accelerate eradication efforts," http://www. who.int/mediacentre/news/notes/2005/np03/en/index.html; Sanofi Pasteur, "Sanofi Pasteur's New Polio Vaccine Licensed for Use in Novel Approach Global Eradication Efforts," http://www.sanofipasteur. com/sanofi-pasteur/front/templates/vaccinations-travel-health-v; International PolioPlus Committee," Statements," July 2006.

12. Rotary International, "Renewed Efforts to End Polio in South Asia," October 10, 2006," http://www.rotary.org/newsroom/polio/061010 sasia.html; Vukoni Lupa-Lasaga,"Rotary supports Kenya's response to new polio threat," *Rotary International News* (November 9, 2006), http://www.rotary.org/newsroom/polio/061101 eafrica.html; Rotary International, "India Steps up efforts to end polio," http://www.rotary. org/newsroom/polio/070104 polio india.html.

13. International PolioPlus Committee, "Statements," July 2006; Global Polio Initiative, "Wild Poliovirus Weekly Update, March 7, 2007," http://polioeradication.org/casecount.asp.

14. International PolioPlus Committee, "Statements;" UNICEF Press Centre, Joint Press Release, "5.5 million under five Angolan children will be immunized against polio," http://www.unicef.org/medica/media_37201.html.

15. UNICEF Press Centre, Joint statement, "Despite difficulties, polio immunization drive underway in Iraq," http://www.unicef.org/media/media_36567.html; U.S. Agency for International Development," Top Strategic Accomplishments in Iraq: Improving Primary Health Care," www.usaid.gov/iraq.

16. Centers for Disease Control, "FAQs on Polio Vaccine," http://www.cdc.gov/nip/vaccine/Poliop/polio-faqs-hcp.htm; David M. Oshinsky, *Polio: An American Story* (Oxford: Oxford University, 2005), 279.

17. CDC, "FAQs on Polio Vaccine."

18. Ibid.; Global Polio Eradication Initiative, "FAQs on OPV Cessation," http://www.polioeradication.org/content/fixed/opvcessation/opvc_QA.asp; Phone interviews with Sona Bari, World Health Organization (Geneva, Switzerland), October 3, 4, 6, 11, 13, 2006; Bernard Seytre and Mary Shaffer, *The Death of a Disease: A History of the Eradication of Poliomyelitis* (New Brunswick: Rutgers University Press, 2005), 139.

19. Pigman, *Conquering Polio*, 3, 40-46; Rotary International, "History of PolioPlus," http://www.rotary.org/foundation/polioplus/information/history.html.

20. Global Polio Eradication Initiative Funding Update, "Financial Resource Requirements for 2007–2009," http://www.polioeradication.org/fundingbackground.asp; International PolioPlus Committee, "Statements," July 2006.

21. Rotary International, "History of PolioPlus," http://www.rotary.org/foundation/polioplus/information/history.html.

22. UNICEF Supply Division, "Supplies for UNICEF Priorities", 4–8; International PolioPlus Committee, "Statements." July 2006.

23. UNICEF Supply Division, "Supplies for UNICEF Priorities", 6.

24. Global Polio Eradication Initiative, "Advisory Committee for Polio Eradication 2006, Context: International concern over four endemic countries," http://www.polioeradication.org/content/general/2006ACPE asp; "Global Polio Eradication Initiative, "2005 Annual Report," full report, www.polioeradication.org/content/publications/AnnualReport2005 ENG01.pdf.

25. International PolioPlus Committee, "Statements," July 2006; Global Polio Initiative, "FAQs on OPV Cessation;" http://www.polioeradication.org/content/fixed/opvcessation/opvc QAQ asp.

26. Vukoni Lupa-Lasaga, "New WHO leader announces antipolio action," *Rotary International News* (January 30, 2007), http://www.rotary.org/newsroom/polio070130 who.html.

Frank—Our Life before Polio

1. United States Army, "History of the Adjutant General's Corps," http://agsssi-www.army.mil/corphist.htm.

2. March of Dimes, "50th Anniversary Backgrounder"; David W. Rose, *Images of America: March of Dimes* (Charleston, SC: Arcadia Publishing, 2003), 42.

Alice (Jaros) Turek, MD, MPH—Polio the Disease

1. March of Dimes, "Polio Vaccine Timeline and Milestones"; "50th Anniversary Backgrounder."

2. Syracuse, New York, City Hospital, 1950 Disease Statistics, City Hospital Annual Reports.

3. Paul, *History of Poliomyelitis*, 391–394; Rose, *Images of America*, 62.

4. 1953 Bulletin of Onondaga County Medical Society, "Poliomyelitis and the Gamma Globulin Program" February, 1953, 12; Ibid., "Report from Communicable Disease Bureau," 16.

5. Paul, *History of Poliomyelitis*, 394.

6. Ibid., 235; Oshinsky, *Polio*, 117–1211.

7. Modulin, "Poliovirus," 2141–2143.

8. Ibid., 2142; "Poliomyelitis," 101114, http://www.cdc.gov/nip/publications/pink/polio.pdf

9. Modulin, "Poliovirus,"2142–2143

10. Ibid., 2142

11. Ibid., 2143

12. Ibid., 2142

13. Ibid., 2142–2143

14. Ibid., 2143; March of Dimes, "50th Anniversary Backgrounder."

15. Modulin, "Poliovirus," 2142–2143.

16. "March of Dimes. "Statement on Support for Polio Patients in Iron Lungs,"received from Christine Scott, March of Dimes Buffalo, NewYork, Office.

17. Ibid.

18. Oshinsky, *Polio*, 10–12.

19. Ibid., 19–23; Paul, *History of Poliomyelitis*, 148–160.

20. Ibid.

21. Ibid.

22. Ibid.

23. "In Search of the Polio Vaccine," The History Channel (DVD).

24. Oshinsky, *Polio*, 162; March of Dimes, "50th Anniversary Backgrounder."

25. Syracuse, New York, City Hospital, Annual Report, 3;Onondaga County Medical Society, 1906–1956, Sesquicentennial Syracuse 1956, 65.

26. Oshinsky, *Polio*, 8–23; Paul, *History of Poliomyelitis*, 188.

27. Seytre and Shaffer, *Death of a Disease*, 31; Oshinsky, *Polio*, 162.

28. Modulin, "Poliovirus," 2143.

29. Ibid.

30. 1953 Bulletin of Onondaga County Medical Society (February 1953), 33; (May 1953), 17; (June 1953), 4; NOAA National Data Centers, U. S. Department of Commerce, National Oceanic and Atmospheric Administration: Local Syracuse Climatological Data, October and November 1953 Daily Record.

31. Frank T. Flood Jr., New York State Certificate of Death Registration Number 2348.

Frankie—Heaven

1. 1953 Bulletin of Onondaga County Medical Society, June 1953, "Report of the death of a six-year-old girl from bulbar poliomyelitis (May 11, 1953)", 4.

Janice—Frankie's Wake

1. Obituary: Frank T. Flood Jr., *Syracuse Post Standard,* November 2, 1953, 9: NOAA, October and November 1953 Daily Report.

2. Memory Book for Frank T. Flood Jr.

3. Ibid.

4. Ibid.

Mrs. Louise DeMartino—United We Stand

1. Memory book for Frank T. Flood Jr.

2. Ibid.

3. "89% of Eligible Children Get Polio Shots at DeWitt," *Syracuse Post Standard, May 3, 1954, 6.*

Frank and Dorothy—Not Again

1. Syracuse, New York, City Hospital Annual Report, 1952, 3.

Janice—City Hospital, Therapy

1. Modulin, "Poliovirus," 2144; Flashback! Polio Cure Elusive; Vaccine Only Hope, *Syracuse Post Standard,* January 9, 1978, 12; Paul, *History of Poliomyelitis,* 335–345.

2. Ibid.

3. Ibid.; Sister Kenny Rehabilitation Institute, "About Sister Kenny Rehabilitation Institute." http://www.allina.com/ahs/ski.nsf/page/aboutus; Kathryn Black, *In the Shadow of Polio: A Personal and Social History* (Reading, MA: Addison-Wesley Publishing Co., 1996), 80–110.

4. Syracuse City Hospital Annual Reports 1949, 1950, 1951, 1955, 1956.

5. Photo with Captions: "First of the DeWitt Polio Epidemic Victims," *Syracuse Post Standard,* January 13, 1954, 8.

Mrs. Russell (Betty) Wightman—March of Dimes, 1953 Memories

1. Oshinsky, *Polio An American Story,* 24–42, 53

2. Ibid., 43–60, 67–69

3. Smithsonian National Museum of American History, "Whatever Happened to Polio?" http://americanhistory.se.edu/news/pressrelease.cfm?key 29&newskey=174; Franklin D. Roosevelt Presidential Library and Museum, "Birthday Balls: Franklin D. Roosevelt and the March of Dimes," http://www.fdrlibrary.marist.edu/bdayb2.html.

4. March of Dimes, "Eddie Cantor and the Origin of the March of Dimes," http://www.marchofdimes.com/aboutus/20311 20401.asp.

5. Ibid; Rose, *Images of America,* 10–12; Black, *Shadows of Polio,* 25, 103.

6. Ibid., 25

7. Rose, *Images of America*, 17, 21, 44, 49, 77–85.

8. Ibid., 77, 81; Oshinsky, *Polio*, 189.

Dave—Surgical Care

1. A. J. Ingram, "Anterior Poliomyelitis," in *Campbell's Operative Orthopaedics* 5th ed., vol. 2, ed. A.H. Crenshaw (St. Louis: The C.V.Mosby Company, 1971), 1517–1684.

2. Ibid.

3. Ibid.

4. Ibid.

5. Ibid.

6. Ibid., 1839–1886.

7. Obituary: Cheryl Munson, *Syracuse Herald Journal*, April 25, 1960, 12

8. Obituary: Patricia Munson, *Syracuse Herald Journal*, November 7, 1967, 16.

Mrs. Betty Anne Read and Mrs. Jeanne LaVoy—Mothers Unite

1. Oshinsky, *Polio*, 87–90.

2. Ibid.; Rose, *Images of America*, 8.

3. Memory Book for Frank T. Flood Jr.; Black, *Shadow of Polio*, 105–107.

4. Undated newspaper, based on article details, written in early 1957, before the annual Mother's March and after 1956 total polio cases had been reported by the Onondaga County Health Department.

5. Memory Book for Frank T. Flood Jr.

6. Rose, *Images of America*, 42–58.

7. Oshinsky, *Polio*, 86.

8. Rose, *Images of America*, 42–58.

9. Ibid., 51; Black, *Shadow of Polio*, 108; Oshinsky, *Polio, 189.*

10. Rose, *Images of America*, 85.

11. Paul, *History of Poliomyelitis*, 324–334; Rose, *Images of America*, 37–39.

12. Black, *Shadow of Polio*, 117–121.

13. Ibid.,109.

14. Ibid.,100–101,107–110; Paul, *History of Poliomyelitis*, 308–323; Oshinsky, *Polio*, 65.

Alice (Jaros) Turek, MD, MPH—The 1954 Salk Vaccine

1. Modulin, "Poliovirus," 2141.

2. Oshinsky, *Polio*, 43–91, 188.

3. Ibid., 94–95, 112–116.

4. Ibid., 117–127, 128–160; Paul, *History of Poliomyelitis*, 404–425; Paul A. Offit, *The Cutter Incident: How America's First Polio Vaccine Led to the Growing Vaccine Crisis* (New Haven and London: Yale University Press, 2005), 4– 43 ; Rose, *Images of America*, 59.

5. Paul, *History of Poliomyelitis*, 404–411, 434–435; Oshinsky, *Polio*, 117–121.

6. Ibid. 157–160; Offit, *The Cutter Incident*, 19–43.

7. Oshinsky, *Polio*, 174–187.

8. Ibid., 86, 165,169–172.

9. Ibid., 171–173.

10. Ibid., 177–186; Paul, *History of Poliomyelitis* 426–429.

11. Oshinsky, *Polio*, 155, 186, 229.

12. Christopher J. Rutty, "40 Years of Polio Prevention! Canada and the Great Salk Vaccine Trial of 1954-55," Health Heritage Research, http://www.healthheritageresearch.com/salk.htm. Originally published in *Abilities,* 19 (Summer 1994), 26, 28

13. Offit, *The Cutter Incident,* 44–52.

14. Ibid., 51–52.

15. Oshinsky, *Polio,* 79–91, 161–173; Nina Gilden Seavey, Jane S. Smith and Paul Wagner, *A Paralyzing Fear: The Triumph Over Polio In America* (New York: TV Books, 1998); Black, *Shadow of Polio,* 24–30, 32, 38, 45–46, 74, 81, 163–164, 214, 226, 232–233, 256.

Mrs. Louise DeMartino—Parental Request to Participate

1. "89% of Eligible Children Get Polio Shots at DeWitt."

2. Offit, *The Cutter Incident,* 49–51; Oshinsky, *Polio,* 194–197.

3. Ibid., 190–191.

1,829,916 Polio Pioneers—The 1954 Salk Vaccine Trials

1. Offit, *The Cutter Incident,* 44-54,60-61,113-118; Oshinsky, *Polio,* 188–213.

2. Ibid.; Arnold S. Monto, "Francis Field Trial of Inactivated Poliomyelitis Vaccine: Background and Lessons for Today." *Epidemiological Reviews by The Johns Hopkins University School of Hygiene and Public Health,* 21, 1 (1999), 7–23, http://epirev.oxfordjournals.org/cgi/reprint/21/1/7 (pdf file).

3. Paul, *History of Poliomyelitis,* 426–428; Oshinsky, *Polio,* 185-187; Martin Bland, *An Introduction to Medical Statistics,* 3rd ed. (Oxford, England: Oxford University Press, 2000), 13–14.

4. Rose, *Images of America,* 66; Oshinsky, *Polio,* 197–199.

5. Ibid., 190.

6. Ibid., 197–198.

7. Ibid., 197; Paul, *History of Poliomyelitis*, 426–440; Monto, "Francis Field Trial", 16, http://epirev.oxfordjournals.org/cgi/reprint/21/1/7 (pdf file).

8. "89% of Eligible Children Get Polio Shots at DeWitt."

9. Ibid.

10. Ibid.

Alice (Jaros) Turek, MD, MPH—Salk Results, Cutter Situation

1. Oshinsky, *Polio*, 201–203; Offit, *The Cutter Incident*, 54.

2. Paul, *History of Poliomyelitis*, 426–440; Oshinsky, *Polio*, 199–204; Offit, *The Cutter Incident*, 54.

3. Oshinsky, *Polio*, 203–204.

4. Ibid., 205

5. Ibid., 205–213.

6. Ibid., 215–221.

7. Offit, *The Cutter Incident*, 58–82, 101.

8. Rose, *Images of America*, 69; Oshinsky, *Polio*, 215–216.

9. Offit, *The Cutter Incident*, 58–104.

10. Ibid., 58–104, 103–131.

11. Oshinsky, *Polio*, 221–228; Offit, *The Cutter Incident*, 86–89.

12. Ibid., 98; Oshinsky, *Polio*, 225–227; Rutty, "40 Years of Polio Prevention!", 26, 28.

13. Offit, *The Cutter Incident*, 115–120; "Syracuse First in State to Put Vaccine to Use," *Syracuse Post Standard*, May 17, 1955; Oshinsky, *Polio*, 232–243.

14. Ibid., 238; Offit, *The Cutter Incident*, 124; March of Dimes, "50th Anniversary Backgrounder."

15. Ibid.; Paul, *History of Poliomyelitis*, 436–440; Offit, *The Cutter Incident*, 105, 154–191; Oshinsky, *Polio*, 241–242.

16. Oshinsky, *Polio*, 275.

Bonne (Paltz) Hall and Bob Paltz—Vaccination in the Late 1950s

1. "Syracuse First in State."

2. Offit, *The Cutter Incident*, 80.

3. "Older Children Not Showing Up—20,516 Get Salk Shot Since Program's Start," *Syracuse Post Standard*, February 1956.

4. "Syracuse Had Only 4 Polio Victims in 1956," *Syracuse Post Standard*, January 27, 1957.

5. "High School Pupils Will Get Free Salk Vaccine," *Syracuse Herald Journal*, January 20, 1957.

6. "Free Polio Vaccine Shots for 28,000 Within 30 Days," *Syracuse Herald Journal*, January 29, 1957, 2.

7. "Parents Asked to OK Polio Shots for All Junior and Senior Pupils," *Syracuse Herald Journal*, February 16, 1957.

8. Ibid.

9. Immunization Action Coalition, "Historic Dates and Events Related to Vaccines and Immunization," http://www.immunize.org/timeline/.

10. Luft, Eric, *SUNY Upstate Medical University: A Pictorial History* (North Syracuse: Gegensatz Press, 2005), 134.

11. Oshinsky, *Polio*, 255–256, 268; Rose, *Images of America*, 74.

Mrs. Pat Marshall Coolican—March of Dimes, Changes

1. Rose, *Images of America*, 23, 25, 38–40, 55, 70.

2. Ibid., 72–73

Alice (Jaros) Turek, MD, MPH—The Sabin Vaccine

1. Paul, *History of Poliomyelitis*, 468; The History of Polio, A Hypertext Timeline.

2. Ibid; March of Dimes, "Polio Vaccine Timeline and Milestones."

3. Ibid., 440–456; Oshinsky, *Polio*, 243–254.

4. Ibid.

5. Ibid., 254.

6. Ibid., 261–263.

7. Ibid., 265–266.

8. Ibid., 266–268.

9. Immunization Action Coalition, "Historic Dates."

10. Ibid.

11. Luft, *SUNY Upstate Medical University*, 134.

12. Offit, *The Cutter Incident*, 124–127; Oshinsky, *Polio*, 272–273.

13. Paul, *History of Poliomyelitis*, 464–465.

14. Ibid., 465–469.

15. Offit, *The Cutter Incident*, 127.

16. March of Dimes, "50th Anniversary Backgrounder."

17. Immunization Action Coalition, "Historic Dates."

Janice—Life Direction

1. March of Dimes, "Polio Vaccine Timeline and Milestones"; The History of Polio, A Hypertext Timeline.

2. Sarah L. Ream, "Decrease in Grief Intensity for Deceased Twin and Non-Twin relatives: An Evolutionary Perspective," California State University Abstracts, http://psych.fullerton.edu/nsegal/twins.html;

"Bereavement Support, Surviving Co-Multiples, Twinless Twins, Lone Twin," http:// multiplebirthsfamilies.com/article/ber_q16html; Nancy L. Segal, "Research on Twin Loss"; Nancy L. Segal, "Circumstances Surrounding Twinloss: A Review of studies and relevant texts"; "Twin Loss Study at Minnesota Center for Twin and Adoption Research," http://www.twinlesstwins.org/dnn/TwinGrief/TwinLossAtAnyAge/ResearchOnTwinLoss/ta.

Dave—Medical Care Update

1. Jacquelin Perry and Mary Ann Keenan, "Post-Polio Corrective Surgery: Then and Now," Paper presented at 6th International Post-Polio and Independent Living Conference, June 1994, http://www.post-polio.org/ipn/pnn/11-3A.html.

2. J. Ingram, "Anterior Poliomyelitis," in *Campbell's Operative Orthopaedics*, 5th ed., vol. 2, ed. A.H. Crenshaw (St. Louis: The C.V. Mosby Co., 1971), 1628–1629; Irwin M. Siegal and Ensor E. Transveldt, "Post-Polio Corrective Spinal Surgery Now," *Post-Polio Health International Polio Network News*, 11, 3, part A (Summer1995), http://www.post-polio.org/ipn/pnn11-3A.html.

3. Ibid.

4. "Appliances for Paralysis in Developing Countries," http://www.worldortho.com/database/polio/polio/pg11.html

5. Ingram, "Anterior Poliomyelitis," 1528–1581, 1588–1602.

Dave—Post-Polio Syndrome

1. Julie Silver, *Post-Polio Syndrome: A Guide for Polio Survivors and Their Families* (New Haven and London: Yale University Press, 2001), 21–26; Mayo Clinic, "Post-polio Syndrome," http://www.mayoclinic.com/health/post-poliosyndrome/DS100494/DSECTION=1

2. Ibid.; Post-Polio Health International, "Polio and Post-Polio Fact Sheet." http://www.post-polio.org/ipn/fact.html

3. Mayo Clinic, "Post-Polio Syndrome."

4. Ibid.

5. Henrik Gonzalez, Katharina Stibrant Sunnerhagen, Inger Sjoberg, Georgios Kaponides, Tomas Olsen, and Kristian Borg, "Intravenous immunoglobulin for post-polio syndrome: a randomized controlled trial," *The Lancet*,5 (2006), 493–500.

6. Mike Mitka, "Aging Brings New Challenges for Polio Patients," *Journal of the American Medical Association*, 296, 14 (2006), 1718–1719.

7. Mayo Clinic, "Post-Polio Syndrome."

8. Ibid.

9. Ibid.

10. Ibid.

11. Ibid.

12. Ibid.

13. Ibid., Julie K. Silver, *Post-Polio*.

14. Ibid.

15. Post-Polio Health International, "Polio and Post-Polio Fact Sheet."

Alice (Jaros) Turek, MD, MPH—Changes, Eradication Update

1. CDC, "FAQs on Polio Vaccine."

2. Ibid.

3. CDC, "Poliovirus Infections in Four Unvaccinated Children-Minnesota, August-October 2005," Morbidity and Mortality Weekly Report, October 21, 2005, 1053–1054, http://www.cdc.gov/mmwr/preview/mmwrhtml/mm5411a6.htm.; CDC, "Outbreak Notice Update: Recent Outbreaks of Poliomyelitis, as of January 29, 2006," http://www.cdc.gov/travel/other/poliomyelitis recent outbreaks 20.

4. Immunization Action Coalition, Unprotected People #82 Polio, "Unvaccinated U.S. adult traveling abroad contracts vaccine-associated

paralytic polio through contact with a child vaccinated with OPV," http://vaccineinformation.org, www.immunize.org (pdf file).

5. International PolioPlus Committee, "Statements," July 2006, www.rotary.org (pdf file); CDC, "Programs in Brief: Immunizations," http://www.cdc.gov/programs/immun10.htm.

6. S.B. Omer, W.K.Y. Pan, A. Halsey, S. Stokely, L.H. Moulton, A.M. Navar, M. Pierce and D.A. Salmon, "Non-medical Exemptions to School Immunization Requirements: Secular Trends and Association of State Policies with Pertussis Incidence," *Journal of the American Medical Association* 296 (2006), 1757; CDC, "Immunizations."

7. CDC, "FAQs on Polio Vaccine."

8. Ibid.; CDC, "Outbreak Notice Update."

9. GlaxoSmithKline "What is Pediarix?" http://www.pediarix.com/what_is_pediarix.htm.

10. CDC, "FAQs on Polio Vaccine."

11. Sanofi Pasteur Press Release, September 26, 2005, "FDA Accepts for Filing License Application for New Pediatric Combination Vaccine, PENTACEL," http://www.sanofipasteur.us/sanofi-pasteur/front/index.jsp?siteCODE=AVP_US&lang=EN&

12. Sabin Institute, "The Albert B. Sabin Annual Awards," http://www.sabin.org/awards/annual_awards.html; Sabin Institute, "Our Mission," http://www.sabin.org/about/sabin_mission.html.

13. International PolioPlus Committee"Statements," July 2006; Global Polio Eradication Initiative "FAQs on OPV Cessation."

14. Oshinsky, *Polio*, 279–282.

15. Duke University, News & Communications, May 25, 2001, "Scientists have combined two genetically engineered viruses to attach brain tumors," http://dukenews.duke.edu/2001/05/mm_scientistshave.html.

Appendix A: Polio History Timeline and Unsung Heroes

1. The list of "Unsung Heroes" was compiled by making note of some of the many researchers who gave of their time and talent to develop the polio vaccines.

2. I have used the following sources for the timeline: March of Dimes, "50th Anniversary Backgrounder"; University of Pittsburgh Medical Center, "Timeline Development of the Salk Polio Vaccine at the University of Pittsburgh," http://newsbureau.upmc.com/MediaKits/Polio50Years/PolioTimeline2004.htm; University of Pennsylvania, Health, Medicine, and American Culture, 1930–1960, "Research Timeline 1796–1998," http://ccat.sas.upenn.edu/goldenage/wonder/w_time.htm; The History of Polio, A Hypertext Timeline, http://www.cloudnet.com/~edrbsass/poliotimeline.htm

Appendix B: Post-Polio Health International, including International Ventilator Users Network

1. Post-Polio Health International, "History of Post-Polio Health International (PHI)," http://www.post-polio.org/hist.html.

2. Ibid.; Post-Polio Health International, "Gini Laurie, Founder, Remembered in Missouri History Museum (MHS)," http://www.post-polio.org/hist-mhs.html; Post-Polio Health International, "Independent Living—The Role of Gini Laurie," http://www.post-polio.org/hist-gini.html.

3. Ibid.

4. Ibid.; United States Equal Opportunity Employment Commission, "Facts About the Americans with Disabilities Act," http://www.eeoc.gov/facts/fs-ada.html.

5. Post-Polio Health International, "History."

Appendix C: Rotary International PolioPlus

1. Pigman, *Conquering Polio*.

2. Ibid.

3. Ibid.

4. "Back in Service Restored Iron Lung," *Syracuse Post Standard,* April 12, 2003, C-2 E-Mail text of article to author from Molly Elliott, July 28, 2006. Photo of iron lung taken by photographer Dick Blume.

Appendix D: March of Dimes

1. March of Dimes, "50th Anniversary Backgrounder"; March of Dimes, "Building on Success," received from Christine Scott; Rose, *Images of America.*

2. Ibid.

3. Ibid.

4. "Caring is a Common Thread," *Syracuse Post Standard,* July 12, 2006, B-3.

Appendix E: University of Pittsburgh

1. *Defeat of An Enemy* (Pittsburgh: University of Pittsburgh, 2005).

Appendix F: World Health Organization

1. Information obtained from phone interviews with Sona Bari, World Health Organization, Geneva, Switzerland.

Appendix G: UNICEF

1. "United Nations Children's Fund: The Nobel Peace Prize 1965," http://nobelprize.org/nobel_prizes/peace/laureates/1965/inicef-history.html; UNICEF, "History of the Organization," www.unicef.org.

Appendix H: Smithsonian Exhibit—Whatever Happened to Polio?

1. Smithsonian, "Whatever Happened to Polio? Clinical Trials"; Smithsonian National Museum American History Press Release April 11, 2005, "The Smithsonian's National Museum of American History Marks 50th Anniversary of the Polio Vaccine," http://americanhistory.si.edu/news/pressrelease.cfm?key=29&newskey=174; Smithsonian, "Whatever Happened to Polio? Franklin D. Roosevelt"; Pamphlets available at the exhibit.

Appendix I: Advisory Committee for Polio Eradication Recommendations

1. Global Polio Initiative "Advisory Committee."

Appendix J: Contact Information—WHO, Rotary, CDC, UNICEF

1. From 2006 Global Polio Eradication Initiative online reports

Appendix K: Received and Confirmed Donor Contributions to Polio Eradication Efforts, 1988–2008

1. Rotary International, "History of PolioPlus."

Appendix L: Tribute to Survivors

1. The partial list of famous polio survivors was taken directly from Jann Hart-man's Web page, *Famous People Who Had Polio.* She has requested that the following links be listed: http://www.geocities.com/arojann. geo/poliopeople.html http://www.geocities.com/Heartland/Ranch/5212/ poliopeople.html E-mail acknowledgement regarding use of this material in this book received from Janice Hartman, March 5, 2007.

Consulted Works

Interviews

Individuals interviewed are noted in the Introduction. In addition, phone and e-mail discussions took place with: Sona Bari of the World Health Organization; Stuart Caplin, MD (my obstetrician and fellow polio survivor); Molly Elliott of the *Syracuse Post Standard*; Jann Hartman of "Famous People Who Had Polio"; Maxine F. Kidder, RN, PNP; Dr. Eric Luft, Curator of the Health Sciences Library at SUNY Upstate Medical University; and Benoit Rungeard of Sanofi Pasteur. All medical information contained in this book has been interpreted for a lay readership through discussions with my husband, David Nichols, MD, and Alice (Jaros) Turek, MD, MPH.

Books, Book Chapters, and Journal Articles

Black, Kathryn. *In the Shadow of Polio: A Personal and Social History.* Reading: Addison—Wesley Publishing Co., 1996.

Bland, Martin. *An Introduction to Medical Statistics*, 3rd ed. Oxford: Oxford University Press, 2000.

Blume, Stuart, and Ingrid Geesink. "Essay on Science and Society: A Brief History of Polio Vaccines." *Science Magazine* (June 2, 2000). http://www.sciencemag.org/cgi/content/full/288/5471/1593 (accessed July 12, 2006).

Cohen, Jeffrey I. "Enteroviruses and Reoviruses." In *Harrison's Principles of Internal Medicine,* 16th ed., edited by Dennis L. Kasper, Anthony S. Fauci, Dan L. Longo, Eugene Braunwald, Stephen L. Hauser, and J. Larry Jameson, 1143–1144. New York: McGraw-Hill, 2005.

Crenshaw, A.H., ed. *Campbell's Operative Orthopaedics.* 5th ed., vol. 2. St. Louis: The C.V. Mosby Company, 1971.

Davis, Fred. *Passage through Crisis: Polio Victims and Their Families.* Indianapolis: The Bobbs-Merrill Company, Inc., 1963. Defeat of an Enemy. Pittsburgh: University of Pittsburgh Press, 2005.

Gonzalez, Henrik, Katrina Stibrant Sunnerhagen, Inger Sjoberg, Georgios Kaponides, Tomas Olsson, and Kristian Borg. "Intravenous immunoglobulin for post-polio syndrome: a randomized controlled trial." *The Lancet*, 5 (2006), 493–500.

Gould, Tony. *A Summer Plague: Polio and Its Survivors.* New Haven: Yale University Press, 1995.

Halberstam, David. *The Fifties.* New York: The Random House Publishing Group, 1993.

Ingram, A. J., "Anterior Poliomyelitis." In *Campbell's Operative Orthopaedics.* 5th ed. vol.2, edited by A. H. Crenshaw, 1517–1684. St. Louis: The C.V. Mosby Company, 1971.

Kallen, Stuart A. *A Cultural History of the United States through the Decades: The 1950s.* San Diego: Lucent Books, 1999.

Kasper, Dennis L., Anthony S. Fauci, Dan L. Longo, Eugene Braunwald, Stephen L. Hauser, and J. Larry Jameson, eds. *Harrison's Internal Medicine.* 16th ed.,vol.1. New York: McGraw-Hill, 2005.

Kehret, Peg. *Small Steps: The Year I Got Polio.* Morton Grove, IL: Albert Whitman & Company, 1996.

Kluger, Jeffrey. *Splendid Solution: Jonas Salk and the Conquest of Polio.* New York: G.P. Putnam's Sons, 2004.

Last, John M. and Robert B. Wallace. *Maxcy-Rosenau-Last Public Health and Preventive Medicine.* 13th ed. Norwalk: Appleton & Lange, 1992.

Luft, Eric. *SUNY Upstate Medical University: A Pictorial History.* North Syracuse, NY: Gegensatz Press, 2005.

Lupa-Lasaga, Vukoni. "India steps up efforts to end polio." *Rotary International News* (January 4, 2007), http://www.rotary.org/newsroom/polio/ 070104 polio india.html (accessed March 5, 2007).

——. "New WHO leader announces antipolio action." *Rotary International News* (January 30, 2007), http://www.rotary.org/newsroom/polio/ 070130_who.html (accessed March 5, 2007).

——. "Renewed Efforts to end polio in South Asia." *Rotary International News* (October 10, 2006), http://www.rotary.org/newsroom/polio/ 061010_sasia.html (accessed November 9, 2006).

——. "Rotary supports Kenya's response to new polio threat." *Rotary International News* (November 9, 2006), http://www.rotary.org/newsroom/polio/ 061101_eafrica.html (accessed November 9, 2006).

Mandell, Gerald, John Bennett, and Raphael Dolin. *Principles and Practice of Infectious Diseases.* 6th ed., vol. 2, Philadelphia: Elsevier Churchill Livingston, 2005.

Mason, Martha. *Breath: Life in the Rhythm of an Iron Lung, a Memoir.* Asheboro, NC: Down Home Press, 2003.

Mee, Charles L. *A Nearly Normal Life.* Boston: Little, Brown Co., 1999.

Mitka, Mike. *"Aging Brings New Challenges for Polio Patients."* Journal of the American Medical Association 296, 14 (2006): 1718–1719.

Monto, Arnold S. "Francis Field Trial of Inactivated Poliomyelitis Vaccine: Background and Lessons for Today," *Epidemiological Reviews by Johns Hopkins University School of Hygiene and Public Health,* vol.21, no.1 (1999): 7–23. http://epirev.oxfordjournals.org/cgi/reprint/21/1/7 (pdf file last accessed March 7, 2007).

Modulin, John F. "Poliovirus." In *Principles and Practice of Infectious Diseases,*6th ed., edited by George L. Mandell, John E. Bennett, and Raphael Dolin, 2141–2148. Philadelphia: Elsevier Churchill Livingstone, 2005.

Offit, Paul A. *The Cutter Incident: How America's First Polio Vaccine Led to the Growing Vaccine Crisis.* New Haven and London: Yale University Press, 2005.

Omer, S.B., W. K. Y. Pan, Halsey, A., Stokely, S., Moulton, L.H., Navar, A.M., Pierce, M. and D.A. Salmon "Non-medical Exemptions to School Immunization Requirements: Secular Trends and

Association of State Policies With Pertussis Incidence." *Journal of the American Medical Association* 296 (2006): 1757–1763.

Oshinsky, David M. *Polio an American Story.* Oxford: Oxford University Press, 2005.

Paul, John R. *A History of Poliomyelitis.* New Haven: Yale University Press, 1971.

Perry, Jacquelin, and Mary Ann Keenan. "Post Polio Corrective Surgery: Then and Now." Paper presented at Sixth International Post-Polio and Independent Living Conference, June 1994. Available at http://www.post-polio.org/ipn/pnn11-3.html (accessed July 1, 2006).

Pigman, Herbert A. *Conquering Polio.* Evanston, IL: Rotary International, 2005.

Plagemann, Bentz. *My Place to Stand.* New York: Farrar, Straus & Co., 1949.

Rivers, Tom. *Reflections on a Life in Medicine and Science, an Oral History Memoir prepared by Saul Benison.* Cambridge, MA: The MIT Press, 1967.

Rose, David W. *Images of America: March of Dimes.* Charleston, SC: Arcadia Publishing, 2003.

Rutty, Christopher J. "40 Years of Polio Prevention! Canada and the Great Salk Vaccine Trial of 1954–55." Health Heritage Research. http://www.healthheritageresearch.com/salk.htm (accessed July 11, 2006). (Paper originally published in *Abilities* 19 (Summer 1994): 26, 28.

Sass, Edmund J. *Polio's Legacy: An Oral History.* Edited by George Gottfried and Anthony Sorem. New York: University Press of America, 1996.

Seavey, Nina Gilden, Jane S. Smith, and Paul Wagner. *A Paralyzing Fear: The Triumph Over Polio in America.* New York: TV Books, 1998.

Segal, Nancy L. "The Importance of Twin Studies for Individual Differences Research." *The Journal of Counseling and Development*

68: 612–622. Available online at http://psych.fullerton.edu/ nseagal/twins.html (accessed March 8, 2007).

———. and Sarah L. Ream. "Decrease in Grief Intensity for Deceased Twin and Non-Twin Relatives: An Evolutionary Perspective." *Personality and Individual Differences* 25: 317–325. Available online at http://psych.fullerton.edu/nseagal/twins.html (accessed March 7, 2007).

Seytre, Bernard, and Mary Shaffer. *The Death of a Disease: A History of the Eradication of Poliomyelitis.* New Brunswick, NJ: Rutgers University Press, 2005.

Shell, Marc. *Polio and Its Aftermath: The Paralysis of Culture.* Cambridge, MA: Harvard University Press, 2005.

Smith, Jane. *Patenting the Sun: Polio and the Salk Vaccine.* New York: William Morrow & Co., 1990.

Silver, Julie K. *Post-Polio: A Guide for Polio Survivors and Their Families.* New Haven: Yale University Press, 2001.

Wilson, Daniel J. *Living with Polio.* Chicago: University of Chicago Press, 1949.

Web Site Source Material

For current and continuously updated information on the global eradication of polio, see the Web sites of the Centers for Disease Control and Prevention, the Global Polio Eradication Initiative, Rotary International PolioPlus, and the World Health Organization. Because Web sites change content frequently, some material referenced in this text may no longer be accessible online. All online articles have been preserved in hard copy by the author.

"Appliances for Paralysis in Developing Countries." http://www. worldortho.com/database/polio/polio/pg11.html

"Bereavement Support, Surviving Co-Multiples, Twinless Twins, Lone Twin." http://multiplebirthsfamilies.com/article/ber_q16html.

Centers for Disease Control and Prevention. "Current Trends National Childhood Vaccine Injury Act: Requirements for Permanent

Vaccination Records and for Reporting of Selected Events After Vaccination." http://www.cde.gov/mmwr/preview/ mmwrhtml/0000005.htm (accessed March 11, 2007). Yale University Press, 2001.

——. "Epidemiologic Notes and Reports: Poliomyelitis—United States, Canada." Morbidity and Mortality Weekly Report, Dec. 19, 1997: 1194– 1195. http://www.cdc.gov/mmwr/preview/ mmwrhtml/00050429.htm (accessed January 29, 2006).

——. "FAQs on Polio Vaccine." http://www.cdc.gov/nip/vaccine/Polio/ polio-faqs-hcp.htm (accessed March 6, 2007).

——. "Outbreak Notice Update: Recent Outbreaks of Poliomyelitis as of January 29, 2006." http://www.cdc.gov/travel/other// poliomyelitis_recent_outbreaks_20 (accessed January 29, 2006).

——"Poliomyelitis." http://www.cdc.gov/nip/publications/pink/polio.pdf (accessed July 11, 2006).

——. "Poliovirus Infections in Four Unvaccinated Children— Minnesota, August–October 2005." Morbidity and Mortality Weekley Report, October 21, 2005: 1053–1054. http://www.cdc. gov/mmwr/preview/mmwrhtml/mm5441a6.htm (accessed August 7, 2006).

——. "Programs in Brief: Immunizations." http://www.cdc.gov/ programs/immun10.htm (accessed July 14, 2006).

——. "Travelers' Health: Yellow Book, Health Information for International Travel, 2005–2006, Chapter 8—International Travel with Infants and Young Children: Vaccine Recommendations for Infants and Children." http://www/2.ncid.cdc.gov/travel/yb/utils/ ybGet. asp?section=children&obj=child-vax. (accessed March 6, 2007).

Duke University. News and Communications, May 25, 2001. "Scientists have combined two genetically engineered viruses to attack brain tumors." http://www.dukesnews.duke.edu/2001/ (accessed March 4, 2007).

"Famous Polio People." http://www.geocities.com/Heartland/ Ranch/5212/poliopeople.html and http://www.geocities.com/ arojann.geo/poliopeople.html (accessed February 12, 2006).

Franklin D. Roosevelt Presidential Library and Museum. "Birthday Balls: Franklin D. Roosevelt and the March of Dimes." http://www.fdrlibrary.marist.edu/bdayb2.html (accessed July 12, 2006).

GlaxoSmithKline. "What is Pediarix? http://www.pediarix,com/what_is_pediarix.htm (accessed March 5, 2007).

Global Polio Eradication Initiative. "Advisory Committee for Polio Eradication 2006, Context: International concern over four endemic countries." http://www.polioeradication.org/content/general/2006ACPE.asp (accessed November 10, 2006).

———. "Annual Report 2005." www.polioeradication.org/content/publication/ AnnualReport2005_ENG01,pdf.

———. "FAQs on OPV Cessation." http://www.polioeradication.org/content/fixed/opvcessation/opvc_QA.asp (accessed March 12, 2007).

———. "Funding Update, Financial Resource Requirements for 2007–2009." http://www.polioeradication.orgfundingbackground.asp (accessed March 7, 2007).

———. "Funding Update: Global Eradication Initiative Financial Resource Requirements for 2006–2008," http://www.polioeradication.org/fundingbackground.asp (accessed February 12, 2006).

———. "Monthly Situation Reports" January 2006, Data as of January 17, 2006. http://www.polioeradication.org/content/general/current_monthly_si (accessed January 29, 2006).

———. "Monthly Situation Reports December 2005." File://C:/Documents%20and%Settings/Dave/Local%20Settings/ (accessed February 12, 2006).

———. "Monovalent oral polio vaccines fact sheet," www.polioeradication.org/content/meetings/MediaMaterials_12OctMediaEvent/mOP/FactSheetfinal2005.pdf.

———. "Polio cases from 1 January 2005, as of 07 February 2006, Global cases of poliovirus: 1906." http://www.polioeradication.org/casecount.asp (accessed February 12, 2006).

——. "Stakeholders reach broad consensus to Complete polio eradication but without rapid injection of funds, global polio eradication effort is threatened." February 27, 2007. http://www.polioeradication.org/content/general/LatestNews200702.asp (accessed March 4, 2007).

——. "Wild Poliovirus Weekly Update." January 9, 2007. http://www.polioeradication.org/casecount.asp (accessed January 10, 2007).

——. "Wild Poliovirus Weekly Update." March 7, 2007. http://www.polioeradication.org/casecount.asp (accessed March 7, 2007).

——. "Wild Poliovirus Weekly Update." April 25, 2007. http://www.polioeradication.org/casecount.asp (accessed April 27, 2007). History of Polio, a Hypertext Timeline, The. http://www.cloudnet.com/-edrbass/poliotimeline.htm (accessed July 10, 2006).

Immunization Action Coalition. "Historic Dates and Events Related to Vaccines and Immunization." http://www.immunize.org/timeline (accessed July 12, 2006).

——. Unprotected People #82 Polio. "Unvaccinated U.S. adult traveling abroad contracts vaccine-associated paralytic polio through contact with a child vaccinated with OPV." www.vaccineinformation.org and www.immunize.org (pdf file).

International PolioPlus Committee. "Statements on Current Facts and Figures Relative to Polio Eradication and the Role of Rotary International in the Global Effort." March 2006. www.rotary.org (pdf file accessed April 21, 2006).

——"Statements on Current Facts and Figures Relative to Polio Eradication and the Role of Rotary International in the Global Effort." July 2006. www.rotary.org (pdf file accessed August 2, 2006).

March of Dimes. "Eddie Cantor and the Origin of the March of Dimes." http://www.marchofdimes.com/aboutus/20311 20401.asp (accessed July 1, 2006).

——. "Post-Polio Syndrome." http://www.marchofdimes.com/professionals/681 1284.asp (accessed July 30, 2006).

Mayo Clinic, "Post-Polio Syndrome." http://www.mayoclinic.com/health/post-poliosyndrome/DS00494/ DSECTION=1 (accessed July 1, 2006).

Multiple Births Families. "Bereavement Support, Surviving Co-Multiples, Twinless Twins, Lone Twin." http://www.multiplebirthsfamilies.com/article/ber_q16html (accessed January 21, 2007).

Nobel Prize "The United Nations Children's Fund: The Nobel Peace Prize 1965." http://nobel.prize.org/nobel_prizes/peace/laureates/1965/unicef-history.html (accessed December 26, 2006).

Palca, Joe. National Public Radio. July 10, 2006, "Children's Health: Salk Polio Vaccine Conquered Terrifying Disease." http://www.npr.org/templates/story/story. php?stpryId=4585992&sourceCode=RSS (accessed July 10, 2006).

"Polio Eradication: The Largest Medical Experiment in History." www.polio.info (pdf file).

Polio History Timeline. "The History of Polio, A Hypertext Timeline." http://www.cloudnet.com/-edrbsass/poliotimeline.html (accessed July 10, 2006).

Post-Polio Health International. "Gini Laurie, Founder, Remembered in Missouri History Museum (MHS)." http://www.post-polio.org/hist-mhs.html (accessed August 9, 2006).

———. "The History of Post-Polio Health International (PHI)." http://www.post-polio.org/hist.html (accessed August 9, 2006).

———. "Independent Living—The Role of Gini Laurie." http://www.post-polio.org/hist-gini.html (accessed August 9, 2006).

———. "Information about the Late Effects of Polio" http://www.post-polio.org/ipn/aboutlep.html (accessed July 19, 2006).

———. "Polio and Post-Polio Fact Sheet." http://www.post-polio.org/ipn/fact.html (accessed July 19, 2006).

Ream, Sarah L. California State University, Abstracts. "Decrease in Grief Intensity for Deceased Twin and Non-Twin Relatives: An Evolutionary Perspective." http://psych.fullerton.edu/nsegal/twins.html (accessed March 7, 2007).

Relief Web International Press Releases. "Nigeria polio update: Enhanced activities planned due to increased incidence in parts of northern Nigeria (Source 5/1/06 WHO Report)." http://www.reliefweb.int/rw/rwb./nsf/db900SID/ KHII-6PE5K8?/OpenDocument (accessed December 26, 2006).

Rotary International. "History of PolioPlus." http://www.rotary.org/foundation/polioplus/information/history.html (accessed November 9, 2006).

———. "History of PolioPlus: Donor Profile for Received and Confirmed Contributions, 1988–2008." http://www.rotary.org/foundation/polioplus/information/history.html (accessed February 12, 2006).

———. "India steps up efforts to end polio." http://rotary.org/newsroom/polio/ 07014 polio india.html.

———. "Renewed Efforts to End Polio in South Asia." October 10, 2006. http://www.rotary.org/newsroom/polio/061010 sasia.html. (accessed November 9, 2006).

Sabin Institute. "The Albert B. Sabin Annual Awards." http://www.sabin.org/awards/annual_awards.html (accessed March 5, 2007).

———. "Our Mission." http://www.sabin.org/about/sabin_mission.html (accessed March 5, 2007).

Salk Institute for Biological Studies. "A Brief History and Overview of the Salk Institute," http://www.salk.edu/about/history (accessed July 27, 2006).

Sanofi Pasteur. Press Release. September 26, 2005. "FDA Accepts for Filing License Application for New Pediatric Combination Vaccine, PENTACEL." http://www.sanofopasteur.us/sanofipasteur/front/ index.jsp?siteCode=AVP_US&lang. (accessed March 5, 2007).

———. "Preventable Diseases, Poliomyelitis." http://www.sanofipasteur.us/sanofi-pasteur/front/index. jsp?siteCode=AVP_US&lang (accessed March 5, 2007).

———. "Sanofi Pasteur's New Polio Vaccine Licensed for Use in Novel Approach Global Eradication Efforts." http://www.sanofipasteur.

com/sanofi-pasteur/front/templates/vaccinations-travel-health-v (accessed October 24, 2006).

Segal, Nancy L. "Circumstances Surrounding Twinloss: A Review of studies and relevant texts." http://www.twinlesstwins.org/dnn/TwinGrief/TwinLossAtAnyAge/ResearchOnTwinLoss (accessed March 7, 2007).

———. "Research on Twin Loss." http://www.twinlesstwins. org/dnn/TwinGrief/TwinLossAtAnyAge/ResearchOnTwinLoss (accessed March 7, 2007).

Siegel, Irwin M. and Ensor E. Transfeld. "Post-Polio Corrective Spinal Surgery Now." *Post-Polio Health International Polio Network News*, 11, 3, part A (Summer1995). http://www.post-polio.org/ipn/pnn11-3A.html (accessed July 1, 2006).

Sister Kenny Rehabilitation Institute. "About Sister Kenny Rehabilitation Institute." http://www.allina.com/ahs/ski.nsf/page/aboutus (accessed March 4, 2007).

Smithsonian National Museum of American History. Press Release, April 11, 2005. "The Smithsonian's National Museum of American History Marks 50th Anniversary of the Polio Vaccine." http://americanhistory.se.edu/ news/pressrelease.cfm?key=29&newskey=174 (accessed July 19, 2006).

"Whatever Happened to Polio? Clinical Trials." http://americanhistory.si.edu/ polio/virusvaccine/clinical.htm (accessed July 14, 2006).

———. "Whatever Happened to Polio? Franklin D. Roosevelt." http://americanhistory.si.edu/polio/howpolio/fdr.htm (accessed July 12, 2006).

United Nations International Childrens Fund (UNICEF). Press centre, Joint Statement. "Despite difficulties, polio immunization drive underway in Iraq." http://unicef.org/media/media_36567html (accessed March 6, 2007).

———. "History of the Organization." www.unicef.org.

———. Supply Division Annual Report 2004. "Supplies for UNICEF Priorities." Online report www.unicef.org (pdf file)

———. "Immunization plus: Africa polio campaign at critical stage." http://www.unicef.org/immunization/index_25959.html (accessed December 26, 2006).

———. Press centre, Joint Press Release. "5.5 million under five Angolan children will be immunized against polio." http://www.unicef.org/media_37201.html (accessed December 26, 2006).

United States Agency for International Development, December 2006 "Top Strategic Accomplishments in Iraq: Improving Primary Health Care." www.usaid.gov/iraq (pdf file accessed March 7, 2007).

United States Army. "History of the Adjutant General's Corps." http://agsssi-www.army.mil/corphist.htm (accessed March 5, 2007).

United States Equal Employment Opportunity Commission. "Facts About the Americans with Disabilities Act." http://www.eeoc.gov/facts/fs-ada.html (accessed August 9, 2006).

University of Michigan, "A letter from the Dean, Spring 2005" Online report.

University of Pennsylvania. Health, Medicine, and American Culture, 1930– 1960. "Research Timeline 1796–1998." http://ccat.sas.upenn.edu/goldenage/wonder/w_time.htm (accessed August 6, 2006

University of Pittsburgh Medical Center. "Timeline Development of the Salk Vaccine at the University of Pittsburgh." http://newsbureau.upmc.com/ MediaKits/Polio50Years/PolioTimeline/2005.htm (accessed July 10, 2006).

World Health Organization (WHO). Media Centre. "Gates Foundation funds new polio vaccine to Accelerate eradication efforts," http://www.who.int/ medicacentre/news/notes/2005/np03/en/index.html (accessed March 7, 2007).

———. Media Centre. "The global polio eradication initiative." http://www.who.org.int/mediacentre/events/2006/g8summit/polio/en/index.html (accessed March 7, 2007).

———. Media Centre. "Global polio eradication now hinges on four Countries." http://www.who.int/mediacentre/news/release/2006/pr56/en/index.html (accessed November 10, 2006).

———. Media Centre, Joint News Release. WHO/Rotary International/ CDC/ UNICEF. "New emergency immunization plan launched to protect horn of Africa, as polio is confirmed in Somalia, 13 September 2005." http:// www.who.int/mediacentre/ newsreleases/2005/pr42/en/ (accessed January 29, 2006).

———. Media Centre, Joint News Release. WHO/CDC/Rotary International/ UNICEF. "Polio endemic countries hit all-time low of four, 1 February 2006." http://www.who.int/mediacentre/ news/release/2006/pr05/en/ index.html (accessed March 4, 2007).

———. Media Centre."Poliomyelitis." http://www.who.int/mediacentre/ factsheets/fs114/en/index.html (accessed March 4, 2007).

World Ortho. "Poliomyelitis: Appliances for paralysis in Developing Countries." http://www.worldortho.com/database/polio/pg11.html (accessed July 1, 2006)..

Newspaper Articles

"Back in Service Restored Iron Lung," *Syracuse Post Standard,* April 12, 2003, C-2

"Emergency Plan Ready as Number of Cases Mount." *Syracuse Post Standard,* September 17, 1950.

Fear Then Stalked the City, Polio Controlled but Protection Still Needed." *Syracuse Herald Journal,* August 20, 1967.

"Flashback! Polio Cure Elusive; Vaccine Only Hope and 3902 School Children of Syracuse Received Salk Shots in Field Trials." *Syracuse Post Standard,* January 9, 1978, 12.

French, Lorae M. "Caring is a Common Thread." *Syracuse Post-Standard,* July 12, 2006, B-3.

"Free Polio Vaccine Shots for 28,000 Within 30 Days." *Syracuse Herald Journal,* January 29, 1957, 2.

"89% of Eligible Children Get Polio Shots at DeWitt." *Syracuse Herald Journal,* May 3, 1954, 6.

"High School Pupils Will Get Free Salk Vaccine." *Syracuse Herald Journal,* January 20, 1957.

Obituary: Frank T. Flood, Jr. *Syracuse Post Standard,* November 2, 1953, 9.

Obituary: Cheryl Munson. *Syracuse Herald Journal,* April 25, 1960, 12.

Obituary: Patricia Munson, *Syracuse Herald Journal,* November 7, 1967, 16.

"Older Children Not Showing Up—20,516 Get Salk Shot Since Program's Start." *Syracuse Post Standard,* February 1956.

"Parents Asked to OK Polio Shots for All Junior and Senior Pupils." *Syracuse Herald Journal,* February 16, 1957.

"Syracuse First in State to Put Vaccine to Use." *Syracuse Post Standard,* May 17, 1955.

"Syracuse Had Only 4 Polio Victims in 1956." *Syracuse Post Standard,* January 27, 1957.

An additional newspaper article was provided by the Onondaga County Historical Society, with the title and date of the article missing. Based on details found in the article, it was written in early 1957.

DVD

The History Channel: In Search of the Polio Vaccine.

Miscellaneous Source Material

Emerson Respirator Instructions and Parts & Price List: J.H. Emerson Company: Cambridge, MA.

Frank T. Flood Jr. New York State Certificate of Death Registration Number 2348, received from the Onondaga County Office of Vital Statistics.

March of Dimes. "Building on Success," received from Christine Scott, March of Dimes, Buffalo, NY Office.

———. "50th Anniversary Backgrounder: Polio Epidemic Statistics, Salk Polio Vaccine, From Polio to Prematurity, the March of Dimes Today," received from Christine Scott, March of Dimes Buffalo, NY Office.

———. March of Dimes brochures and pamphlets received from Christine Scott, March of Dimes, Buffalo, NY Office.

———. "Polio Vaccine Timeline and Milestones," received from Christine Scott, March of Dimes Buffalo, NY Office.

———. Report from National Office, Research and Grants for California.

During the last 10 years.—Verbal report received from Christine Scott, Buffalo, NY Office.

———. "State of Polio Today, Polio Facts," received from Christine Scott, March of Dimes Buffalo, NY Office

———."Statement on Support for Polio Patients in Iron Lungs," received from Christine Scott, March of Dimes Buffalo, NY Office.

Memory Book for Frank T. Flood, Jr. supplied by Schumacher-Whelan Funeral Home; Syracuse, NY (1953).

New York State Department of Health. Basic Vital Statistics New York State Excluding New York City. *1900–1967 Cases and Deaths from Poliomyelitis and Tuberculosis, 28.*

NOAA National Data Centers, U.S. Department of Commerce, National Oceanic and Atmospheric Administration: Local Syracuse Climatological Data. October and November 1953 Daily Record.

Onondaga County, New York, Medical Society, 1906–1956, Sesquicentennial, Syracuse, 1956.

Syracuse, New York, City Hospital Annual Reports—1949, 1950, 1951, 1952, 1955, 1956 Disease Statistics. Requested information provided by Dr. Eric Luft, Curator of the Health Sciences Library SUNY Upstate Medical University (loose sheets with only a few pages recorded in library records).

1953 Bulletin of Onondaga County Medical Society. "Poliomyelitis and the Gamma Globulin Program," February 1953; "Report from Communicable Disease Bureau," February and May 1953; "Report from the Bureau of Communicable Diseases," June 1953.

1954 Bulletin of Onondaga County Medical Society. "Poliomyelitis in Syracuse 1954—First Report," September 1954; "Poliomyelitis in Syracuse in 1954—Second Report," October 1954; "Poliomyelitis in Syracuse in 1954—Third Report," November 1954.

Resource Material Related to Twin-Loss

Recommended books, as listed by two Web sites dedicated to the support of individuals who have lost their birth partner (s):

Case, Betty J. *Living without Your Twin.* Portland, Oregon: Tibbutt Publishing, 2001.

Kubler-Ross, Elisabeth. *On Children and Death.* New York: Collier Books, 1983.

Sandbank, Audrey C., ed. *Twin and Triplet Psychology.* New York: Routledge, 1999.

Segal, Nancy L. *Entwined Lives.* New York: Penguin Books, 2000.

Wolfelt, Alan D. *A Child's View of Death.* Fort Collins: Center for Loss and Life Transition, 1991.

Woodward, Joan. *The Lone Twin: Understanding Twin Bereavement and Loss.* New York: Free Association Books, 1998.

Organizations for twins:

Twinless Twins
P.O. Box 980481
Ypsilanti, Michigan 48198
www.twinlesstwins.org Also: www.multiplebirthsfamilies.com

Photo Credits

Syracuse Post Standard has given permission for the publication of photos from the following articles:

"Back in Service Restored Iron Lung Machine." April 12, 2003, C2. Photographer: Dick Blume. The photo was not used in the book. E-mail text of article sent to author by Molly Elliott on July 28, 2006, at 2:50 PM.

"First of the DeWitt Polio Epidemic Victims." January 13, 1954, 8. Photo of Janice Flood with Mrs. MacDougall. Reproduced with permission by Dave Nichols.

"89% of Eligible Children Get Polio Shots in DeWitt." May 3, 1954, 6. Photo of Janice Flood receiving shot from Dr. John Holmes. Reproduced with permission by Dave Nichols.

Society Page. December 4, 1949. Photo of Janice feeding Frankie. Reproduced with permission by Dave Nichols.

1952 Moses DeWitt Elementary School kindergarten class photo: Verbal permission received from Jamesville DeWitt Central School District Superintendent, Dr. Alice Kendrick.

Photo of iron lung. August 8, 2006. Permission received from Hugh Bonner, Dean of the College of Health Professions at SUNY, Upstate Medical University. The iron lung is housed in Silverman Hall. Photographer: Deborah Rexine, Medical Photography.

Dr. Jaros: Photo supplied by Dr. Turek

Dr. (Jaros) Turek: Photo taken by Dave Nichols, February 24, 2007.

Dr. Kalamarides: Photo supplied by Mr. John Kalamarides.

All other photos have been taken from Flood Family files.

47388728R00173

Made in the USA
Lexington, KY
05 December 2015